GREAT FEUDS
IN HISTORY

GREAT FEUDS
IN HISTORY

*Ten of the Liveliest
Disputes Ever*

Colin Evans

JOHN WILEY & SONS, INC.
New York · Chichester · Weinheim · Brisbane · Singapore · Toronto

This book is printed on acid-free paper.

Copyright © 2001 by Colin Evans. All rights reserved

Published by John Wiley & Sons, Inc.
Published simultaneously in Canada

This publication is designed to provide accurate and authoritative information in regard to the subject matter covered. It is sold with the understanding that the Publisher is not engaged in rendering professional services. If professional advice or other expert assistance is required, the services of a competent professional person should be sought.

Library of Congress Cataloging-in-Publication Data

Evans, Colin
   Great feuds in history : ten of the liveliest disputes ever / Colin Evans.
     p. cm.
   Includes bibliographical references and index.
   ISBN 0-471-38038-5 (cloth : alk. paper)
   1. Celebrities–History–Anecdotes. 2. Vendetta–History–Anecdotes. I. Title.

D110.5 .E83 2001
909–dc21
00-043919
Printed in the United States of America

10 9 8 7 6 5 4 3 2 1

CONTENTS

ACKNOWLEDGMENTS

I wish to thank the following for their invaluable assistance in the preparation of this book:

Research staff at the National Archives; the Library of Congress; the British Library, London; and the British Newspaper Library at Colindale, London.

Among the many individuals who steered me in the right direction, the following deserve special mention: David Anderson, bibliophile extraordinaire, unfailingly generous with help and ideas; Christopher Duke, the consummate research librarian. Jeff Golick wielded the fine editorial hand at Wiley, while Sonia Greenbaum and Kimberly Monroe took admirable care of the copyediting duties. Special thanks to Ed Knappman, my agent, who offered the encouragement and feedback in the early stages that did so much to shape this book. That being said, responsibility for any errors is mine alone.

As always, the final thank-you is for Norma.

GREAT FEUDS
IN HISTORY

INTRODUCTION

Ever since Cain and Abel got into it over the relative merits of sacrificial offerings, feuds among the mighty and the famous have always exercised a powerful hold on the public imagination. If we are honest, most of us experience at least a tingle of delight when confronted by the spectacle of two celebrities clawing each other to shreds. Quite why this should be is a question best left to the psychologists and beyond the scope of this book; on the other hand, if you have an appetite for some of the juiciest, most bruising personal battles in history. . . .

Individuals with the desire and the talent to shape history have never gone seeking bushels under which to hide their lights. They have a keen appreciation of their own worth and expect others to share that view; which is all well and good until they collide with someone similarly minded. If neither is prepared to bend or give way, then a feud is possible, though by no means certain. For a feud—a dyed-in-the-wool, hard-core feud—to really blossom, both contestants need to be punching roughly the same weight. An example: say Lyndon Baines Johnson had gotten wind that he was being trashed by some Capitol Hill minnow, chances are a single phone call from the Oval Office would have been enough to induce a knee-trembling silence. But make the offending voice that of Robert F. Kennedy and we are dealing with a whole different ballgame. Kennedy could hurt Johnson, and the latter knew it; here we have that all-important vital ingredient for a classic feud.

In the same way, even Joseph Stalin, the ultimate gangster-politician, was forced to put his murderous instincts temporarily on hold in the early days of his dispute with Leon Trotsky. Trotsky was simply too powerful to be whacked. Of course, Stalin had the patience of an ice fisherman and ultimately prevailed, but not before providing the twentieth century with its deadliest and politically most significant feud.

1

Not all of the feuds covered here were fought on the world stage. Buried deep in the mazy forests and hidden valleys of the southern Appalachians, a couple of backwoods families raised internecine warfare to a near art form as they swarmed all over each other like killer bees. Although the Hatfields and the McCoys tried like crazy to draw a blind over their homicidal interplay, eventually they were outed by their own notoriety, their names a byword for feuding no matter where it occurs. And they exhibited exactly the same traits as their historically more significant counterparts. Old Randolph McCoy never was too much on book learning and may never have heard of Oliver Cromwell, but when it came to grudge bearing, this shambling hillbilly and England's republican supremo were blood brothers. While the methods they employed might have been very different, they shared an identical goal—dominance, an all-consuming desire to trample and pulverize their opponent into humiliating submission.

In recent years the face of feuding has altered beyond all recognition, thanks mainly to modern communications. When Queen Elizabeth I began the long, slow barbecue of her cousin Mary, Queen of Scots, royal tactics were a mystery to all except a few court insiders; nowadays, the gossip mags and the Internet would pick up on such devilry in a matter of days, if not hours. Secrecy gave Elizabeth the luxury of time, a valuable commodity in any campaign; it also gave Mary enormous scope for intrigue and she certainly made the most of it.

In these pages you will uncover the darker side of some of history's greatest figures. Shocking and often violent, these are personalities who demand and deserve closer inspection, for without them the cozy, familiar world that we know today would look startlingly different. Because the main thrust of this book is personal conflict, the broader themes of politics, religion, and military confrontation, where they appear, act only as a backdrop, a canvas for our central leitmotiv. Deciding which feuds to include caused considerable anguish, but I hope the reader will agree that all the final selections merit their place.

For ease of reading the chapters have been organized in chronological order, and each one is prefaced with a brief rundown on the nuts and bolts of that particular feud, rather like the "Tale of the Tape" that sportswriters use to display the relative physical merits of each boxer in a championship bout. For, make no mistake, all of the feuds covered within these pages were genuine knock-down, drag-'em-out brawls, and no one wanted to win on points: it was a KO or nothing. Most were fought literally to the death—the executioner's sharpened ax, a duel on the Hudson, Appalachian gunfights, NKVD assassins stalking their prey halfway around the world, snipers in Memphis—the list goes on.

Even those feuds that ended without direct carnage contained more than their quota of tragedy: Scott's disastrous trek into oblivion, Patton's grotesquely incongruous demise, the Duchess of Windsor's slide into maudlin alcoholism. The pursuit of greatness, it seems, exacts a harsh toll.

It is a five-hundred-year journey from a black-draped scaffold in an English medieval castle to the floor of a crowded Los Angeles hotel kitchen, but that is the path we will follow. A word of caution: tread carefully—there has been an awful lot of blood spilled along the way.

CHAPTER 1

Elizabeth I versus Mary

Years of feud:	1561–1587	
Names:	Elizabeth Tudor	Mary Stuart
Strengths:	Resolute and determined in a male-dominated society	Boundless charm, inspirational
Weaknesses:	Jealous, spiteful, hypocritical	Hotheaded, amoral, probably an accessory to murder
At stake:	A crown and the religious direction of a nation	

In 1517, a thousand years of spiritual certainty were thrown out the window when a disaffected German friar named Martin Luther nailed his Ninety-five Theses, denouncing abuses by the Roman Catholic church, to the church door in Wittenberg, a small town in Saxony. With this simple act of defiance, Luther toppled the world off its religious axis. As the tidal wave of Reformation surged across northern Europe, it lapped the shores of England. Here, the formidable bulk of the Catholic king, Henry VIII, at first formed a bulwark against the Protestant offensive—not for nothing was he called "Defender of the Faith"—but as his domestic circumstances deteriorated over the next decade, the wily monarch spotted an opportunity. Desperate for a male heir and fed up with Pope Clement VII's refusal to grant him an annulment from the irritatingly miscarriage-prone Catherine of Aragon, Henry decided in 1533 that the time had come for a

5

little freelance faith founding of his own. As a result, Henry got the divorce he'd been seeking for years and a new wife, his already pregnant mistress, Anne Boleyn. Meanwhile, his subjects had to wrestle with the nuances of a brand-new religion, the Church of England.

For the next three hundred years the rift between Catholic and Protestant would dominate the fabric of British life; not that it mattered much to poor Anne Boleyn. Although, like her predecessor Catherine, she did manage to produce a daughter, she signally failed to deliver the son that Henry craved. A succession of miscarriages and the lusty sovereign's roving eye sealed her fate.

The daughter Anne left behind was one of the most remarkable women in history, and yet for the first quarter century of her life, Elizabeth Tudor floundered in a sea of tumultuous uncertainty. Was she a princess or wasn't she? Was she, as the Vatican averred, a bastard, or did she have a lawful claim to royal succession? Even more uncertain: would she be allowed to stake that claim, or would circumstances conspire to hasten her in the footsteps of her mother, to trek those few wretched yards from cell to headsman's ax on Tower Hill?

Shoved unceremoniously into the shadows by her father, Elizabeth saw her dire situation hit rock bottom in 1553, when her demented half sister, Mary Tudor, daughter of Henry VIII and Catherine of Aragon, succeeded to the throne, determined to restore Catholicism as the only true faith in the land. During her five-year reign, "Bloody Mary" burned over 250 Protestants at the stake, and brought enormous pressure to bear on Elizabeth to convert to Catholicism. As an act of obedience Elizabeth did attend one mass, but complained the whole time of feeling ill, an early indication of her independence of spirit. As it happened, Mary's brutal suppression of Protestantism backfired badly, turning public opinion against her and toward her redheaded half sister. Elizabeth judged that patience would bring its own reward: Mary's health was on the slide and couldn't hold up forever.

On November 17, 1558, Mary died, and a nation rejoiced as Elizabeth became Queen of England. But to the north, in Scotland, it was a very different matter.

Unlike her newly crowned English cousin, Mary Stuart, the devoutly Catholic Queen of Scots, possessed impeccable royal credentials. As the daughter of James IV of Scotland and Margaret, sister of Henry VIII, she had, according to many, far better title to the English throne than did Elizabeth. It was all a question of legitimacy. In the eyes of Rome, Henry's divorce from Catherine had been a flagrantly illegal act, the precursor to the even greater sin of bigamy; and as the product of that bigamous union, Elizabeth was viewed as a heretic usurper by the royal houses of France and Spain, which regarded Mary as England's lawful monarch.

Europe had always formed Mary's power base. At age five she had been betrothed to the French dauphin and had spent most of her childhood in France, enjoying a life of pampered opulence. In April 1558, at the age of fifteen, she married the dauphin. Seven months later the young couple shared the trepidation felt by most of Europe when Elizabeth succeeded to the English throne.

For Elizabeth this was an unsettling time. Anxious, eager for international recognition, she suffered a crisis of confidence the following year when, after a fatal riding accident to his father, the dauphin unexpectedly found himself King Francis II of France. In the twinkling of an eye, Mary was queen of not one but two nations, Scotland and France. Sandwiched uncomfortably in between the two lay England.

As unappetizing as this prospect might have been, Elizabeth could probably have coped had it not been for the fact that Francis II died abruptly in 1561. Widowed and rootless, Mary decided to return to the Scottish kingdom she had not seen in a dozen years, news that sent a chill through the English court.

Elizabeth, still single, could smell danger: if she died without issue, then Mary, with the support of France and Spain, was a shoo-in for the English throne. Just one year earlier the Treaty of Edinburgh had been drafted specifically to prevent this eventuality. Under its terms Mary agreed to renounce all claims to the English throne, yet she had declined to ratify the treaty, a refusal that now took on even more ominous overtones.

Elizabeth panicked. Quite apart from the dynastic threat posed by her cousin, there existed the possibility of religious conflict north of the border, sparked by rumors that Mary had told the pope that she intended to restore Catholicism in her Scottish kingdom. For these reasons, in the summer of 1561 Elizabeth refused Mary a safe-conduct through England on her way home to Scotland. Although Elizabeth later changed her mind, by that time Mary, seething from the slight, had taken ship from France and landed at Leith, the port of Edinburgh, on August 19.

The battle had been joined.

The queen who returned to Scotland brought a dash of European elegance to the drab Edinburgh court, even if at first she struggled to remember the Scots tongue of her childhood and knew no English at all. In essence she was a cultivated Frenchwoman, a lover of music, dancing, ballets and masques, able to produce exquisite needlework and embroidery, all the attributes thought desirable in a sixteenth-century monarch.

Elizabeth could afford to scoff at such humdrum accomplishments. Intellectually, she was several times removed from her cousin and scorned the suffocating restrictions ordinarily placed on young royal women at this time. She studied geography, history, math, astronomy, calligraphy, and had a genuine gift for languages, enough for her tutor, Roger Ascham, to write: "She talks French and Italian as well as she does English. When she writes Greek and Latin, nothing is more beautiful than her handwriting."[1] Like Mary, she was an accomplished horsewoman, fond of hunting and archery, and she was able to play the lute and virginals (an early form of harpsichord) to an impressive standard.[2]

Clearly, Elizabeth was a well-rounded woman, fully developed both cerebrally and physically, able to hold her own in any company. All of which begs the question: why was she so intimidated by her cousin? The answer was as old as time itself.

The statuesque Queen of Scots was a sexual sorceress. She possessed, according to the dour Calvinist preacher John Knox, "some enchantment, whereby men are bewitched,"[3] and throughout her life she never lost this spellbinding power. At almost six feet in height and with a great shock of chestnut hair, Mary cut an extraordinary figure, but it was her mesmerizing charm, with its constant hint of intimacy, that won over princes and servants alike.

Prior to Francis's death, Elizabeth had been the most desirable royal match in Europe, inundated with suitors all clamoring for her hand in marriage. Mary's premature widowhood changed all that. Younger, more beautiful, suddenly she was the hot matrimonial ticket and no one expected the sensuous Scot to remain single for long. Her choice of husband was a matter of paramount concern to Elizabeth, who feared the arrival of a powerful foreign Catholic prince in the neighboring kingdom. At the same time, Mary's undeniably strong claim to the English throne posed a continuing threat to Elizabeth's security, leading to an intense rivalry between the two female sovereigns that would dominate Anglo-Scots relations for the next quarter century.

"Uneasy Lies the Head . . ."

First, Elizabeth needed to resolve the problem of succession. Snuff out Mary's claim, argued her counselors, by quickly marrying some foreign prince and producing an heir of her own. Elizabeth scowled her disapproval. Being the daughter of Henry VIII had given her a unique insight into the precariousness of royal wedlock. Following her own mother's execution, she had seen four stepmothers come and go; hardly surprising, then, that she developed so skeptical a view of marriage. She attempted to mask this distrust with flowery phrases, telling one ambassador, "Love is usually the offspring of leisure, and as I am so beset by duties, I have not been able to think of love."[4] On another occasion, when pressed to take a husband, she snapped, "I am married already to the realm of England."[5]

There was another reason for her reticence: an abiding distrust of heirs. A keen student of history, Elizabeth knew just how often monarchs were undone by their own flesh and blood. Years spent idling on the royal sidelines were powerful incubators of resentment, and she wasn't prepared to risk that.

The upshot of all these prejudices meant that she became wonderfully skilled at deflecting suitors. Plenty made it to her bedchamber door, some even crossed the threshold, but none—so she would always claim—gained access to the royal bed. Elizabeth had no intention of reducing herself to the role of a royal broodmare.

Power also played its part. Six years after her succession, when informing a Scottish emissary, Sir James Melville, of her intention to remain single, he at once replied, "I know the truth of that, Madam, you need not tell it me. Your Majesty thinks if you were married you would be but Queen of England; and now you are both King and Queen."[6]

It was a shrewd observation. Elizabeth had both hands on the reins of power and had absolutely no intention of letting go.

Mary's attempt to loosen that grip had already faltered. Hers had been an awkward homecoming. After the languid sophistication of France, Scotland seemed stuffy and vulgar, run by an uncouth Protestant clique prepared only to tolerate her as the lesser of two evils. They were still smarting from the snub delivered by Elizabeth's refusal to marry the Earl of Arran and ally herself with them. For them, Mary's Catholicism was a price worth paying—just.

It was an uneasy alliance. Highly strung and fun loving, Mary failed entirely to grasp the somber Scottish character, while the Scots had nothing but contempt for her perceived giddiness and habit of taking to her bed for days on end, incapacitated by depression. Hardest of all, it was impossible to eradicate the suspicion that she was merely an opportunistic foreigner.

Government spies kept Elizabeth constantly informed about her rival's distress. Her feelings toward Mary were ambivalent: on the one hand she feared her as a dangerous opponent, and on the other she felt enormous kinship to another ruling sovereign and a cousin. After much soul-searching, kinship won out. Elizabeth decided that if Mary declared herself willing to renounce her pretensions to the English throne, then a mutually beneficial accommodation could be reached. Against ministerial advice, Elizabeth insisted that she and the Scottish queen should meet face-to-face: only that way could the vexed questions of succession and possible misunderstandings over the Treaty of Edinburgh be resolved.

Mary was similarly minded. Although bitterly resentful of the way in which Elizabeth had promoted Protestantism in her kingdom, she accepted the desirability of a friendly personal relationship. This is why she paid close heed when the Scots lords suggested that she offer a deal with her cousin: in return for Mary renouncing her claim to the English throne, would Elizabeth be prepared to recognize her as heiress presumptive?

It was worth a shot, and at the end of August 1561, Mary dispatched longtime supporter William Maitland of Lethington to sound out whether Elizabeth was willing to revise the terms of the Treaty of Edinburgh. After a warm welcome, Maitland wasted little time in laying Mary's cards on the table.

Elizabeth did not hide her disappointment. "I looked for another message from the Queen your sovereign. I have long enough been fed with fair words," she said. "When I am dead, they shall succeed that have most right." After grudgingly conceding that she knew of no better title than Mary's, she allowed her perennial insecurity over the thorny topic of heirs to resurface. "More people worship the rising than the setting sun," she grouched, saying that Mary's best chances of succession lay in demonstrating to the English people that she was a good neighbor.[7]

Maitland left the meeting with one deep conviction: if it came to personal negotiations between Elizabeth and Mary, then the latter would be eaten alive. In terms of judgment, political acumen, and all-round hustle, the Scottish queen was a raw neophyte compared with her streetwise English counterpart.

In September, Maitland again met with Elizabeth, and this time he dropped heavy hints that if Mary was not named heiress to the crown, she might be tempted to snatch it by force, adding ominously that "although Your Majesty takes yourself to be lawful, yet are ye not always so taken abroad in the world."[8]

So unnerved was Elizabeth by this stark appraisal that Maitland was able to wring from her the assurance that she would review and alter the wording of the Treaty of Edinburgh, much to the chagrin of Sir William Cecil, Elizabeth's ultracautious Secretary of State and her closest adviser. He distrusted Mary and told Elizabeth so in such candid terms that she regretted her rash concessions.

Chastened by Cecil's stinging rebuke, Elizabeth pinned her hopes on a summit meeting between herself and Mary. Mary responded warmly, expressing delight at the prospect of meeting her "dear sister" face-to-face and sighing that "she wished one of them was a man, so that their kingdoms could be united by marital alliance."[9] Plenty of others were thinking along much the same lines.

Against a rising tide of disapproval on both sides of the border, Elizabeth pushed ahead with plans for the meeting. There was more than politics at work here; she wanted to see for herself if Mary's famed beauty lived up to the advance billing, while praying that it did not. Her jealousy was boundless. On one occasion when a foreign diplomat carelessly mentioned in her presence that Mary was reputed to be very lovely, Elizabeth spat back that "she herself was superior to the Queen of Scotland."[10]

After much negotiation the meeting was arranged for the fall of 1562 in northern England. Then disaster struck. News reached England that civil war had broken out in France; moreover, Elizabeth learned to her dismay that Mary had offered aid to her Catholic relatives in their genocidal pursuit of the Protestant Huguenots. Elizabeth had no alternative but to cancel the meeting, with a promise that it would be revived at some later date. Mary, bawling like a baby, ran to her bed in disappointment and didn't get up for days.

Smallpox Scare

Elizabeth, too, was soon abed, not from depression but from that scourge of medieval Europe—smallpox. For days her life hung in the balance; then, as if by a miracle, she clawed her way back. Even more miraculous, the angry pustules had left little trace on her complexion, a rare and fortunate outcome that led Mary to write, expressing her delight "that your beautiful face will lose none of its perfections."[11]

Not only had Elizabeth's brush with death resurrected concerns about the succession, it had concentrated her mind wonderfully on the marital aspirations of her cousin. Ideally, she would have preferred Mary to remain single; given the unlikelihood of that scenario, she fretted long and hard over who might be the next King of Scots.

Most of all she dreaded an alliance with one of the major Catholic royal houses, Spain, Austria or France, any of which might pose problems for the newly Protestant England. When rumors linking Mary's name to that of Don Carlos, the simpleton heir to the Spanish throne, reached her court, Elizabeth cracked the whip. Such a choice, she told Mary, was unacceptable. "Consider well your steps,"[12] she warned.

Elizabeth's arrogance reached breathtaking proportions. In the spring of 1563, she began compiling a shortlist of suitable marriage candidates for her cousin. The first name out of the hat astounded her courtiers. Admittedly, Sir Robert Dudley had a well-advertised weakness for redheads, but hadn't most of his affection—and rather more, if court gossip was to be believed—been directed at and received by that other flameheaded royal, Elizabeth herself?

Maitland listened askance to Elizabeth's suggestion, which he found insulting, and said that if Dudley was such a good catch, maybe she should marry him herself. His skepticism was mirrored in Scotland, with Mary tartly refusing Elizabeth's request for a meeting.

Elizabeth's fixation on her unseen rival festered to the point of obsession. When another Scottish emissary, Sir James Melville, was sent south to pursue the Dudley question, Elizabeth plagued him with a barrage of childish queries all designed to establish whether Mary was more attractive than herself. When pressed to say more, he replied tactfully that Elizabeth was the fairest queen in England, and Mary the fairest queen in Scotland. Still, this didn't satisfy Elizabeth, who archly demanded that he climb off the fence and make a choice. Backed into a corner, he bravely mumbled that Mary was the fairer.

Elizabeth glowered. A glutton for flattery, she was unused to such candor. Sulkily, she next demanded to know if Mary was taller than herself. On learning that she was, Elizabeth trumpeted her celebration: "Then she is too high; for I myself am neither too high nor too low!"[13]

With all the juvenile angst of a spotty adolescent, Elizabeth kept pestering Melville about her rival's social graces, forcing him into one reluctant admission after another. Yes, Mary was an accomplished huntress; yes, she read good books; yes, she played the lute and virginals. At this, Elizabeth pounced. How well does she play?

"Reasonably well for a queen," groaned the unfortunate Melville.[14]

That night Elizabeth arranged an elaborate charade whereby Melville was inveigled into a chamber where she was playing the virginals. Ostensibly startled by the intrusion, she quizzed

Melville on why he had stumbled unannounced into the royal quarters. Melville, aware that he had been set up, took the diplomatic line. "I heard such melody as ravished me and drew me within the chamber."[15] Elizabeth motioned him to kneel by her side and demanded to know whether she played better than Mary. On this occasion he could, in all honesty, agree that she did.

It turned into a long night for Melville. All his representations about Dudley went unheeded as he was coerced into yet more opinion passing, this time on Elizabeth's dancing. With escape the only thought on his mind, the poor fellow conceded that Elizabeth was the better dancer, then bolted for the door.

Melville returned to Scotland, where he wasted little time in informing Mary of his decidedly poor opinion of Elizabeth. She was, he said, conniving and manipulative in the extreme.

Mary weighed her options carefully before informing Elizabeth that she would not consider marrying Dudley unless Elizabeth promised to settle the succession on her. To general astonishment, Elizabeth did not refuse point-blank, stating that if Mary married Dudley, she, Elizabeth, would shower him with honors and promote Mary's claim from behind the scenes. However—and it was a *big* however—Elizabeth refused to make public this strategy until such time as she herself was married or had announced her intention to remain single, which decision was expected soon. This was too much for the emotional Mary, who again took to her bed, sobbing and depressed.

At this juncture Elizabeth further muddied the already murky waters of succession by pressing the claims of yet another potential suitor for Mary's hand—this time one of the most eligible bachelors in the kingdom.

Still in his teens, Lord Darnley was tall and devastatingly handsome, with the porcelain features of an angel, and his arrival in Edinburgh on February 13, 1565, caused a sensation. Mary just melted. Throwing two such highly sexed individuals together was bound to generate sparks, and so it proved. Reports of the liaison's steamy success filtered south and prompted yet another about-face from Elizabeth, as she now doubted the wisdom of her matchmaking and urged Mary to show caution. Setting aside her fury at this meddling interference, Mary promised in late

May to delay any wedding for three months. However, on July 29, she married Darnley and proclaimed him King of Scots, much to the dismay of the local nobility, who loathed his bullying arrogance.

When told the news, Elizabeth raged that Mary had broken her promise, and any hope of a rapprochement between the two queens vanished into the ether. Henceforth, it would be open, if undeclared, war.

For all her fabled sexuality, Mary was clueless when it came to choosing her men; and in Darnley she made her biggest blunder of all. Feckless and afflicted with an insatiable libido, he was an unmitigated disaster, both as husband and king. Admittedly his immaculate pedigree—he was Elizabeth's second cousin—had strengthened, if anything, Mary's claim to the English throne, but he treated her abominably, and before long his visits to the local stews, where he drank and caroused in the company of other women, were the subject of scandalous gossip.

Just months into the wedding and Mary, too, was seeking alternative companionship, showering her attentions on her Italian secretary, David Rizzio. Rumors of the alleged affair filled Darnley with a murderous rage, and, on March 9, 1566, he and five others burst into the room where Mary and Rizzio were dining, dragged him into an antechamber, and stabbed him to death.

When, just over three months later, on June 19, Mary gave birth to a son, James, winks and nudges were the order of the day in Edinburgh, with whispers that the father was Rizzio, not Darnley. Certainly this is what Darnley believed.

With her lover dead and her marriage in complete disarray, Mary thirsted for revenge. An unlikely ally came in the shape of the Earl of Bothwell, a swaggering rogue whom she found irresistible. Bothwell's ear was ever attentive to Mary's pleading, and he may have heard more than he imagined.

Mysterious Explosion

On the evening of February 9, 1567, Darnley was staying at an Edinburgh lodging house called Kirk o' Field, just a few hundred yards along the Royal Mile from Holyrood Palace, where Mary resided. A couple of hours after midnight, the still night air was torn by an enormous explosion that reduced Kirk o' Field to rubble. Among those killed were Darnley and his valet, whose bodies, both clad in nightgowns, were found in the gardens. Judging from marks around their throats, they had been strangled and the explosion was merely a subterfuge to cover up the crime.

Whatever the truth of this incident, most Scots believed that Mary and Bothwell had conspired in Darnley's death, as did Elizabeth's spies in Edinburgh. A tepid inquiry failed to uncover anything conclusive, and on April 24 Bothwell bore Mary off to Dunbar, where, so she later claimed, he raped her, though this appears to have been a face-saving fabrication on Mary's part, designed to arouse sympathy and deflect attention from her own misdeeds.

After Bothwell's marriage was dissolved on the grounds of his adultery with a maid, he was free to marry Mary, which he did on May 15 at Holyrood. Despite Mary's continued protestations of innocence in the Darnley affair, few believed her, certainly not Elizabeth. She was shocked to the core by the way in which Mary had surrendered herself to Bothwell. According to a courtier, Elizabeth "had great misliking for the Queen's doing, which she doth so much detest that she is ashamed of her."[16]

Once again, Mary's inability to divorce the pleasures of the bedchamber from the obligations of office proved calamitous. For all his virile charm, Bothwell was a brute, and while Mary was prepared to make allowances for her husband's excesses, the Scots lords were not and they acted swiftly to rid themselves of this perceived embarrassment. A brief battle at Carberry Hill on June 15 delivered Mary into their hands, and they sent Bothwell packing to Denmark, where he was imprisoned and died insane eleven years later.

Although the lords assured Mary that they meant her no harm, her return to Edinburgh triggered enormous public outrage. Crowds yelled insults as she passed, calling her a whore and a murderer. With her reputation and her reign in tatters, Mary was thrown into jail and forced under pain of death to abdicate in favor of her thirteen-month-old son, who became King James VI of Scotland.*

*Later King James I of England.

Elizabeth heard of these events with deep concern. Whatever Mary had done—and Elizabeth was entirely bereft of sympathy on a personal level—she was still an anointed sovereign, to whom her subjects owed loyalty and obedience, and their treatment of her had set a dangerous precedent. Inspired by this fear, Elizabeth impulsively threatened an invasion of Scotland to free Mary, until wiser heads pointed out that this might jeopardize Mary's life.

Vindication for Elizabeth's prescience came soon, with ballads praising the Scots' action being heard across the land in English taverns and marketplaces. Driven by a fear of revolt in her own kingdom, Elizabeth stepped up the campaign to free her imprisoned cousin.

Not that Mary was languishing idly behind bars. Far from it. Using her formidable powers of persuasion on a love-struck custodian, on May 2, 1568, she managed to escape from captivity. Thousands rallied to her side, but a crushing defeat at Langside on May 13 at the hands of the Scots lords' army finished her. Three days later, rancorous and vengeful, she crossed the border into England, hoping for the military aid that would enable her to crush her enemies for good.

Her arrival on English soil plunged the country into crisis. Elizabeth's insistence that Mary should be restored immediately appalled Cecil, who argued that it was dangerous folly to support a queen who had schemed and plotted against her for years and was in every sense her enemy; better to return her to Scotland, posthaste. Elizabeth refused on grounds that it would mean certain death. Nor could she send Mary to the Continent—with her bewitching charm she might beguile some powerful Catholic prince into marriage and become a force for rebellion.

Having run out of options, Elizabeth reluctantly ordered that Mary should remain as her "guest" and under constant observation. As an added insult, she refused to meet Mary "by reason of the great slander of murder whereof she was not yet purged."[17] On this point she was unmovable: until formally cleared of Darnley's murder, Mary was persona non grata at court.

An incident early on gives a revealing insight into the darker side of Elizabeth's character. Upon hearing that Mary had fled Scotland with a paltry wardrobe, she dispatched a bundle of clothes so shoddy that the embarrassed emissary declared that it must have been a mistake; surely these were garments intended for a maidservant. The slight was heartless and deliberate. Now that she had Mary in her clutches, Elizabeth intended squeezing her like a lemon, ready to wring the last drop of humiliation out of her distress. In the acrid exchange of letters that followed, Mary complained constantly of her straitened circumstances, prompting Elizabeth to snarl, "Have some consideration of me, instead of always thinking of yourself!"[18]

Schooled in the hotbed of French royal intrigue, Mary had an insatiable appetite for conspiracy, and from almost her first day on English soil she plotted against Elizabeth, contacting Catholic supporters across Europe. To the Queen of Spain she promised to "make ours the reigning religion"[19] in England, but before that eventuality she had to overcome the ticklish problem of the "Casket Letters." Coming to light at a suspiciously opportune moment, these documents purported to contain intimate correspondence between Mary and Bothwell, which, if genuine, provided strong evidence that the couple had connived at Darnley's murder. Forgery or authentic? Opinion is still divided. Certainly most people at the time, including Elizabeth, believed them to be genuine. However, the investigating inquiry that was established was denied its star witness: Mary pulled rank and refused to testify, a simple expedient that prevented the tribunal from being allowed to find her guilty, much to the relief of Elizabeth, who ordered the letters suppressed.

Mary was clearly too dangerous to be set free. "The Queen of Scots," Cecil warned Elizabeth, "is, and always will be, a dangerous person to your estate."[20]

For this reason, in January 1569, Mary was moved to Tutbury Castle, a dank and dismal pile in the Midlands, and placed in the custody of the Earl of Shrewsbury, who was under strict orders not to fall prey to Mary's honeyed charm. Elizabeth, still no closer to fathoming her cousin's hypnotic appeal, had irritably observed to the French ambassador that there must be something "divine about the speech and appearance of the Queen of Scots, in that one or the other obliges her very enemies to speak for her."[21]

Mary's ability to rouse support did indeed appear to flirt with the supernatural. When, in November, a small pro-Mary rebellion rose in the north, Elizabeth reacted swiftly, issuing a death warrant for Mary, to be enacted if she were found to be behind the uprising. But by December 20 the rout was on and most had fled north of the border, to Scotland. A second, larger rebellion was similarly quashed, except that this time Elizabeth ordered harsh reprisals. Hundreds were hanged, while lands and possessions were confiscated and distributed to loyal noblemen.

Still, Mary would not be subdued. From Tutbury she smuggled a message to the Spanish ambassador, predicting that if his king would help, "I shall be Queen of England in three months, and mass shall be said all over the country."[22]

Ironically, Mary was more popular on the Continent than in her homeland. Most Scots wanted nothing to do with her, and it was left to Pope Pius V, a fanatical reactionary, to fire the next round on behalf of the imprisoned queen. On February 25, 1570, he issued a papal bull excommunicating Elizabeth, effectively urging Catholics to rise up against her and replace her with Mary. Designed to subvert and undermine Elizabeth's position, the papal bull produced the exact opposite, hardening the attitude of Protestants, who deeply resented the introduction of politics into a hitherto purely religious matter.

Inevitably this attack revived debate about Elizabeth's marital status. Much of the harmful speculation could be silenced, counseled her advisers, if only she would marry and produce an heir. Their logic was undeniable, and at age thirty-seven Elizabeth's biological clock was ticking fast if she wanted an heir. But did she? And, indeed, could she?

As already noted, her antipathy toward heirs was declaredly based on a suspicion of intrigue, but Mary had reason to suspect another explanation entirely for Elizabeth's parental aversion. According to her jailer's wife, the Countess of Shrewsbury, a gossipy former lady-in-waiting to the English queen, Elizabeth was "not like other women,"[23] implying that she was sterile. If true, this would explain much in Elizabeth's reign; after all, given her grim upbringing, who knew better than she the perils that might befall a barren queen in a childless marriage? And if she was infertile, then cultivation of her subsequent role as the Virgin Queen was a masterstroke, for not only did it have the effect of enhancing, almost deifying, her reputation, it also tightened her grip on power. By eschewing the advice of her counselors to marry, Elizabeth was sending clear signals that she intended being there for the long haul.

Such long-term planning was not within Mary's compass; she was driven by impulse and enforced quarantine had done nothing to temper her recklessness. Convinced that her freedom would never be achieved by legitimate means, she continued to intrigue and in 1571 enlisted the aid of Roberto Ridolfi, an eloquent Florentine banker and papal agent, who was charged with persuading the Catholic houses of Europe to raise an army and liberate Mary. Discovery of the plot, with its plan to assassinate Elizabeth, pushed Mary to the brink of execution. Instead, Elizabeth exacted a more subtle revenge, ordering publication of the damning Casket Letters.

Across the Channel, Charles IX bemoaned his former sister-in-law. "Alas, the poor fool will never cease until she loses her head. They will put her to death. It is her own fault and folly."[24] Fearing for her life, Mary at first cringed and denied all knowledge of the Ridolfi Plot; later she regained enough of her regal poise to write Elizabeth a letter of savage recrimination. Elizabeth's snapping response—Mary ought to be grateful that she had not been treated more severely—left the Scots queen in no doubt as to the peril of her situation.

Elizabeth's ambivalence toward her treacherous cousin continued to amaze. In 1572, to the bafflement of her advisers and both Houses of Parliament, she refused to sign a bill that would automatically debar Mary from succeeding to the English throne, saying that it was not to "her whole and perfect liking."[25]

She also resisted calls for Mary's head. Far better, she reasoned, if someone else could be lured into doing the dirty work. To this end, she attempted to have Mary returned to Scotland to stand trial for murdering Darnley, a move guaranteed to end at the block. But the Scots lords would only agree if English soldiers were present at the scaffold, and since this would implicate Elizabeth in Mary's death, she grumpily abandoned the plan.

By now Mary had relinquished all hope of regaining the Scots throne and instead focused her entire attention on England. She saw herself as a champion of Catholicism, overthrowing the heretic Elizabeth and restoring the true religion. She had no scruples about her conduct and little grasp of reality. "I will not leave my prison save as Queen of England,"[26] she once declared, and events showed she meant it.

Prince of Spies

Over the next few years Mary plotted ceaselessly, unaware that her every move was being monitored. Sir Francis Walsingham, a fanatical Protestant and the first great spymaster of history, had agents everywhere and they regularly intercepted and decoded Mary's ciphered messages. Elizabeth's mood darkened with every decrypt, and she slashed her cousin's allowance upon learning that much of it was spent on bribes to couriers.

When the French ambassador complained about her mistreatment of Mary, Elizabeth, who had just received word of Mary's latest round of plotting, hissed that her cousin was "the worst woman in the world, whose head should have been cut off years ago, and who would never be free as long as she lived."[27]

Longevity was a subject close to Elizabeth's heart. In January 1583, at the age of fifty, she finally abandoned all notions of marriage, sadly telling her courtiers, "I am an old woman, to whom paternosters will suffice in place of nuptials."[28] With her best bargaining tool—her hand in marriage—gone, Elizabeth's only hope was to outlive the Queen of Scots.

Desperation now began to infect Mary's reasoning. In the spring she and her allies conceived a half-witted plan whereby she would be reinstated in Scotland as joint ruler with her son, James, with herself holding the lion's share of power. James dismissed the idea out of hand.

A dangerous escalation came in November 1583, when Walsingham's agents arrested a Catholic spy named Francis Throckmorton, whom they had been watching for six months. A search of Throckmorton's London house revealed inflammatory pamphlets and lists of papist aristocratic sympathizers and of harbors where foreign ships could land in safety. Under torture he revealed that the conspiracy's purpose had been to set Mary on the throne of England, and that Mary had been involved from the outset. For his pains Throckmorton was executed at Tyburn.

The clamor for Mary's head reached pandemonium level, but

Elizabeth was deaf to all pleas. Much as she hated her cousin, her reverence for the Divine Right of monarchy was impregnable.

By 1584, Mary was still only in early middle age, but all those years of captivity had levied a harsh toll on her famed beauty: the supreme seductress of Europe was now fat and rheumaticky, with prematurely gray hair. Despite being moved to the slightly more agreeable surroundings of Sheffield Castle, she remained a closely guarded prisoner; every letter was read, every visitor scrutinized. At the same time, on Elizabeth's orders, she was still kept in the manner of a queen: each night her household of forty-eight persons dined on sumptuous meals. It was a surreal existence, enlivened only by her continual intrigue.

As a punishment, Walsingham, an implacable foe of the imprisoned queen, whisked her back to Tutbury, which she hated. An ultimatum was issued: cease plotting or risk the consequences. Mary's sugary denial of any such involvement fooled no one; within forty-eight hours she wrote Philip II of Spain, urging him to move against England.

Pressure mounted on Elizabeth to remedy this wearisome problem. Anxious to avoid the embarrassment of a trial, she in turn pressured James to share his throne with his mother. James, selfish and petulant, just scoffed. In March 1585, he wrote his mother, saying that it would be impossible to ally himself with someone who was "captive in a desert."[29] Mary, devastated by the betrayal, relayed her disappointment to Elizabeth. "Was there ever a sight so detestable and impious before God and man, as an only child despoiling his mother of her crown and royal estate?"[30]

Demands for Mary to be kept under stricter surveillance were met in April when Sir Amias Paulet was appointed her new guardian. Austere, totally impervious to his charge's wiles, Paulet tightened security to the point where Mary found it almost impossible to send or receive any letters, forcing her supporters to ever more desperate measures.

In December 1585, a trainee Catholic priest, Gilbert Gifford, was arrested at Rye on his arrival from France and confessed to having been sent to establish contact with Mary. In a brief interrogation, Walsingham spelled out Gifford's rather limited career options—turncoat or gallows. He opted for the former. With

Walsingham pulling all the strings, Gifford forwarded a message from the French embassy to the ecstatic Mary, who, believing she had an avenue of communication at last, grasped the opportunity with both hands.

News of this development enabled Elizabeth to chide the French ambassador. "You have much secret communication with the Queen of Scotland, but believe me, I know all that goes on in my kingdom."[31]

The Babington Plot

Deeply conscious of the virulent anti-Mary fever abroad in the land, Elizabeth gave Walsingham his head. In May 1586, his agents tracked another Catholic priest named John Ballard to a meeting with Anthony Babington, a wealthy northern supporter of Mary. Ballard assured Babington that a Spanish invasion of England was being prepared for that summer, and that to guarantee its success Elizabeth would have to be assassinated. Babington undertook to carry out the deed himself with the aid of some friends. As the plot reached a more advanced stage, he decided to take Mary into his confidence. A letter, dated July 6, outlined the coup's aims in unambiguous terms. Addressing Mary as "My dread Sovereign Lady and Queen," he wrote that "six noble gentlemen, all my private friends," would "dispatch the usurper,"[32] while he himself would rescue Mary from imprisonment and help her accede to the throne of England.

On July 17, in a coded letter, Mary sealed her own fate by openly endorsing the plot and sanctioning Elizabeth's murder.

Walsingham swooped. On August 4, Ballard was sent to the Tower, Babington and his cohorts panicked and went into hiding, and a few days later Mary was arrested. Her jailer, Paulet, received a letter from Elizabeth. "Let your wicked murderess know how with heavy sorrow her vile deserts compelleth these orders, and bid her from me ask God forgiveness for her treacherous dealings towards the savior of her life many a year, to the intolerable peril of my own."[33]

Within days Babington and his fellow plotters were rounded up, tried, and sentenced to death. Their subsequent execution was hideously barbaric—they were hanged, then castrated and disemboweled while still conscious—on the express orders of the wrathful Elizabeth, who was determined to set an example.

She was far less emphatic about Mary. Much as she hated her cousin, whom she regarded as an adulterous murderess, she had no wish to have her executed, fearing it would undermine her own authority. But her council members were now in a blood frenzy.

With the clamor for Mary to be tried for treason building non-stop, Elizabeth finally caved in, although right up to the eve of Mary's trial, which began October 12, 1586, at Fotheringay Castle, she was still throwing out lifelines, as the following letter makes clear:

To MARY, Queen of Scots

You have in various ways and manners attempted to take my life and to bring my kingdom to destruction by bloodshed. I have never proceeded so harshly against you, but have, on the contrary, protected and maintained you like myself. These treasons will be proved to you and all made manifest. Yet it is my will, that you answer the nobles and peers of the kingdom as if I were myself present. I therefore require, charge, and command that you make answer for I have been well informed of your arrogance.

Act plainly without reserve, and you will sooner be able to obtain favor of me.

ELIZABETH.[34]

After a two-day examination, during which Mary acquitted herself well, the court adjourned to convene again at London's Star Chamber on October 25, at which time Mary was convicted of treason. Both Houses of Parliament urged Elizabeth to pass sentence of death without delay.

Still she procrastinated. While her ministers tore at their hair in frustration, Elizabeth hedged for weeks, then months. She even wrote secretly to Mary, saying that if she confessed then her life might yet be spared. Mary flung the offer back in her face, unrepentant in her claims of innocence. In one last sly move, designed to absolve herself from public blame, Elizabeth even investigated the possibility of having Mary covertly murdered, so that her death could be announced as due to natural causes. When this plan foundered, on February 1, 1587, Elizabeth yielded to overwhelming pressure and signed the death warrant.

One week later, on the morning of February 8, Mary, Queen of Scots, was beheaded in the Great Hall at Fotheringay. She died bravely and well, seemingly relieved that her torment had come to an end.

All of London rejoiced on news of the execution; only Elizabeth appeared sad. Her grief and remorse, though genuine, were as much for herself as for Mary, for deep in her heart she believed she had violated God's law. To ward off the threat of retaliation from Europe, she deliberately affected to appear as ravaged as possible by emotion and regret, in hopes that her enemies would say that one so moved by the death of the Queen of Scots could not possibly have ordered it.

It was a vain and, as events proved, unnecessary ploy. Elizabeth's victory was absolute: after a quarter of a century she had finally eliminated her bête noir, a woman whom she never met, and it was time to savor the fruits of victory.

Few would deny Elizabeth's place in history as one of the first truly "modern women," emancipated, powerful, not just some sexual chattel, but a vibrant, independent ruler who left her country in far better shape than she found it. There can be no greater praise. By the time of her death on March 24, 1603, at the age of sixty-nine, she was universally regarded as one of England's greatest monarchs, loved by her subjects, lauded by poets and artists as Gloriana, the Virgin Queen.

Which brings us back to her battle with Mary. It stank of hypocrisy. In cynically using religious differences to mask what was an intensely personal feud—after all, had she not herself once said, "There is only one Christ Jesus and one faith; the rest is a dispute about trifles"?[35]—Elizabeth fooled no one. Had Mary been a frumpish pennyweight, she would hardly have deigned to notice her; but to a plainish monarch, grown fat on flattery, this Celtic enchantress, unattached and dangerous, took on a demonic form and had to be destroyed. In this Elizabeth succeeded brilliantly, even if she never quite eradicated the suspicion that like other powerful women in history, she found problems emanating from the opposite sex rather easier to solve than those arising from her own.

CHAPTER 2

Parliament versus Charles I

Years of feud:	1625–1649	
Names:	The Houses of Parliament	Charles Stuart
Strengths:	A rough-and-ready attempt at democracy, not bad by seventeenth-century standards	Immense personal courage
Weaknesses:	Unforgiving and vengeful	Woeful political judgment
At stake:	The Divine Right of monarchy	

Republicanism has been around an awfully long time. Ever since the Romans kicked out their last king around 509 B.C., clearing the way for history's first republic, the notion of representative or nominated government has held a powerful allure for peoples everywhere, yet for most of recorded history that dream has remained maddeningly elusive. In Europe only tiny San Marino—perched like an aerie atop the Apennine Mountains and entirely surrounded by Italy—bucked the trend. The system of government that it instituted in the fourteenth century exists to the present day, making it the oldest continuous republic in the world. Elsewhere it was the old familiar ragbag of kings, queens, potentates, tsars, emperors or kaisers that held sway. Magna Carta (1215) was an early attempt by some highly motivated English barons to rein in the sovereign's powers, but no single country tried seriously to overthrow a monarchical monopoly until the mid-seventeenth century, when the elected body of England posed the big question: who rules this country, king or Parliament?

On July 17, 1604, a royal cavalcade set out from Dunfermline in Scotland, bearing a rare and precious cargo. Prince Charles, three years old and the second son of the recently crowned king James I, was about to enter England for the first time. As the entourage meandered slowly south to the East Midlands, it passed within a few miles of the sleepy rural town of Huntingdon. There another youngster, eighteenth months older than the prince, was already taking preschool lessons from a governess, studying his Bible, perhaps practicing the florid copperplate handwriting that would one day have such a bearing on the young prince's life.

We don't know if the young Oliver Cromwell was aware of the momentous events unwinding just a horse ride from his home; more likely he had his mind on other things: raiding apple orchards, wrestling with his friends, hunting and fishing, all the usual pursuits of a robust young country boy.

Sadly, poor Charles was denied any such license. A sickly child with stunted limbs, his every waking hour was closely monitored, especially after his elder brother, Henry, died in 1612, catapulting the diminutive Charles into the unexpected role of heir to the English throne.

That succession came about in 1625, by which time, through a regime of rigorous physical exercise, Charles had shed the frailty of his youth to become an excellent horseman, a regular athlete. He was also diffident and reserved, traits much appreciated by subjects long weary of his dead father's knockabout boorishness. Most welcomed the transition. Now all the new king needed was a queen, and here Charles made his first mistake.

No one minded that Henrietta Maria, daughter of France's King Henry IV, was only fifteen when she became Charles's wife, or that the newlyweds seemed largely indifferent to each other—after all, royal marriages had always been more about contract than commitment—no, what troubled courtiers and populace alike was her faith: she was a staunch Catholic. Almost a century earlier, Henry VIII had severed all links with Rome and established the Church of England. It had been an uneasy schism, and as many worshipers soon found to their cost, Protestantism was a multihued faith: pick the wrong shade and life could be downright miserable, even fatal.

James I had thrown his weight behind Anglicanism, which in tone, vestment, and ritual was modeled closely on Rome. Down at the other end of the Protestant spectrum lay the gloomy Puritans, straitlaced and austere, rabidly opposed to any form of religious ostentation, convinced that pleasure was the invention of the Devil. Fun-loving James despised them and would, he gloated, harry them out of the land. Many, most notably the Pilgrim Fathers, took him at his word and abandoned England to settle in the New World.

James's death changed nothing. Those Puritans that remained were left to contend with an Anglican king who not only showed no disinclination to abandon his father's intolerance, but had married a queen who brazenly celebrated mass at court. Rumbles of discontent began to grow.

Public opinion didn't count for a jot with Charles. A dyed-in-the-wool "Divine Rightist," he intended to rule the country absolutely, with no limits to his power, much like the monarchs of France were doing. So far as Charles was concerned, he had been put on this planet by God to rule England and nothing would be allowed to come between himself and that belief, certainly not those elected upstarts at Westminster. When the new king faced his first Parliament in 1625, he walked into a bear pit, although most of the brickbats were aimed at the Duke of Buckingham, the hugely influential royal adviser Charles had inherited from his dead father. An inveterate meddler, especially in foreign affairs, Buckingham had now wrapped his tentacles around the impressionable king.

Figuratively, at least, Buckingham lingered in the shadows while Charles stood before Parliament and demanded that it grant him tonnage and poundage (an import/export tax) for life, as had been accorded to preceding monarchs. He badly needed the funds to make good on his promise to Henrietta's brother, King Louis XIII, to assist in the suppression of the chief Huguenot stronghold of La Rochelle, just one of the many bloodthirsty conflicts between Catholics and Protestants that had wracked Europe since the outbreak of the Thirty Years' War in 1618.

When Parliament thumbed its nose at Charles's demands, he angrily dissolved the assembly.

His dealings with the second Parliament (February 6–June 15,

1626) were no more fruitful. Dominating all other business was an attempt to impeach Buckingham, whose disastrous military exploits in Europe were threatening to bankrupt the nation. When the noted parliamentarian Sir John Eliot compared Buckingham with Sejanus, the homicidal favorite of the Roman emperor Tiberius, the implication was unmistakable. Intentionally or not—and it is hard to imagine that such a slur was accidental—Charles had been cast in the role of Tiberius the tyrant. It was an insult he never forgave. With relations worsening daily, Charles came to Buckingham's rescue by once again dismissing the legislature.

What followed was a sulky twenty-month hiatus, during which the country had no Parliament. Charles and Buckingham persisted in their flamboyant foreign policy, attempting to finance their foolishness with a mix of private loans and heavy-handed coercion that amounted to nothing more than mugging by monarchy. When five knights, thrown into jail for refusing to hand over money to the royal exchequer, applied for a writ of habeas corpus, Charles, anxious not to have the legality of his actions tested in open court, instructed the jailer to inform the knights they were incarcerated "by His Majesty's special commandment."[1]

It was a grievous blunder. Charles's political judgment—rarely astute—had failed him completely as furious members of Parliament (MPs) added complaints of arbitrary imprisonment to the old standby of arbitrary taxation.

Blinkered by his own stupidity and heartened by news that impeachment proceedings against Buckingham had been dropped, Charles, as always in urgent need of money, agreed to a third Parliament. When it met on March 17, 1628, the atmosphere fairly crackled with tension. Again and again MPs took the floor to complain that Charles's arrogance in policy matters amounted to a flagrant renunciation of Magna Carta, a dissatisfaction best captured by the leading parliamentarian, John Pym, who thundered, "There is no sovereign power but the law."[2]

The upshot of all this rancor was a Petition of Right, four simple demands that went to the heart of the Commons's grievances: no taxation without consent of Parliament; no imprisonment without due cause; no billeting of soldiers or sailors with householders against their will; and no martial law except for military offenses. Grudgingly Charles agreed to the petition, which, after a mammoth struggle in the Lords, finally passed both Houses in late May.

Bloody Murder

In the brief parliamentary recess that followed, anti-Buckingham sentiment reached a fever pitch and peaked on August 23, when a disgruntled army lieutenant, John Felton, stabbed England's most powerful statesman to death on the streets of Portsmouth, not for reasons of politics, but just because he, Felton, had been passed over for promotion.

While the country rejoiced and Charles grieved, Henrietta seized her chance. Hitherto theirs had been a loveless marriage; but now Charles needed her, especially her counsel. Capitulation to Parliament was not an option, she urged; fight them at all costs. It soon became apparent that the Petition of Right might as well not even exist, for all the heed that Charles paid it. Laws, not petitions, were needed to keep this monarch in check, or so most MPs reckoned. Six months of pent-up fury gushed out when, on January 23, 1629, the third Parliament reconvened at Westminster.

For the first time Charles faced Parliament without Buckingham. In the early rounds, he performed well—the stammer that had plagued him since childhood was in check, and he chose his words carefully—but when he renewed his demands for tonnage and poundage, parliamentary warning antennae twitched furiously. Frustrated and choleric, Charles began ordering peremptory adjournments whenever debates turned awkward, much to the chagrin of his opponents. When, on March 2, the Speaker told the House of Commons that the absent king had decreed yet another adjournment, bedlam erupted. Fights broke out, doors were locked, and two MPs ran to grab hold of the skedaddling Speaker, saying, "You shall sit till we please to rise!"[3]

Eventually, the Commons voted to adjourn until March 10. On that day Charles went to the House of Lords, and in a cunning, divisive speech, he drew a sharp distinction between the majority of "dutiful subjects" and those "few vipers" who had fomented this discord. After warning the assembled nobles that "those vipers must look for their reward of punishment,"[4] he once again dissolved Parliament.

Charles was in good spirits as he disrobed afterward, joking that never again would he don these ceremonial garments. Attendants noticed a new lightness in his attitude; he smiled more often than of late, delighted to have finally shrugged off the burdens of a meddlesome Parliament. Henceforth he would rule the country by Personal Rule.

Among the swarm of MPs who had watched this drama unfold from below the bar that separated the House of Commons from the House of Lords was the newly elected member for Hunting-don, a man already marked out by his religious zealotry, and a man who more than anyone else would come to embody the malignant feud between king and Parliament. Although those epochal events lay many years in the future, his fiery charisma had already caught the eye and ear. That same year one MP had taken a fellow member aside and pointed out the newcomer. "That slovenly fellow which you see before us, who hath no orna-ment in his speech: I say that sloven, if we should ever have a breach with the king (which God forbid) in such a case will be one of the greatest men of England."[5]

As political predictions go, it was one of the best.

Cromwell's Rise

There was nothing in Oliver Cromwell's background to suggest that here was someone who would change the course of world history. His beginnings were mundane, drab even. He was born into a modestly affluent Puritan family—his father was a farmer— on April 25, 1599, and other than the fact that he attended the local grammar school, very little is known of his childhood.

At age seventeen, like many young men of his social standing, he went to university—in his case, neighboring Cambridge—only to drop out a year later upon the death of his father. Sometime later he turned up in London, where he appeared to have acquired a smattering of law at one of the Inns of Court, although there is no evidence to suggest that he intended a career in law; rather, he was acquiring some basic legal knowledge essential for the gentleman farmer with land to manage.

While in London he met and married Elizabeth Bourchier, and after the ceremony, in August 1620, the newlyweds returned to Huntingdon to set up housekeeping. The children came in quick profusion, nine in all, with each new arrival only accentuating the precariousness of farming as a way of life. It was too mercurial, too reflexive for someone like Cromwell, who thrived on order and discipline. The endless belt-tightening and deprivation wore away his already meager reserves of optimism, and he plunged into the melancholia that would haunt him for the rest of his life.

Sometime in his late twenties, his mood didn't change but his ideas did, as beneath the wide-open fenland skies the doleful and indecisive young country squire underwent a religious conversion of Damascene proportions. Puritan piety was elbowed to one side by a burning fundamentalist zeal. Cromwell emerged from the experience as one of the "godly," hard-line Protestants dedicated to furthering (or completing) the Reformation begun by Henry VIII. "Blessed be His Name for shining upon so dark a heart as mine," he wrote later, adding his belief that God had made him His "chosen vessel."[6] Seized by a sense of divine destiny and resolved to stamp out forever the baneful influence—perceived or otherwise—of Catholicism, he put himself forward for election and gained a seat in the Parliament of 1628.

He joined Westminster at the most turbulent time in its history. As we have seen, discontent with Charles was near the boiling point, and it is significant that Cromwell's first recorded contribution to Parliament, a motion that the business of the king of Earth should play second fiddle to that of the king of Heaven, served only to inflame these tensions. As a commoner, Cromwell would have been barred from entering the chamber of the House of Lords when Charles came to speak on that momentous day in March 1629, but never in his wildest dreams could he have imagined that when the king's stinging harangue concluded, the doors would close on the Houses of Parliament, not to reopen for another eleven years.

Like most MPs, Cromwell returned home, to his farm in Huntingdon, and there we once again lose him in the mists of antiquity. Many myths have grown up around his activities in this period—berating drunks outside local inns, preaching brimstone-laden sermons to awestruck peasants—but the provable facts are scarce. What we do know is that he moved twice, first in 1631, when he was forced to sell his property in Huntingdon and lease a smaller farm in nearby St. Ives, and then again in 1636, when he inherited a large estate in Ely from his maternal uncle, Sir Thomas Steward. The legacy's principal benefit was to arrest what had been an alarming decline in Cromwell's fortunes. Now he was a considerable landowner, a man with plenty of clout in the community, and he intended milking that influence for all its worth.

Charles, too, had been improving his lot. Personal Rule suited him: financing royal activities through the selling of commercial monopolies and the occasional arbitrary tax hike allowed him to extricate the country from its prohibitively expensive overseas wars, setting the stage for a period of peaceful prosperity. Indeed, had Charles confined himself to secular matters, then fate might have rewarded him very differently, but he was a fussy monarch, obsessed with the spiritual well-being of his subjects, and that meant ramming Anglicanism, with all its popish overtones, down the throats of an increasingly Puritan population.

All at once non-Anglicans found themselves being whipped for their beliefs. But Charles's bullying tactics came a cropper when he tried to force the English Book of Common Prayer onto a predominantly Presbyterian Scottish population that wanted little to do with its neighbors to the south, and no part at all of Rome. When protest riots broke out in Edinburgh, Charles's response was typically dim and clumsy. Displaying the political naïveté that marred his entire reign, he bluntly ordered Scotland to accept the new book. Go to hell, was the response, coupled with a call to arms.

Although no all-out war ensued, a series of border skirmishes soon dissipated the funds that Charles had accumulated during ten years of financial prudence. Having grossly underestimated Scottish resolve and strength, and teetering on the brink of bankruptcy, he was forced to bite the bullet and issue a writ for a new Parliament.

It met on April 13, 1640. After some nifty carpetbagging,

Cromwell had managed to wangle himself a seat as a member for Cambridge, and he was again standing below the bar as Charles addressed the House of Lords with his demand for higher taxes to finance a military action against the recalcitrant Scots.

Parliament just snorted its contempt. The notion of sanctioning tax hikes to promote what they themselves so vehemently opposed was risible, and an avalanche of condemnation left the king in no doubt that he had backed a loser. The Short Parliament, as it became known, lasted just three hectic weeks until, thwarted at every turn, Charles ordered its dissolution.

Chaos ensued. As rioting spread across the land, churches were desecrated, terrified Catholics fled for their lives, then a Scottish army crossed the border on August 20, pushing southward with primeval ferocity, sweeping aside everything in its path. A hastily negotiated treaty did halt the Scots, but they were allowed to remain on English soil—at a cost of £850 a day to the English exchequer—until the final arrangements were made. Charles's hand was forced. Like it or not, the king needed Parliament—fast.

The so-called Long Parliament, which would sit for thirteen years, assembled on November 3. Over the next fourteen months it steadily dismantled all the powers that Charles had arrogated, steadfastly refusing to authorize any royal funding until the headstrong monarch was brought to heel. The Triennial Act (1641) assured the summoning of Parliament at least every three years, a formidable challenge to royal prerogative; while the Tudor institutions of fiscal feudalism (manipulating antiquated fealty laws to extract money), the Court of the Star Chamber and the Court of High Commission, were declared illegal. In a twinkling, power had shifted from the traditionally aristocratic House of Lords to the emerging middle-class House of Commons, composed mainly of merchants, tradesmen, and Puritans.

Charles's humiliation was compounded doubly by rumors that Pym was drawing up articles of impeachment against Henrietta for conspiring with Irish Catholics. Urged on by a wife in genuine fear for her life, Charles retaliated by impeaching Pym and four other MPs on charges of treason. On the night of January 4, 1642, backed up by an armed retinue, Charles entered the House of Commons—the first king to do so—to arrest the five suspects. The members stood aghast as Charles trampled generations of parliamentary privilege underfoot by striding into the chamber. "Gentlemen," he explained, "you must know that in cases of treason no person hath a privilege."[7]

Then he looked about him. Pym and company, forewarned by one of Henrietta's confidants, had made their escape by boat along the river. "I see all the birds are flown,"[8] Charles muttered weakly, unsure what to do next. Outmaneuvered, made to look hopelessly inept, he crept empty-handed from the chamber, his ears burning to derisive chants of "Privilege! Privilege! Privilege!"[9]

The streets of London were no less brutal, with crowds jeering the monarch at every turn. In order to escape the mob, Charles abandoned Whitehall for the comparative safety of Hampton Court. On that very day, January 10, Pym and his fellow MPs reentered the House of Commons to a rousing heroes' welcome.

Suddenly, even Hampton Court didn't feel so safe to the imperiled monarch, and after taking stock of his situation he rode for Dover. There he packed Henrietta and the crown jewels off to the Continent for safekeeping before returning to the outskirts of London, only to find the capital almost entirely in the hands of his enemies. Fast running out of options, Charles wheeled north, seeking to rally support as he rode.

Throughout spring and summer, the country polarized into either supporters of Parliament (small landowners and Puritans mainly) or defenders of the crown (aristocrats and Anglicans). Besides class and religious differences, the protagonists also split on roughly geographical lines, with the northern and western provinces aiding the king's supporters, or Cavaliers, while the more financially prosperous and populous southern and eastern counties rallied behind the parliamentary forces, which became known as Roundheads owing to their close-cropped haircuts.

Gradually, Charles mustered a three-thousand-strong army, and after roaming the country in search of an operational headquarters, he finally settled on Nottingham. On the blustery evening of August 22, 1642, the defiant monarch unfurled his standard against the forces of Parliament.

The Civil War had begun.

The First Civil War

When war broke out, Cromwell was a forty-three-year-old raw-boned farmer and minor politician, little known outside his hometown, yet within a decade this impulsive Puritan would be hailed as one of history's greatest military strategists, fit to stand comparison with Alexander, Hannibal, or Caesar. How Cromwell acquired this hitherto unsuspected battlefield brilliance has led many to wonder if he honed his combat skills fighting Catholics in Europe during the Thirty Years' War. It is a tempting speculation, nothing more.

Certainly his contemporaries had little idea of Cromwell's genius for warfare, for when the first great battle took place at Edgehill on October 23, the man from East Anglia was a lowly captain whose Huntingdon troop, comprising just sixty horse, watched impotently from the sidelines as the Royalist leader, Prince Rupert, led his cavalry in a dashing charge that gouged huge holes in the Roundheads' left wing. As the Roundheads scattered like chaff in the wind, the Cavaliers, instead of turning to rout the enemy infantry that remained, set off in whooping pursuit, an error that permitted the Roundheads—Cromwell's troops among them—to regroup and inflict heavy casualties on the Royalists. When nighttime fell, both sides were claiming victory, but on balance the day belonged to the Roundheads. The Royalist advance on London had been halted in its tracks.

Cromwell digested the day's events with an icy precision that he rarely brought to other aspects of his life. Hotheaded indiscipline had cost the Cavaliers a crushing victory, of that he was certain; if Parliament could somehow raise an army of dedicated and disciplined soldiers, the king might yet be beaten.

Chewing over this mouthwatering prospect, Cromwell returned home for the winter to help organize the Eastern England Army. He was a draconian disciplinarian, demanding and receiving absolute subservience from his men; he was not averse to administering stiff fines to soldiers who swore or got drunk, and publicly flogging anyone caught attempting to desert. Offsetting Cromwell's iron-fisted rule was his revolutionary disregard for military tradition. In Cromwell's army, talent, not bank balance, dictated the course of a man's career, which meant that lowly farmhands who displayed military initiative suddenly found themselves given command over men of much higher birth.

Cromwell was seeking a military meritocracy. And he got it.

For the most part, though, the summer of 1643 brought nothing but despondency to the parliamentarians. Their unity was fragile, based on an uneasy coalition between the hawks, who were willing to wage war until the last drop of Royalist blood was shed, and the doves, who were pushing for a negotiated settlement with the king. Cromwell, both feet firmly in the hawkish camp, provided what few moments of triumph that parliamentary troops enjoyed that grim summer as he revolutionized battlefield strategy. His favored tactic was to strike with his cavalry at the heart of the advancing army, smash through the lines, then wheel either left or right, milling the infantry into a disoriented mob, creating confusion and utterly destroying them.

His first test of strength had come in May 1643 at Grantham, in Lincolnshire. Tackling a Royalist army twice its size, Cromwell's force succeeded in routing the enemy, killing nearly 100 men and losing only 2.

Despite Cromwell's emergence as the premier military strategist on either side, morale slipped among most parliamentary troops as dismal weather and bad food began to sap their enthusiasm, already depleted by frequent and infuriating wage delays. Cromwell, nauseated by his pennypinching superiors, often resorted to paying his soldiers out of his own pocket, a munificence that, unsurprisingly, elevated him to near godlike status in their eyes. By September 1643, he had 1,400 men under his command.

Royalist fortunes, too, had been mixed. In July, Charles had been joined at Oxford by Henrietta, who in a five-month march from the north of England had amassed a sizable force to fight for the crown, and together, king and queen attempted to re-create Whitehall in the heart of the English countryside while blood seeped into the fields all around them. Some progress was made in the west, but by the winter of 1643 Charles was still holed up in Oxford, no nearer to capturing London than he had been one year earlier.

The new year brought a significant shift in the strategic balance of the war, when an army of twenty thousand Scots crossed into England, ready to fight for Parliament. Their irresistible advance unnerved Charles, who dispatched Prince Rupert north to relieve the city of York as it came under siege from the parliamentarians. Headstrong and inspirational, Rupert succeeded brilliantly, driving off the intruders; but instead of consolidating his position, he pursued the much larger parliamentary forces to Marston Moor, some seven miles to the west.

Here the two armies lined up for battle. Suddenly, across the fields of stubbly corn, came an eerie chorus, the sound of psalms bursting forth from the throats and hearts of the parliamentary forces. Rupert looked up. "Is Cromwell there?"[10] he asked anxiously, clear indication of the fear generated by the farmer turned fighter. In just eighteen months Cromwell had been promoted from captain to lieutenant general, and now the Civil War's undisputed battlefield master tactician had galloped to Marston Moor, ready to urge his men forward. Rupert knew he was in for the fight of his life.

The battle began on July 2 and lasted barely two hours. In the ferocious hand-to-hand fighting, Cromwell sustained a neck wound from a pistol shot fired at such close range that he was temporarily blinded by the flash of exploding gunpowder. Though stunned and momentarily incapacitated, he refused to leave the battle and soon regrouped his men to attack the Royalist cavalry from the rear, eventually driving them from the field.

It was the bloodiest day of the Civil War, with nearly four thousand Cavaliers dead and a further one thousand taken prisoner. Those Royalists that did escape the horrors of Marston Moor fled south to rejoin Charles as the monarch retreated to lick his wounds.

Cromwell's heroic indefatigability earned him the nickname "Ironsides," a term of admiration that was soon extended to all the men under his command. He threatened to sweep all before him, and yet with total victory in sight he found himself balked by a combination of vacillation and petty jealousy. When Cromwell tried to press his commanding officer, the Earl of Manchester, into adopting a more aggressive strategy, he was fobbed off with the excuse "If we beat the king ninety-nine times, yet he is still the king . . . but if the king best us once we shall all be hanged."[11]

"If this be so," Cromwell spat contemptuously, "why did we take up arms at first?"[12]

It was a reasonable question. Unfortunately Manchester, like many parliamentarians, wanted a negotiated settlement, whereas Cromwell demanded a more radical solution, dead set against any arrangement that permitted Charles to reestablish an absolute monarchy.

Extraordinary as it may sound, in between battlefield heroics, Cromwell would don his political cap and return to the even more treacherous waters of the House of Commons, where his endless tirades against governmental shilly-shallying served only to widen the breach between Parliament and the army.

Eventually, a compromise was cobbled together that stopped the bickering overnight. The Self-Denying Ordinance, passed on April 3, 1645, obliged military commanders to resign their seats in Parliament. Cromwell, unwilling to abandon his increasing influence as a politician, opted to stay at Westminster, but his eyes must have glittered with anticipation when creation of the New Model Army was announced.

Parliament Gets Its Army

Funded by regular, assured taxes and consisting of 24,000 troops, the New Model Army would be a national force loyal to Parliament alone, and with a disciplinary structure that replicated Cromwell's blueprint exactly. Under the provisions of the new law, Cromwell, as an MP, was barred from taking command of the army; that honor went to Sir Thomas Fairfax, an old and trusted ally, but by the strangest of coincidences, Cromwell's former post of lieutenant general was left conveniently vacant.

News of this New Model Army reduced Charles and his generals to hoots of derisive laughter. The notion that ill-bred fighting men, no matter how well trained, could defeat aristocratic Royalists was just too absurd to contemplate, and as the opposing forces neared each other at Northampton in June, that Royalist confidence seemed well placed. Cromwell's absence had sent panic through the New Model Army. The call went out. No Hollywood screenwriter could have scripted it better. In the nick of time, the great general galloped in at the head of six hundred horse, to a huge roar from the assembled troops. *"Ironsides is come!"*[13]

Across a shallow valley Charles, in full armor, also rode

proudly before his legions, exhorting them to sell their lives dearly if necessary. He and Cromwell squared off boldly. On the morrow, these two unshrinking titans, each convinced he was God's chosen instrument, would decide a nation's destiny on a few acres of soil called Naseby.

Despite an overwhelming numerical advantage, the New Model Army began badly. At the outset, it was a virtual rerun of Edgehill: Rupert's cavalry cut a swath through the parliamentary ranks, until once again overexuberance got the better of them. While the Cavaliers pursued their quarry far beyond the battlefield, Cromwell bided his time, then ordered his better disciplined parliamentary horse to charge the opposite flank. Once they got in behind the Royalist infantry, it became a massacre. Sabers, pikestaffs, muskets, all took a dreadful toll as the earth ran crimson. Hundreds were cut down. By the time Rupert's exhausted cavalry panted back, the battle was already lost. Realizing the hopelessness of their position, the remaining Cavaliers ran for their lives, as did the king.

Although Charles lost the battle, most of his army, and great personal wealth as well, most damaging of all was the capture of private papers that revealed his secret negotiations with Irish troops, irrefutable proof that the Protestant king had been conspiring with Catholics.

Naseby was Cromwell's finest hour, and he harbored not a scintilla of doubt as to where the credit lay. In a letter to Parliament, which was also read in churches in and around London, he wrote: "This [victory] is none other but the hand of God; and to Him alone belongs the glory."[14] Victorious generals are always popular, and soon a cult of Cromwellism sprang up, with one parliamentary newspaper lauding him as the "active and gallant commander Lieutenant General Cromwell,"[15] before going on to describe the awe in which other MPs viewed the Roundhead leader.

Though Charles held out for another year, Naseby effectively crushed the Royalist cause, and the surrender came in June 1646. But when exultant Roundhead troops entered Oxford expecting to nab their quarry at last, they were flabbergasted to find him gone, off to Scotland, from where he continued to barter for the most favorable terms.

Implacably opposed to any negotiated settlement with the

artful monarch, Cromwell relinquished his military command for the cut and thrust of politics, but he had no stomach for the pointless, petty factionalism that was the lifeblood of Westminster and only succeeded in rekindling his depression. He tumbled into a torpor that dragged on for months, made worse by reports that Parliament had refused to address a string of mainly financial grievances advanced by his former army colleagues. Now that the New Model Army had achieved the government's purpose, their ungrateful paymasters wanted nothing more to do with it.

At the same time, Cromwell watched moodily as the moderates conjured up ever more tortuous means of trying to settle with the troublesome monarch. So far as he was concerned, too much blood had been shed for Parliament to countenance anything else except total surrender.

Charles's shiftiness was also beginning to get under Scottish skins. Once they realized that he had no intention of adopting Presbyterianism, as had been hinted, they washed their hands of him. In February 1647, aware that his position had become untenable, Charles surrendered himself into parliamentary custody, only then to be abducted by a group of disaffected army officers, headed by George Joyce, who were looking for some political leverage in their ongoing dispute with Westminster. Joyce set out his complaints in a letter to Cromwell, informing him what they had done.

On June 4, Cromwell rode to Childersley, near Cambridge, and there, in a garden, vanquished king and victorious general came face-to-face for the first time. They eyed each other appraisingly. Charles decided he had little to fear; in spite of his parlous situation and diminutive stature, he retained a certain regal elegance that the rough-hewn Cromwell could never hope to match. When Cromwell tried to distance himself from Joyce's strong-arm kidnapping tactics, the king just laughed. "Unless you hang up Joyce, I will not believe what you say!"[16]

Despite his heartfelt contempt for monarchy in general, Cromwell found that he liked Charles personally, and he was later moved to tears when he witnessed the king being reunited with his children. Yet he continued to distrust him, as did Parliament, which dispatched the king to Hampton Court.

From his writings it is clear that the worst Charles feared was forced abdication—reflected in his efforts to guarantee the succession of his son, the Prince of Wales—and his first few months of leisurely incarceration seemed to bear out this belief. But slowly opinion hardened against him, with Cromwell especially fast losing patience with the king's endless equivocation. Charles, fearing for his life, began to hatch plots.

King Flees Palace

On November 11, he made his escape from Hampton Court with such facility that many suspected a parliamentary lifeline had been tossed out, in expectation or hopes that the royal annoyance would take his mischief to the Continent. Unfortunately for all concerned, he reappeared at Carisbrooke Castle, in the Isle of Wight, and from there, in what amounted to virtual semicaptivity, he continued his tiresome negotiations. News in January 1648 that Parliament had passed a vote of No More Addresses to the King forced a rethink. Escape, this time to much farther afield, now dominated royal thoughts.

Not that Charles was entirely friendless. By spring his position looked brighter. A sympathetic army had been raised in Scotland, ready to cross the border in his support; Irish troops had promised help; and a popular uprising was under way in Wales. Almost without anyone noticing, the country slid into yet another civil war.

For the second time in under a decade, brother fought brother and families were torn asunder as king and Parliament renewed their opposition on the battlefield. The outbreak of hostilities in March 1648 sparked calls, soon answered, for the mighty Cromwell to resume command of the army, and he quickly demonstrated that he had lost none of his martial effectiveness. After easily suppressing the Royalist uprising in Wales, he rode hard northward to repel the invading Scottish army. A series of running battles through the month of August culminated with Cromwell finally shattering the dispirited and divided Scots at Preston. As usual, his dispatch to Parliament was fulsome in its claims of divine intervention.

Superficially, the victory did seem miraculous, considering the

Scots' numerical superiority. As Cromwell wrote, "Only give me leave to add one word, showing the disparity of forces [21,000 Scots vs. 8,600 English] . . . that you may see and all the world acknowledge the hand of God in this business."[17] In truth, English success owed more to Scottish ineptitude than to divine intervention, but the effect on public opinion of a such a victory, achieved against such odds, was incalculable.

It was a brief, bloody war that marked the end of organized Royalist resistance in England, and yet it hardly changed a thing as Charles continued to shift and twist with foxlike cunning. On December 1, the patience of the army snapped and Fairfax sent a body of troops to remove Charles from the Isle of Wight and bear him across the Solent to Hurst Castle.

Yet another ominous indicator of the army's newfound strength came five days later, when a Colonel Thomas Pride prevented Presbyterian members from entering the House of Commons. With the army flexing its governmental muscle and ready to push through its own agenda, no peaceful solution involving the king seemed possible and talk of criminal indictment was on everyone's lips. One London broadsheet openly questioned who should succeed the disgraced monarch. "For (say the Saints) shall not we be happy when we ourselves make choice of a good and upright man to be king over us?"[18] Fairfax or Cromwell? Both were "honorable and victorious [men], in whom God hath miraculously manifested his presence,"[19] but the sheer magnitude of Cromwell's colossal personality and achievements tipped the scales overwhelmingly in his favor. Nor was he disinclined to be swept along by the tidal wave of extremism that he himself had unleashed. Every drop of his previously held respect for Charles had evaporated in the face of endless royal chicanery. Now Cromwell wanted the king dead. Nothing else would do.

On December 17, Charles was bundled into Windsor Castle, which had been converted into a prison for captured Cavaliers. While he was there the mood in London darkened nastily. An incendiary sermon preached at Westminster by Hugh Peter first compared certain army leaders to Moses, then implored them to "root up monarchy, not only here, but in France and other kingdoms round about."[20]

This belligerence was echoed by the Commons when, on January 1, 1649, it passed an ordinance charging that the king be tried for treason on grounds that he had waged war against Parliament and the country. First, the ordinance had to pass the House of Lords. By its inherent nature this aristocratic arm of the legislature was more favorably disposed to the monarch, so few were surprised when it rejected the motion out of hand.

The Commons, determined to assert its primacy, retaliated by passing the bill a second time, together with an ordinance establishing a High Court of Justice of commissioners, parliamentarians, and soldiers to try the king.

King Tried for Treason

At its first meeting on January 8, only 52 commissioners were present out of the 135 originally summoned, less than an quorum. When someone pointed out this discrepancy to Cromwell, his fearsome temper erupted. "I tell you we will cut off his head with the crown upon it!"[21]

But others, too, doubted the commission's legitimacy. Many had stayed away. Even Cromwell's old ally, Fairfax, was absent, as were all the prominent lawyers of the time. Only John Bradshaw, a legal lightweight from the north of England, was willing to chair the dubious proceedings.

On January 19, a coach and six brought Charles from Windsor Castle to London and the lofty splendor of Westminster Hall. Rumors of a Royalist attempt to free the king led to tight security measures: cellars were searched for bombs; guards were posted on roofs; Bradshaw even had his hat reinforced with metal plates!

Into this cauldron stepped King Charles I. Dressed entirely in black, except for his white collar and cuffs, he picked his way daintily to the dock that had been specially prepared for him out of public view, and listened as Solicitor General John Cook listed the charges of high treason, recounting a litany of battles from the civil wars and Charles's attempts to further Royalist aims.

When Cook was done, Charles sniffed his disdain, demanding to know by what authority he had been brought here. "I am your king. I have a trust committed to me by God, by old and lawful descent. I will not betray that trust to a new unlawful authority."[22]

Asked to plead, Charles refused. For him the issues were clear-cut: the king was God's representative on earth and the

Bible called upon all subjects to obey their king. He refused to recognize this illegal court.

In the often brutal exchanges that followed, one of the commissioners, Colonel John Hewson, rushed forward and cried out "Justice!"[23] then spat in the king's face.

"Well, sir," remarked Charles, wiping away the insult, "God hath justice in store for both you and me."[24]

The next day Bradshaw again attempted to get Charles to respond to the charge, but when the defendant launched yet another round of delaying tactics, he was hauled bodily, yelling at the top of his lungs, from the chamber while the commissioners decided what should be done with him.

All eyes fell on Cromwell. Although he was the most powerful commissioner in attendance, he had taken little verbal part in the trial, but his was always the hand at the tiller. By Friday he had bludgeoned the court into acquiescence—sentence would be passed next day.

On January 27, Charles was brought back into Westminster Hall to hear his fate. As Bradshaw began to read aloud the verdict, a masked woman in the gallery cried out, "It is a lie . . . Oliver Cromwell is a tyrant!"[25]

Every head turned. Cromwell thought he recognized the voice as that of Lady Fairfax, wife of his fellow general, but the woman escaped in the melee. Murmurs of unease filled the great hall. All through the tribunal Cromwell had fought, at times unsuccessfully, to maintain a quorum, and now matters threatened to spiral out of control. When a fellow commissioner, John Downes, pleaded for some compromise to be reached with the king, Cromwell's exasperation got the better of him. Charles was, he roared, "the hardest-hearted man on earth," and then he redirected his bile toward the trembling Downes, branding him "a peevish, troublesome fellow."[26]

Poor Downes just dissolved in tears.

Cromwell was terrifying in his implacability. He was "God's instrument," and the iron will that had catapulted him from rural obscurity to international prominence in scarcely a decade, that enabled him to crush armies and topple dynasties, was merciless. There would be no compromise, no backtracking, no arguments, no king.

That same day Charles was sentenced to death. In all, fifty-nine names were appended to the death warrant. Cromwell's signature, firmly written unlike some, came third on the list, while others complained that he had grabbed hold of several reluctant commissioners and physically forced their trembling hands to sign.

On January 30, Charles stepped from a window at the Banqueting Hall in Westminster onto a wooden scaffold that had been draped in black. He remained defiant to the end, proclaiming his unshakable belief in the right of monarchy, declaring, "A subject and a sovereign are clean different things."[27]

Then he laid his head on the block.

That night, so the story goes, Cromwell, his face hidden by a cloak, went to view the king's mutilated corpse. Gazing down into the coffin, he is reputed to have muttered, "Cruel necessity."[28] It is hard to imagine any truth in this tale. In those final days Cromwell's pursuit of the ultimate penalty for Charles bore all the hallmarks of monomania—indeed, without his bullying, it remains moot whether the tribunal would have ordered the king's execution—which makes the notion of a regretful Cromwell frankly unbelievable. He had inherited Parliament's feud with the king and made it a bitter personal crusade: God had decided to work through him, and that was an end to it. All that was left now was to finish the job.

Literally at a stroke, the British political landscape changed overnight. As undisputed leader of the Commonwealth, Cromwell soon acquired as much, if not more, executive power as the monarch he had deposed. In December 1653, he accepted the title Lord Protector of the Realm, and only after considered and considerable deliberation did he decline the offer of the crown. Not that it mattered: in all but name Oliver Cromwell was king.

He remains an enigma, schizophrenic almost. An advocate of tolerance within the Protestant faith, he had an abhorrence of Catholicism that lurched into the fanatical and led him to slaughter thousands in Ireland, sowing seeds of hatred that would fester for centuries. Like Charles he wrangled with Parliament, and like the dead monarch he dissolved the legislature when it suited him. Power was both seductive and destructive, and he soon found himself bombarded with cries of "Tyrant!" and "Traitor to the Revolution," and as the criticism grew sharper, more vitriolic, he retreated from public life. His later years were blighted by the depression that had always diminished his life. Now it deepened into darkest despair.

Cromwell died on September 3, 1658, as much from disillusionment as anything. Earlier this scourge of monarchy had boasted that were he ten years younger, "There was not a king in Europe I would not make to tremble,"[29] but he did think enough of one Royalist tradition—succession—to ensure that his son, Richard, would assume the mantle of Lord Protector. It was a disaster for all concerned. Unable to escape from the shadow of his father—who could?—he survived barely a year before scampering off to the Continent, thus heralding the restoration of Charles II to the throne in 1660.*

England's flirtation with republicanism was brief yet momentous. In time the violent dislocations of 1642–1660 would lay the groundwork for a fledgling America to shrug off an unwanted oppressor, and encourage other European nations, most notably France and Russia, to follow in England's footsteps and bloodily dispose of unwanted monarchies. But for now the great revolutionary experiment was over.

Had it not been for Charles's pigheaded intransigence, none of this might have happened. A subtler, more thoughtful monarch would have yielded a bit here, gained a tad there; instead, he chose confrontation and paid a dreadful price.

As for Cromwell, while he undoubtedly changed the course of world history, he changed his own country surprisingly little. The relationship between Britain and its monarchs has always been turbulent and will probably continue to remain so; but despite all the squabbling, there is a coziness and familiarity to the crown that seems to suit the British psyche, perhaps fueled by a suspicion that when it comes to spawning tyrants, the ballot box and the bluebloods are running neck and neck.

---

*On January 29, 1661, Cromwell's corpse was exhumed and decapitated. The head was impaled on a pole and exhibited outside Westminster Hall, until finally decomposing in 1684.

CHAPTER 3

Burr versus Hamilton

Years of feud:	1791–1804	
Names:	Aaron Burr Jr.	Alexander Hamilton
Strengths:	Conciliatory, a masterful political campaigner	The ultimate Renaissance Man, who found all things easy
Weaknesses:	Sneaky as a rattler and just as venomous	Pompous, intolerant, hypocritical
At stake:	The U.S. presidency	

History has dealt a kindly hand to the Founding Fathers. In the popular imagination they remain a rosy-cheeked, avuncular bunch, wholesome and heroic, selflessly devoted to the common good. Too often the greatness of their achievement has obscured the fact that many of the central players were hard-bitten political horse traders of immense hubris and ambition, with back-stabbing skills to rival anything found in the Roman Senate. If the hurly-burly of American Revolutionary politics was one of rhetoric, reason, and rigorous debate, then it was also a time of vicious score-settling.

With so many supercharged egos in direct competition, feuds flowered at the drop of a hat. Plots were hatched, careers were ruined, sometimes even blood was spilled. Decidedly, it was not a time for the fainthearted. A nation was being forged, and the direction that nation should take was a constant source of dispute. In the violent bickering that followed, one voice was heard louder and more eloquently than any other.

Alexander Hamilton has strong claims to be considered the cleverest person yet spawned by the American political system. Writer, lawyer, soldier, philosopher, politician, he performed all these tasks with an effortless insouciance that made contemporaries blink in amazement. Even the formidable Thomas Jefferson—no slouch in the polymath stakes—was overawed, muttering to James Madison in 1795: "Hamilton is really a colossus . . . without numbers, he is a host within himself."[1]

Being so clever did have its drawbacks. In the first place, hardly anyone outside his family seems to have liked him. Nourished by a keen appreciation of his own brilliance, he made enemies as easily as breathing. Jefferson, Madison, John Adams, James Monroe, even his former mentor, George Washington, all fell foul of this prickly genius. So far as Adams was concerned, Hamilton would always be that "bastard brat of a Scotch peddler."[2] Hamilton soaked up more than his share of barbs, in the knowledge that when it came to trading insults he could spear all comers with gimlet sharpness. He wounded nobody, however, quite so often or with such malice as the man who would become the third vice president of the United States, Aaron Burr Jr.

Woodrow Wilson once said of Burr, he had "genius enough to have made him immortal, and unschooled passion enough to have made him infamous,"[3] and it is hard to disagree with that assessment. In the end, greatness passed him by and he had to settle for notoriety. It could have, and should have, been so much more. Born into the patrician class—his father was the second president of Princeton University—Burr could trace his lineage back to the Puritan settlers, usually a cast-iron guarantee of induction into the close-knit political circles of the times. Yet throughout his career Burr remained an outsider. Those searching to explain the serpentine twists and feints that hallmarked his career point to his troubled childhood. Always a sickly child, at age two he was orphaned, then farmed out to his uncle, a sadist whose warped notions of parental guidance often resulted in the lad being "beaten like a sack,"[4] so often, in fact, that absconding from home became a way of life.

He was formidably clever, and at age thirteen he entered the College of New Jersey (later Princeton) to study theology, became one of its most brilliant students, and graduated with distinction three years later, in 1772. Temperamentally unsuited to the sacrifices of the cloth, he abandoned the clergy after a couple of years in favor of law, only to have his legal career stymied in April 1775, when the minutemen clashed with British troops at Lexington, plunging America into a fight for its very existence.

War suited Burr; he was very good at it. By the age of twenty-one his dashing skills as a field officer had earned him promotion to the rank of lieutenant colonel, though this scarcely satisfied his vaulting ambition and led directly to numerous clashes with the commander in chief, George Washington, whom he despised as a semiliterate slave owner and planter. Burr served with distinction until ill health forced his resignation in 1779. When fit enough to do so, he resumed his legal studies in Albany.

After raising eyebrows by marrying Theodosia Prevost, the widow of a British officer, in 1782, Burr moved to New York City, where he carved out a lucrative law practice and made important political connections, so that within six months he was elected to the state assembly. It remains an anomaly of Burr's career that he was rather better at seeking office than wielding power. Although he was an active member of the assembly, his efforts were strangely ineffectual, so that it comes as no surprise to find him, at the expiration of his term, returning to the practice of law.

He thrived in the hothouse of the New York bar. A masterly technician, skilled in stripping down a case to its nuts and bolts, always searching for that elusive thread upon which to hang his argument, Burr was a dynamic performer. Whatever he lacked in physical presence—he was shortish and of slender build—he more than made up for in magnetic appeal. Juries were first hypnotized by his "bright, black and piercing" eyes,[5] then seduced by the plausibility of his brief. Success brought great rewards for the young advocate. Although his fees were high, he spent lavishly, and with his wife practically an invalid and requiring constant medical treatment, it meant that he was forever embarrassed by money woes. Negotiations for loans and adjustments of debt were daily chores, and it required most of his boundless energy to keep the family's financial head above water. Such industry meant that between 1794 and 1800 he figured prominently in almost every significant case to arise in New York.

So did Alexander Hamilton.

In character and background, no two men could have been more dissimilar. Unlike Burr, all suavity and sensuous allure, Hamilton was tetchy, famously impatient, and he had no advantages of birth. His had been a struggle from day one. Even the exact year of his birth is uncertain, though most scholars plump for 1755. He was born on the West Indies island of Nevis, the son of Rachel Fawcett Lavine and a rascally Scottish merchant named James Hamilton, who disappeared in 1765. The circumstances of Hamilton's birth were to haunt him all his life. Illegitimacy at this time carried an almost insuperable social stigma, and nothing says more for his extraordinary talents and fortitude than the fact that he was able to, if not quite shrug off this blight, then at least oblige others to look beyond it.

Impressing people was his stock-in-trade. As a youth his prodigious intelligence prompted awestruck neighbors to raise funds in order that he might further his education in America, and in 1774 he entered King's College (now Columbia University), his mind already bubbling with the brewing revolt against Britain.

Not yet out of his teens, Hamilton wrote several widely read pro-Whig pamphlets that stamped his name indelibly on the political map. After the upheaval of Lexington and Concord, when argument gave way to action, he joined the New York Artillery Company with the rank of captain. Two years later, Washington plucked Hamilton from out of the pack, made him an aide-de-camp, and promoted him to the rank of lieutenant colonel.

At a stroke Hamilton had been fast-tracked for success. Unrivaled access to the C-in-C and other members of Washington's inner circle placed him at the epicenter of those tumultuous times and made him an object of jealousy. It also meant he was in the loop when Washington was tangling with the overconfident Colonel Burr, an experience that granted him an early taste of Burr's erratic temperament.

Hamilton was a firecracker, quick-witted and even quicker to take offense. Small in stature, with reddish hair, he burned with high-octane energy, almost manic in his pursuit of status and fame. A brilliant marriage on December 14, 1780, to Elizabeth Schuyler, daughter of General Philip Schuyler, a scion of one of New York's snootiest Dutch dynasties, did wonders for his shaky social status and helped subdue the vicious whispering campaign aimed at his origins. They eventually had eight children.

In 1781, after a spat with Washington, he took a command position under Lafayette in the Yorktown, Virginia, campaign before resigning his commission that November. He then read law at Albany. By 1783, he had established a law office in New York, where he soon became one of that city's finest legal practitioners.

Hamilton's oratorical gifts and reasoning abilities were little short of wondrous, and in an age that set great store by the spoken word, he had few peers—certainly not Aaron Burr. The two clashed often. And yet, oddly enough, in the battle to win over the jury, it was Burr, the plutocrat, who had the greater understanding of human nature and invariably gained the upper hand over his more eloquent rival. A contemporary noted their varying styles: "Hamilton addressed himself to the head only . . . [Burr] first enslaved the heart, and then led captive the head."[6]

Courtroom Battles

Their courtroom confrontations were always tense affairs. Even when representing the same side, which happened often, there was an edginess to the alliance that kept everyone on tenterhooks. Outside the courtroom it was no contest: Hamilton's overpowering intellect kept him at the forefront of post-Revolutionary politics and left Burr trailing in the dust. He was also contemptuous of Burr's bottomless malleability, discerning in it a lack of integrity that he found profoundly distasteful. Gradually, whatever shred of initial grudging respect Hamilton may have felt for his rival was eroded by a deep and lasting distrust.

The 1780s belonged indisputably to Hamilton. A member of the Continental Congress in 1782–1783, he became a vigorous advocate of a strong central government. Then came his most enduring achievement. In collaboration with John Jay and James Madison, he penned a series of letters to the New York press, which were later published in book form in 1788. Of the eighty-five papers in *The Federalist,* fifty-one were written by Hamilton, and the book remains a classic in political science and the mechanics of republican government.

Clearly, Washington couldn't afford to have such talent idling on the bench, which is why in 1789 the newly inaugurated president set aside all personal grievances and appointed Hamilton secretary of the treasury. By coincidence, that same year Burr achieved his first significant public office when Governor George Clinton of New York appointed him attorney general, but this was small beer indeed compared to the weighty problems that Hamilton had inherited.

Independence had been costly. America's post-Revolution finances were in a mess, with millions of dollars in war debt and competitive tariffs between states that hampered economic growth and fostered political discord. In a series of reports Hamilton authored a program designed to shape a powerful, industrial nation. Among his more controversial proposals was the establishment of a national bank, a suggestion guaranteed to cause palpitations to those archproponents of states' rights, Jefferson and Madison.

They flew at Hamilton like scalded alley cats, scorning him as a closet monarchist, a parvenu whose heart was not fully committed to the republican cause. Hamilton sniffed his disdain. Having spent his youth outside the American colonies, he was unfettered by the intense state or regional loyalties that bedeviled so many of his Virginian colleagues; in his view, it was America first, individual states a very distant second. And as for Jefferson and Madison and all those other tiresome Democratic-Republicans, they could all take a hike; he had an economy to run and he intended running it his way alone. Eventually, Hamilton's habit of playing fast and loose with treasury rules would have calamitous personal repercussions, but for now he was inviolate, the natural successor to Washington, or so he thought.

Two years into his term as treasury secretary, a rare cloud darkened his personal horizon when his father-in-law, General Schuyler, was ousted from the post of New York senator, which was then offered to none other than Aaron Burr. Hamilton saw red. Convinced that Burr, skulking in the wings, had stage-managed the coup, Hamilton never forgave him and from that moment the hitherto unspoken hostility between the two erupted into open warfare.

Burr's senatorial career was lackluster. Hated by Hamilton, distrusted by Clinton, he was also rejected by Washington, who dismissed calls for the openly Francophile Burr to be appointed as minister to France and dispatched Monroe instead. Harking back to his subordinate's earlier criticism, Washington also denied Burr the use of official documents that he wished to consult preparatory to writing a history of the Revolutionary War.

In all these setbacks, as so often throughout his career, Burr detected or imagined the hand of Hamilton, and with some justification. In the vipers' nest of late eighteenth-century politics, allegiances and enmities were endlessly flexible, and as much as he loathed Jefferson, Hamilton hated Burr more, intriguing nonstop to foment unrest between the Democratic-Republican leader and the freshman senator. To this end, Hamilton enlisted all manner of unlikely allies, Monroe and Madison included, but through it all Burr's fancy political footwork never let him down. Not only did he survive Hamilton's covert onslaught; he prospered, garnering the support of many Federalists as well as Democratic-Republicans.

From the published correspondence of both men it appears as though Burr was largely unaware of Hamilton's vicious hostility; but it should be remembered that Burr was crafty down to his bootstraps. There was little profit to be gained by badmouthing Hamilton in print; besides, it is entirely possible, even likely, that his literary reticence masked a full awareness of what was going on, as subsequent events would demonstrate.

Hamilton, meanwhile, still had Washington's ear, even more so after 1793, when Jefferson, exasperated beyond endurance by Hamilton's insufferable arrogance, resigned from the cabinet. As Hamilton's star soared, Burr suffered a jolting setback.

The death of his wife in 1794, although not unexpected, shook him to the marrow. What part his countless extramarital affairs played in her decline must remain a matter for conjecture, but judging from the depth of his grief, one can detect a heavy tinge of guilt in Burr's devastation. The most immediate outcome was to draw him even closer to his beloved daughter, also named

Theodosia, with whom he enjoyed an unusually close relationship. While Burr wrestled with personal tragedy, Hamilton went from strength to strength. As the fulcrum of Washington's cabinet, he reached the pinnacle of his power and influence, advising on and directing a wide range of foreign and domestic policy. But the knives were being sharpened. In the press he was depicted as a monster, a nascent Caesar intent on overthrowing the republic and establishing a monarchy, with himself as sovereign ruler. Even more ominously, the Democratic-Republicans pursued allegations that Hamilton and his Federalist cronies had used the Treasury Department and the Bank of the United States for personal gain. They demanded access to financial records, which Hamilton provided; although they did show certain sketchy dealings, the smoking gun that would prove outright fraud was absent, and Hamilton weathered the storm.

Where political enemies failed, family commitments succeeded as mounting debts forced Hamilton to resign from the Treasury Department in 1795 and resume his law practice, not that he had the slightest intention of relinquishing any political clout. Inevitably, though, his power waned. An early indicator of his declining influence came in the 1796 election, when he toiled fruitlessly to prevent fellow Federalist and longtime rival John Adams from gaining the presidency. Even more galling for the disappointed Hamilton, his archenemy, Aaron Burr, used this forum to make the transition from local to national figure. His fourth place in the presidential race didn't look that great on paper, but it definitely marked him as a coming man—if only he could stay solvent. Like Hamilton, Burr was drowning in a sea of debt; numerous speculative land deals had gone sour, forcing him into "the hands of usurers."[7]

Having been thwarted in his attempt to deny Adams the presidency, a vengeful Hamilton now sought to exercise his influence secretly within the cabinet. But crisis loomed as all the financial legerdemain he had employed to juggle the nation's books now came back to haunt him, giving his enemies a priceless opportunity to finish him off for good.

In 1797, a journalist published a story that while he was treasury secretary, Hamilton had colluded with a financial schemer named James Reynolds in a string of highly dubious business ventures. Quoting Reynolds as his source, the journalist asserted that Hamilton had skimmed government funds in order to speculate in the financial market. Hamilton's riposte was quick and astonishing. After hotly denying any allegation of financial chicanery with Reynolds, he caused a sensation by declaring, "My real crime is an amorous connection with [Reynolds's] wife . . . with his . . . connivance . . . brought on by a combination between the husband and wife with the design to extort money from me."[8]

The story Hamilton told was fantastic. It had all begun, he claimed, in the summer of 1791, when he had been staying in Philadelphia. One day a distraught young woman had come knocking at his door, begging him for the coach fare back to New York. Being a good Christian, Hamilton felt conscience-bound to assist a troubled soul in her hour of need and extended a warm welcome. Although he declined to elaborate on the more dubious circumstances of this meeting—rumors persisted that the couple's first assignation had occurred much earlier—suffice it to say that the voluptuous Maria Reynolds delayed her return to New York in order to attend to the treasury secretary's more earthy concerns.

Middle-aged and gullible, Hamilton was a sitting duck as the affair degenerated into a classic "badger game" sting. Sure enough, summer's hot romance cooled in the chill of fall, then turned downright icy in December when Maria's husband, James, suitably outraged, also appeared at Hamilton's house, huffing and puffing that he intended revealing Hamilton's gross adultery to the world. Unless, of course . . .

Hamilton reached for his billfold. Biting back his revulsion, he handed over blackmail totaling $1,000, a small fortune in 1791. Afterward, with plenty of time to ponder the foolishness of his actions, Hamilton moved inexorably toward the belief that he had fallen victim to a trap laid by the abominable Aaron Burr. Naturally, discretion demanded that he not broadcast his suspicions, so for years he kept the shameful secret buried deep in his breast, until Thomas Reynolds went public with his allegations of supposed financial wrongdoing.

The laudable frankness of Hamilton's denials—ready to admit to adultery but not to professional misconduct—made a profound impression on all concerned and actually resulted in his emerging from the whole unsavory episode with his reputation enhanced. Which was more than could be said for Maria Reynolds. During the interim she had divorced Reynolds, and in her haste to remarry, this time to one Jacob Clingman, she had inadvertently tied the matrimonial knot thirty minutes before her divorce became absolute, apparently the result of poor counsel from her lawyer, who was, lo and behold, none other than Aaron Burr!

Hamilton's worst suspicions had been confirmed, and to his dying day nothing would dissuade him from the conviction that Burr was an amoral charlatan, ready to wallow in any sewer in order to achieve his devious purpose.

Soon it was Burr's turn to start hitting the headlines, as his financial dealings also came under the microscope. When it emerged that he had finessed the law to favor one of his investments, a businessman, John Barker Church, whose many insurance and banking interests Burr represented, made his disapproval abundantly clear. Burr reacted furiously. By this stage of his career, his earlier languid equanimity had been supplanted by a hair-trigger intolerance of personal criticism, and he challenged Church to a duel. The two met on September 2, 1799, at Weehawken, on the New Jersey side of the Hudson. After the customary preliminaries, shots were exchanged, but apart from the ball from Church's pistol that passed through Burr's sleeve, no harm was done to either man. With honor duly settled, the protagonists retired for breakfast.

Despite these wearisome hiccups, Burr's political star was in the ascendant and as the presidential election of 1800 drew near, he set his sights squarely on the greatest prize of all.

The Standoff of 1800

Ever since his election in 1796, John Adams had endured a miserable presidency. He had been so weakened by relentless attacks from his own Federalist party, whipped up by Hamilton, that a Democratic-Republican victory looked odds-on. Adams's main opposition was expected to come from Jefferson, but Burr was a canny operator, shrewd at cutting backroom deals, and it was by no means certain that this would be just a two-horse race.

Burr's chances improved out of all recognition when assistance arrived from an unexpected quarter.

Hamilton's hatred of Adams had always bordered on the pathological, and he now chose this moment to commit his vitriolic opinions to paper, which miraculously found its way into the hands of delighted Democratic-Republicans. Publication of the pamphlet revealed the depth of the split in the Federalist party and virtually handed the election on a plate to the Democratic-Republicans.

But which candidate would take office—Jefferson or Burr? Logic dictated that Jefferson was the front-runner, for he had the credentials and the support, but as the votes were tallied, Burr inched ever closer.

Extraordinarily, the result was a tie. Under the convoluted electoral system then in use, Jefferson and Burr received an equal number of electoral votes for the presidency (seventy-three each), easily defeating the two Federalist candidates, Adams and Charles C. Pinckney. Such an impasse threw the outcome into the House of Representatives, which would decide who became the next president.

Having seen off one rival, Hamilton now directed all his formidable energies to scotching Burr's presidential dreams. Flinging himself into the fray with inhuman relish, he organized cabals, whispered in ears, wrote scorching letters, anything to destroy his nemesis. One letter to his close ally, Gouverneur Morris, spelled it out in no uncertain terms: "Jefferson or Burr? The former without all doubt . . . His [Burr's] elevation can only promote the purposes of the desperate and the profligate."[9]

Another letter, this time to James A. Bayard, a Federalist mandarin, gave Hamilton opportunity to further vent his spleen. "I . . . am sure there is no means too atrocious to be employed by him. . . . Disgrace abroad, ruin at home, are the probable fruits of his elevation."[10]

Not everyone approved of Hamilton's savage anti-Burr letter campaign. One recipient, Chief Justice John Marshall, wrote back in disgust, "I can take no part in this business."[11]

On February 11, 1801, the Federalist-dominated House began to deliberate between Burr or Jefferson for president. Although most Federalists instinctively favored Burr over Jefferson,

Hamilton brought his huge personality to bear, browbeating and cajoling, wearing down resistance in one round of voting after another, until he persuaded a few to cast blank ballots. Finally, on the thirty-sixth ballot, Thomas Jefferson became the third president of the United States.

Under the electoral rules then in force, candidates did not run separately for the vice presidency; it was a straight race for the top job, with the runner-up automatically assuming the rank of vice president.

Burr had come within a hairbreadth of the Golden Fleece, only to have it snatched from his grasp by the machinations of just one man—Alexander Hamilton. Nothing now could avert them from disaster.

Whatever satisfaction Hamilton derived from this victory was fleeting, effaced by a cruel personal setback. In November 1801, his son Philip became embroiled in a heated argument at a theater with a Republican named George I. Eacker, who had insulted the Hamilton family name. The challenge was issued and accepted and Philip, just nineteen, fell mortally wounded on the dueling grounds at Weehawken, New Jersey. Hamilton, consumed with guilt, had anguish piled on top of grief as his daughter Angelica, from whom Philip had been inseparable, plunged irretrievably into madness after hearing of her brother's death.

Not even a double tragedy of this magnitude could deflect Hamilton from the obsessive urge that now dominated his life. "I feel it a religious duty to oppose [Burr's] career,"[12] he once wrote to a friend, while another heard how the new vice president was in debt to "about 80,000 Dollars."[13] Shortly afterward, a blizzard of pamphlets hit the New York sidewalks, dripping with venomous accusations that Burr had conspired with certain Federalists to wrest the presidency from Jefferson and his Virginian cohorts. Few doubted Hamilton's directorship of this smear campaign. If the intention was to sow seeds of doubt and hatred among the leaders of the Republican party, then it succeeded marvelously well, as increasingly Burr found himself shoved to the margins of power. Like most occupants since, he discovered that the office of vice president was more puffery than power, an impotent sinecure.

For two years Hamilton piled on the pressure with scarcely a pause for breath. In February 1804, he was at last able to claim victory when the Democratic-Republican caucus nominated Jefferson for president and discarded Burr in favor of George Clinton for vice president.*

Burning with humiliation at having been pitched ignominiously onto the political scrap heap, Burr scrambled to recover. He threw his hat into the 1804 New York gubernatorial race and begged the Federalists for their endorsement. Under Hamilton's stewardship they just brushed him aside. What followed was one of the meanest gubernatorial election campaigns on record. Handbills, accusing Burr of everything from legal malpractice to seduction of "unhappy wretches who have fallen victim to this accomplished debaucher,"[14] flooded the streets. Behind the scenes, Hamilton pulled the strings and stepped up his letter campaign, unleashing his full armory of insults against Burr. "He is as unprincipled and dangerous a man as any country can boast."[15]

Only now did Burr comprehend the full extent of Hamilton's animus. He was deeply shocked. In a raging temper, he approached Hamilton and demanded an explanation. For all his vaunted high principle, Hamilton could muster impressive reserves of hypocrisy and dole out huge globs of soothing verbal balm when necessary—like now. He smooth-talked Burr's concerns into oblivion, stroked his ego, assured him of his lasting friendship, in short he did everything conceivable to ensure that the two parted on the most amicable of terms. Only later did Burr realize how comprehensively he had been duped.

By this time it was too late to save him. Burr's political swan song came on April 25, 1804, when he was defeated for the governorship of New York by the majority Republican candidate, Morgan Lewis. Washed-up politically, Burr thirsted for revenge, and that meant taking dead aim at Alexander Hamilton.

Feud Goes Public

The feud reached critical mass at an Albany dinner party, during which Hamilton delivered yet another of his by now familiar diatribes against Burr. Somehow the tenor, if not the content, of his harangue found its way into the press. One New York

---

*For the first time, the 1804 election had distinct vice-presidential candidates.

newspaper revealed that Hamilton had expressed certain "despicable" opinions of Burr, with the writer hinting tantalizingly that he "could detail . . . a still more despicable opinion which General Hamilton had expressed of Mr Burr."[16]

Mouthwatering for the gossips, the final straw for Burr. On June 17, 1804, he summoned Judge William Van Ness, a close friend of Hamilton's, and insisted upon an explanation for Hamilton's libelous campaign. Dissatisfied with the response, Burr dispatched a letter to Hamilton demanding an unconditional apology and retraction of all the derogatory comments. In the ensuing war of letters, Hamilton obfuscated and hedged but refused to issue the blanket apology that his opponent demanded.

Burr snapped. Twice in the past he had considered challenging Hamilton to a duel, only to be fobbed off. Now, his patience exhausted and complaining that he had "been constantly deceived," he threw down the gauntlet.[17]

Hamilton, too, had once teetered on the brink of challenging a detractor to a duel—such was his testy nature—but the tragedy of his own son, and the guilt he still felt about that episode, had changed him irrevocably. Even so, he felt compelled by the prevailing code of "gentlemanly conduct" to meet the challenge.

Employing the mix of sanctimoniousness and cunning that exemplified his career, he wrote a letter, to be published in the event of his death, in which he loftily declared his intention of withholding his fire no matter what Burr might do. In effect, Hamilton was guaranteeing that if he left the dueling grounds feet first, Burr would have the devil's own job fending off charges of murder.

Once sanctioned by law and custom, dueling had declined in the northern states after the Revolution and was outlawed in New York, hence the trips across the Hudson into New Jersey. As the fateful day approached, both men put their affairs in order and readied themselves for the duel.

Dawn broke misty and pink on the morning of July 11 as Hamilton set off in a small sailboat with his second, Nathaniel Pendleton, and Dr. David Hosack. A three-mile sail along the Hudson River brought them to Weehawken, opposite the end of

Forty-second Street, New York City, where they landed shortly before seven o'clock.

Five years earlier Burr had made this same journey and had been lucky to escape with his life. On that occasion his aim had let him down. He had no intention of repeating the mistake. In the starched, formal manner customary at such a dread occasion, courtesies were exchanged, the two men selected their pistols, then paced off the agreed distance of ten steps.

A public statement issued by Pendleton and James Van Ness recorded the encounter:

> Both of the parties took aim, & fired in succession, the intervening time is not expressed as the seconds do not precisely agree on that point. The pistols were discharged within a few seconds of each other and the fire of Colonel Burr took effect & General Hamilton almost instantly fell.

(In private, Pendleton insisted that Hamilton's pistol discharged only after he was struck by Burr's shot.)

> Colonel Burr then advanced toward General Hamilton with a manner and gesture that appeared to General Hamilton's friend to be expressive of regret, but without speaking turned about & withdrew. . . . We conceive it proper to add that the conduct of the parties in that interview was perfectly proper as suited the occasion.[18]

Hamilton was carried from the dueling grounds, more dead than alive. The next day, weakened by a loss of blood, he succumbed to his wounds and was later buried in Trinity Churchyard in Manhattan.

The feud was over, but Burr's problems had just begun. When told of his stricken rival's stated intention to withhold his fire, he was appalled. "Contemptible disclosure, if true," he told his friend Charles Biddle.[19] From lame-duck vice president to common fugitive in the squeeze of a trigger: this was Burr's fate as he now fled to Philadelphia in order to escape the arrest warrants for murder that were out for him. Eventually, the indictments were dropped and Burr was allowed back into the political fold, though as a spent force.

The curse of Weehawken dogged his every move. In 1807, a

half-witted attempt to establish a "Western Empire" somewhere beyond the Mississippi, with himself as ruler, landed him in court on charges of treason, and although he was acquitted, outraged public opinion hounded him into exile in Europe. In 1812, he crept back into the United States, living out the remainder of his years in obscurity until his death on September 14, 1836.

The most enduring mystery surrounding this feud is what exactly did Hamilton say to provoke Burr to such drastic action? Was it just an ultimately fatal personality clash, or was there something more sinister at work? Certainly Hamilton could be a frightful prig when it came to politics, brutal in his condemnation of opponents and vicious in his attempts to crush rivals and allies, but politics alone can hardly explain the malevolence of his scorched-earth campaign against Burr. Such astringency reeks of a more visceral motive. A good place to start is the "Reynolds Affair." It had come perilously close to ruining Hamilton and, as we have seen, he long suspected that Burr had engineered the whole sordid encounter. It is not difficult to imagine the garrulous Hamilton blurting out his suspicions over port and cigars at the dinner table.

Or maybe there was some rivalry in love? Burr was a serial philanderer whose licentiousness provided a constant source of drawing-room gossip, while even the upright Hamilton occasionally stooped to conquer. Some have even speculated that Hamilton accused Burr of an incestuous relationship with his daughter Theo. While Burr's devotion to his daughter, and hers to him— she once said that life without being the daughter of Aaron Burr was not a life worth living—is beyond doubt, not a scintilla of evidence exists to support this most scurrilous of accusations.

Whatever the motivation, both men remain enigmatic to the core. For all his vast intellectual capacity, Hamilton displayed an almost childlike lack of common sense. All too often the brilliance of his mind was betrayed by the laxity of his tongue. He wore his heart, and just about every other vital organ, on his sleeve, setting Olympian standards for himself and expecting no less of others. Nothing meant more to him than his good name; he was fanatical in pursuit of probity and integrity.

For someone like Burr, sly, skeptical, the archetypal backroom political hustler, such transparency was anathema, yet he, too, allowed his famed street smarts to let him down. In later life, so it's rumored, he agonized over his own recklessness, saying that had he been wiser he would have realized that the world was big enough to accommodate both Hamilton and himself.

One thing is certain: when the wisps of black powder smoke cleared over the palisades at Weehawken that July morning, Burr's life was over just as surely as if he had turned the pistol on himself. Hamilton may never have captured the hearts of Americans in the way that Jefferson and Lincoln were able to, but his enormous contribution to the shaping of the republic and the prophetic accuracy of his vision of the United States as a global power fully earned him the seven-foot statue that graces the Capitol Rotunda.

Alas for Aaron Burr, his reward was to find himself vying with Benedict Arnold for top billing in the American Hall of Infamy, an unfulfilled political might-have-been, misunderstood in his own time and forever damned by history.

CHAPTER 4

Hatfields versus McCoys

Years of feud:	1878–1890	
Names:	The Hatfields	The McCoys
Strengths:	Sharp in business, the most successful of the family logging operations	Fiercely loyal, viewed as the underdogs
Weaknesses:	Hair-trigger tempers and a fondness for violence	Champion grudge bearers
At stake:	Family pride	

In the latter half of the nineteenth century, the United States embarked on the greatest campaign of industrialization that the world has seen. In their eagerness to satisfy the nation's seemingly insatiable appetite for goods and machinery, northern factories gobbled up vast amounts of wood, coal, and minerals. The task of finding and transporting these raw materials fell to the railroad companies, which pushed ever farther westward, deep into the brooding forests of the South Appalachians. Here grew the high-quality hardwoods so much in demand back east. Ultimately, the Appalachian logging industry would be dominated by large timber corporations; but in the 1870s, especially along the valley of the Tug Fork River, which forms the border between Kentucky and West Virginia, tree felling remained very much a family business.

Human nature and business acumen being what they are, some of these close-knit families were more successful than others, and for every fortune earned, there were dozens of farmers who scuffled to scrape a living from the unforgiving terrain. Jealousy and rancor were day-to-day realities. And it is against just such a backdrop that this story unfolds. In time the Hatfield and McCoy feud would convulse townships and counties, set one state against another, add thousands to newspaper circulations, and eventually reach the United States Supreme Court. Almost a century later it would even feature in million-selling country music records. Sorting out fact from fiction in this convoluted saga is no easy task, especially as the killings got more frequent and the headlines got more lurid, but one thing is certain: hardly anyone remembers just how this blood-drenched vendetta actually started.

It all began with a pig.

Sad to say, the feud by which all others in America are judged, and perhaps the single most famous feud in history, had its origins in nothing more quarrelsome or momentous than an old razorback hog.

Now, it should be remembered that along the Tug Valley, a sizable accumulation of hogs meant status and standing in the community, not to mention some serious folding money in the pocket, and the sudden loss of a porcine snuffler was grounds for considerable distress. Which explains why Randolph "Ran'l" McCoy got so riled when one of his hogs went missing one fall day in 1878. A suspicious sort, the fifty-two-year-old Kentucky farmer immediately turned his cold, gray gaze across the mists of the Tug Valley, into neighboring Logan County, West Virginia, home of the hated Hatfields.

There had been bad blood between the two families for years, though no one knows exactly why. Maybe it had something to do with the Logan Wildcats, a guerrilla band formed by William Anderson "Devil Anse" Hatfield back in 1863, after he'd deserted the Confederate Army in favor of a little freelance skirmishing. The Wildcats were a hellacious rabble that largely ignored matters of national military significance in favor of local raids on adjoining farms, most notably the McCoys'. . . .

Or it might have been the killing of Asa Harmon McCoy, an ex–Union soldier hunted down through the snow by bushwhackers and killed in a cave on January 7, 1865. Although blame fell on the Wildcats, no one could be certain if Anse was present at the time of the killing. . . .

More likely the feud was rooted in simple jealousy. Anse Hatfield was several light years removed from being the stereotypical backwoods rube. A shrewd, intimidating businessman with a dangerously quick temper, he and his wife, Levicy, had transformed their branch of the Hatfield clan into the Tug Valley's wealthiest landowners.

Whatever the origin of the bad feeling, there can be no doubt that in this remote corner of the Appalachians, with no railroads, no towns, no industry, and scant law enforcement, there was plenty of time and ample opportunity for grudge bearing.

And Ran'l McCoy could bear a grudge with the best of them.

The McCoys had been among the first wave of pioneers to settle the Kentucky side of the Tug Valley, one of the most rugged and forbidding sections of the Appalachians, a maze of secluded valleys, dark shadowy woods, and craggy hills that kept out the sun. Since the Civil War, Ran'l had struggled to eke out an existence from the forests. Unlike Devil Anse, his efforts to garner a share of the vast timber profits on hand had ended in ruin and soul-destroying poverty. Things got so bad that most of his sons—he and wife, Sarah, produced sixteen children—were reduced to sharecropping on neighboring farms, which in Appalachian terms was just about as low as a man could get.

It was a tough life and it showed. In his dress and austere demeanor, Ran'l McCoy resembled an Old Testament prophet, with his full, flowing beard, shaggy hair, broad shoulders, and threadbare clothes. Home was a rough log cabin on Blackberry Fork in Pike County, and like just about everyone in these parts, he supplemented his meager income by distilling illegal whiskey and raising hogs.

Except that one of his hogs was missing.

Ran'l was ready to bet his life he'd find it rooting around in some Hatfield pen. For the most part, his neighbors were honest, but not those Hatfields. Old Devil Anse and his kin just couldn't keep their hands off other folks' property, despite the fact that they already owned several thousand acres of prime timberland, way more than anyone else.

"Six feet of devil and one hundred eighty pounds of hell,"[1] ran one acid description of the Hatfield patriarch, and few argued the point. Devil by name, devil by nature, and woe betide the fool who crossed Anse Hatfield. They came up against a hook-nosed, bearded troglodyte and his thirteen strapping kids, most of whom had inherited Pa's swaggering belligerence. No doubt about it, the Hatfields were big trouble and, boy, could they brag.

It was this propensity for loose talk that led Ran'l to the home of Floyd Hatfield, Anse's cousin. Sure enough, Ran'l peered into a pen and spotted a hog that looked mighty familiar. When challenged, Floyd angrily pointed out his own brand on the hog's ear and growled at Ran'l to make himself scarce.

Contrary to popular belief, not all mountain disputes were settled with buckshot. Ran'l, a law-abiding man, took his grievance to a local judge, the Reverend Anderson Hatfield, who, despite the name, had a reputation as an impartial jurist.* Because hog rustling was a serious crime, Reverend Hatfield listened closely to what Ran'l had to say and agreed there was a case to answer. Come trial time, the reverend sat a jury divided equally between Hatfields and McCoys, the clearest indication yet that the litigants' mutual animosity was already well established. The star witness was Ran'l McCoy's nephew, Bill Staton. Since Staton's sister had married into the Hatfields, few doubted where his loyalties lay, so it came as no surprise when Staton placed his hand on the Good Book, then swore he'd seen Floyd mark the hog's ear with his own brand. An angry muttering rippled through the McCoy faction seated at the back of the room as Staton slunk off the stand, branded forever as a Judas prepared to sell out his family for a few bucks.

And then, rubbing salt into the McCoy legal wounds, one of "their" supposed jurors, Selkirk McCoy, had the unmitigated gall

---

*Although the names Hatfield and McCoy were widely scattered along the Tug Valley, most were only distantly related. The feud was fought out between two distinct branches of each clan. Before the outbreak of hostilities, the extended families had even intermarried.

to vote for Floyd Hatfield, who won the case and kept the hog. Such seeming betrayal could hardly have shocked the McCoys. Ever since 1872, Selkirk had worked on Anse Hatfield's timber-felling crew, and with jobs scarce and money short, he wasn't about to bite the hand that fed him.

Not that it mattered. Selkirk McCoy, too, went into the books as a traitor.

Although vexed by the outcome, Ran'l agreed to abide by the court's decision. Other family members were not so magnanimous, and before long bullets were flying along the Tug Fork when a group of Hatfields came under fire while out deer hunting.

Bullets Along the Border

No one was killed, but on June 18, 1880, the feud finally exploded into open warfare. Accounts of the incident are contradictory, but it appears that after crossing the Tug Fork into Logan County, West Virginia, Paris and Sam McCoy happened to run into the much-hated Bill Staton. After a blistering exchange of gunfire, which left Paris McCoy with a shattered hip, Sam McCoy finished off Staton with a bullet to the head.

Curiously enough, three months later when Paris McCoy stood trial in Logan County for Staton's death, he was found not guilty on grounds of self-defense. (Two years later, in the spring of 1882, Sam would enjoy similar leniency from a predominantly Hatfield jury, fueling speculation that Anse, who exercised control over the court, had arranged the acquittal in order to defuse the incendiary situation.) The McCoys were bug-eyed at the verdicts, but miffed that their kin had even been tried in the first place.

The next flurry of trouble came during the August 1880 elections for Pike County, Kentucky. Elections were like market days: kids played games, women brought pies and other produce to sell or barter, while the men got drunk and argued. In between times a few votes were cast, but generally it was a carnival atmosphere that encouraged socializing. Which perhaps explains why, although this was McCoy territory, Anse Hatfield and his two oldest sons, Johnse and Cap, suddenly showed up, ready to partake of the local merriment.

From all accounts, Johnse was the most agreeable of the Hatfields, stylish, always flush with money from his moonshining activities, a real charmer. One report describes him as "ruddy faced . . . and sandy haired, with a pair of insinuating blue eyes that set the mountain belles' hearts a-flutter."[2]

One heart that apparently performed cartwheels that day belonged to Roseanna McCoy, Ran'l's twenty-year-old daughter. Tall and slender and with luxuriant black hair, she was quite a looker herself, and pretty soon the romantic sparks were flying. While the others drank whiskey and partied, Johnse and Roseanna disappeared for a little partying of their own. What happened next only they knew, but the tryst left Roseanna quaking in her boots and certain of one thing—if Ran'l found out, he'd tan the hide off her. So that evening she fled with Johnse to live at his home, situated appropriately enough on Mate Creek.

Needless to say, when Ran'l sobered up after the day's carousing, he was not pleased. Losing any daughter in such circumstances was bad enough; losing her to a Hatfield was unpardonable. In a fury he dispatched a tremulous delegation of three McCoy women to Logan County with orders to return his prodigal daughter to the family fold. But Roseanna stood her ground: marriage to the handsome, rich Johnse beckoned and she was thrilled.

If Ran'l had been discomfited by his daughter's decision to elope with Johnse Hatfield, then he was positively apoplectic when, just a matter of months later, the couple split up and Roseanna slunk home. Ran'l took one look at Roseanna's swollen belly and swore vengeance. It wasn't so much that she was pregnant—single mothers were commonplace in the Appalachians at this time—but that she had been with a Hatfield.

Smarting for revenge, a gang of McCoys tracked down and captured Johnse, and things would have been bleak for the errant father had not Roseanna gone to Anse and pleaded for his help. He rounded up a posse of Hatfields and managed to free his feckless son.

At this point the accounts get murky. One version has Roseanna giving birth to a son and keeping him. The other, more commonly accepted story is that, weakened by a bout of measles, the poor young woman miscarried. Either way, she needed to get away from the Tug Valley, which she did, moving to the county town of Pikeville.

But the troubles kept piling up at her doorstep. Before long she heard that Johnse had married her cousin, Nancy McCoy, a high-spirited woman known for her temper and mean tongue. It was the final straw for Roseanna. Her health went into a long decline until, worn out and heartbroken, she eventually died in 1888, having yet to see her thirtieth birthday. The most tragic victim of the Hatfield/McCoy feud, she once tried to explain her mental and physical tailspin to her mother: "It was Pa. Every time Pa looked at me, I couldn't stand the hate in his eyes."[3]

An Uneasy Peace

For now, though, an uneasy peace settled over the Tug Valley. It lasted until Monday, August 7, 1882. The occasion was yet another of those rambunctious election days in Pike County, and this time it was Ellison Hatfield, Anse's brother, apparently loaded on corn whiskey, who enlivened the proceedings by trading insults with Tolbert McCoy. Still seething from the affront to their family pride over Roseanna, Tolbert and two brothers, Randolph Jr. ("Bud") and Pharmer, first came at Ellison with knives, stabbing him twenty-six times, then shot him. Bleeding like a butchered hog, Ellison was borne away by his family, only to die two days later.

Anse Hatfield's vengeance for the murder of his brother was swift and terrible. Rounding up a posse, he hunted down the three guilty McCoys, capturing them near present-day Matewan, West Virginia, on August 9, 1882. After dragging the trio back to the Kentucky side of the Tug Fork, he tied them to some papaw trees, blindfolded them, then drilled them with bullets.

Slaughter on this scale was too savage for the authorities to ignore. So on September 14 a Pike County grand jury under the direction of Judge George Brown issued indictments against twenty men, including Anse. Four days later, Judge Brown issued arrest warrants.

They were legal flimflam, nothing more.

When the next court term convened in February 1883, the sheriff disingenuously claimed he had been unable to serve any of the warrants. Beside each name he wrote, "Not found in this county February 19, 1883,"[4] a tacit admission of official unwillingness to confront the Hatfields, who had continued to cross the Tug Fork into Kentucky, always in heavily armed bands. It was open defiance of an already enfeebled system of justice that saw law officers too scared to arrest and juries too scared to convict. Besides, families in these parts were expected to settle their differences privately, and for this reason the feud was swept under the official rug.

Although a lid had temporarily capped the violence, the resentments still festered, tempers worsened, and trigger fingers got a bit more itchy.

The catalyst for more strife came in fall 1886. For reasons that remain unclear, Jeff McCoy, Nancy's brother, and Josiah Hurley found themselves on the West Virginia side of the river, in whooping pursuit of two Hatfield girls who had holed up in a cabin. The two men burst in and gave their hapless victims a fearful whipping, then took off. Whether anything more sinister took place remains unclear. All Anse's second son, Cap, needed to know was that two members of his family had been grievously misused. Incandescent with rage, he procured for himself an appointment as a special constable for the express purpose of serving the warrant. Using his backwoods skills and intimate knowledge of the terrain, he tracked down Jeff, who somehow managed to escape and head for the Tug Fork with Cap hot on his heels. At the river Jeff plunged into the swirling waters and struck out for the safety of Kentucky. A volley of bullets made the water boil around him, yet he succeeded in reaching the far bank, only to be cut down by a final fusillade that sent him toppling back into the water.

For whatever reason, this incident failed to ignite any overt displays of retribution. In all likelihood the McCoys felt shamefaced about the whole messy business and sided with the generally held view that a vicious woman beater had received his just deserts.

After this, life returned to what passed for normal along the Tug Valley, which remained one of the most inaccessible and isolated valleys in America, a place where each clan communicated through its own "backwoods wireless telegraph," a collection of unusual animal sounds and birdcalls signifying everything from the arrival of a stranger to a family gathering. It was pastoral and remote, untouched by "progress."

But all that was about to change.

The Railroads Come

Early geological surveys of the South Appalachian region had disclosed fantastic reserves of high-quality coal. Getting that coal out of the ground would not prove difficult; getting it to market would—until the Norfolk and Western Railroad Company announced plans to build a line linking Virginia with the Ohio River that would run right through the Tug Valley.

This was a revolutionary announcement. Huge profits were just waiting to be made in land, timber, and coal. Into this feverish climate of property speculation stepped a slippery, quick-witted Pikeville lawyer named Perry Cline, and he had a plan.

As a young boy, Cline, a distant cousin of Ran'l McCoy, had grown up in the Tug Valley, and had inherited the family hatred of all things Hatfield. Compounding his grudge tenfold was the fact that early in his business career he had tangled with Anse Hatfield over ownership of five thousand acres of land along Grapevine Creek. After a protracted legal battle, the dispute was settled out of court, with Cline having to grit his teeth and concede the land to his sworn enemy. At the time the setback didn't mean too much, except a loss of face; now, with the coming of the railroad, that land was skyrocketing in value.

The Kentucky gubernatorial race of 1887 gave Cline his opening. Lured by the chance to line his pockets and settle some old family scores, he approached the Democratic candidate, Simon Buckner, with a proposition. He would deliver the entire McCoy vote if, when elected, Buckner promised to bring the Hatfields to justice. Given the huge number of McCoys scattered all over

South Kentucky, Buckner shook hands on the deal and, sure enough, he romped home at the polls.

On September 10, 1887, the newly elected governor contacted his West Virginian counterpart, E. Willis Wilson, and requested the extradition to Kentucky of Anse Hatfield and nineteen others named in the 1882 indictments. At the same time Buckner sweetened the pot by offering a $500 reward for the capture of the defendants and their return to Pike County. This introduced a whole new factor into the equation: bounty hunters. Pretty soon the Tug Valley began filling up with hard-faced strangers, all carrying rifles, and all eager for easy pickings.

Meanwhile, Governor Wilson, a serious-minded, fair man, refused the extradition request, citing the absence of an affidavit from the Pike County authorities, as required by West Virginia law. Buckner duly filed the missing document with Wilson on October 13.

Three weeks passed with no news. During this hiatus, the Hatfields, smelling trouble and making a mockery of the notion that they were dumb mountain hicks, hired legal counsel to petition Wilson on grounds that they could not receive a fair trial in Pike County.

Irked by the law's delay, on November 5, Cline upped the ante. In a flagrant breach of protocol, he fired off a semiliterate letter directly to Wilson, lambasting the Hatfields as "the worst band of meroders [*sic*] ever existed in the mountains."[5] Furthermore, he obtained bench warrants from the Pike County Court for the arrest of the defendants. To serve the warrants he enlisted Pike County Deputy Sheriff Frank Phillips, who made a series of lightning raids across the Tug Fork that soon bagged the hated turncoat Selkirk McCoy.

"Bad" Frank Phillips was a flamboyant egotist, mean on drink and stuffed full of his own self-importance. Fired by this early success, he, too, began peppering Wilson with bombastic letters, using Cline's letterhead, much to the governor's chagrin.

As for Anse Hatfield, he digested these developments with a sense of impending doom. Anxious that a deal was being cut to extradite him and his family to Kentucky, and unnerved by Phillips's pesky raids and those damn bounty hunters, the patriarch of the Hatfield clan resolved to hit back—with deadly force.

The New Year's Day Massacre

January 1, 1888, was icy cold in the Tug Valley. As dusk fell and the mercury began to plummet still further, Anse rounded up family members and friends alike for a council of war at which he bemoaned the state of constant trepidation in which the Hatfields had been forced to live. As he so movingly put it, he and his family wanted "to occasionally take off their boots when they went to bed."[6] His solution? A preemptive strike against the McCoys. After outlining details of the attack, Anse pulled out of leading the raid on grounds of sickness and handed over stewardship of the campaign to his uncle, Jim Vance.

Under cover of darkness that night, nine masked and armed men crept up on Ran'l McCoy's dwelling on Blackberry Fork, which stood on a heavily wooded hillside. More in hope than expectation, Vance shouted for the occupants to surrender. Suddenly, defying Vance's orders not to shoot, Johnse, erratic as ever, cut loose with a rifle. The retaliatory gunfire was immediate and heavy.

Dodging bullets all the way, Vance and another man, Tom Chambers, edged their way close enough so they could torch the cabin. As the flames took hold, Calvin, Ran'l's son, shouted for his three sisters, Josephine, Alifair, and Adelaide, to help. First, they hurled buckets of water onto the blaze; then, when the water ran out, they resorted to buttermilk.

The gunfight continued to rage. Suddenly, the kitchen door was thrown open. There, framed in the doorway, flames licking at her ankles, stood fifteen-year-old Alifair. Confident that the Hatfields would not harm a woman, she attempted to douse the blaze from outside the burning house. Just then, on orders from Cap and Johnse, one of the Hatfield's cousins, a simple-minded oaf named Ellison Mounts, shot her in the stomach. According to legend, as Alifair lay screaming on the ground, her mother, Sarah, tried to reach her, crying out, "For the love of the Lord, let me go to her!"[7] Johnse, drunk with revenge, was having none of it. He ran forward and pistol-whipped the grieving mother into unconsciousness.

Through the smoke and hellish confusion, Calvin yelled to Ran'l that he would provide covering fire so the old man could escape.

Ran'l, grabbing extra cartridges, defied his sixty-two years and sprinted like a jackrabbit for the labyrinthine woods, where the Hatfields dared not follow. Behind him the crackle of gunfire raged.

Calvin fought bravely, but the odds were overwhelming and soon a Hatfield bullet snuffed out his life.

In their bloodlust the Hatfields burned the house to the ground. The raid had been a disaster for both sides, but especially for the attackers. As they rode off in the darkness, they could hear the wails of the McCoy women, all of whom were witnesses to the carnage. When Ran'l finally emerged from the pigsty where he had been hiding, he saw for the first time young Alifair, cold and dead, her hair frozen to the ground.

Just days later the bodies of Alifair and Calvin were laid next to their three brothers (Tol, Pharm, and Bud), who had been buried in the Blackberry Creek cemetery less than six years earlier. Ran'l McCoy was fast running out of family.

With his wife, Sarah, still clinging to life, Ran'l packed up and moved the McCoys to Pikeville. The awful events of that night unhinged his mind. Forever after, when drunk and sometimes even when sober, he would take to the streets of Pikeville, cursing the Hatfields at the top of his lungs, howling for vengeance.

Over in West Virginia, aware that this latest outburst had been one bloodbath too many, several Hatfields hastily laid the groundwork for any future defense by swearing affidavits to the effect that they were nowhere near Blackberry Fork on the fateful night.

Even more significantly, for the first time news of the Hatfields and McCoys reached the big-city papers, where reports varied widely in their accuracy and impartiality. In the *Pittsburgh Times,* reporter Charles S. Howell thundered, "There is a gang in West Virginia banded together for the purpose of murder and rapine," dominated by a cold-blooded autocrat who had ordered "a succession of cowardly murders by day and assassinations and house-burnings by night."[8]

In West Virginia, unsurprisingly, the *Wheeling Intelligencer* put an entirely different spin on events, declaring, "No more hospitable, honest, or peacefully disposed people live than the Hatfields."[9]

Such partisan reporting helped stoke interstate animosity and led to local militias on either side of the border being mobilized. While muckraking journalists made hay, the governors struggled to work out a compromise.

On January 9, Buckner wrote Wilson, asking if there was any good reason why those indicted for the 1882 killing should not be rendered to Kentucky. Before any reply was forthcoming, "Bad" Frank Phillips organized a large posse that forayed deep into Logan County and fought a pitched battle on Grapevine Creek with thirteen Hatfield supporters. In the shoot-out Phillips's band gained the upper hand, and over several raids they rounded up nine Hatfield supporters and marched them back to Kentucky to stand trial. When Phillips finally nabbed the crafty Vance, he took no chances and shot him in the head.

While the bullets continued to fly, the two governors maintained their correspondence, Wilson reminding Buckner that more than five years had elapsed from the 1882 killings before any extradition request had been made. He also wanted Cline and his troublemaking henchman, Phillips, removed from any impending negotiations. As stances hardened, Wilson dispatched an emissary to Buckner with a demand that he free the nine imprisoned West Virginians. Buckner replied that this was a matter for the courts, not the governor.

Armed Prison Train Runs North

The judicial system finally got involved on February 10, when both states argued their case before a federal court in Louisville, which ordered the jailer of Pike County to produce the prisoners. Under heavy guard, directed by Cline, all nine men were placed aboard a Chesapeake and Ohio Railway train. When they arrived in Louisville on February 16, locals filled the streets, all eager to catch a glimpse of these legendary mountain men. Most were surprised at how well dressed they were, in suits and soft fedoras. Why, three of them even wore collars!

Their stay in Louisville was brief. Writs continued to fly back and forth across the state border, and on March 16 they were all shipped back to Pike County.

Almost unnoticed in all this turmoil was the separation of those two lovebirds, Johnse and Nancy. Once the divorce came through, Nancy returned to her home state of Kentucky, where she married the ubiquitous Sheriff Frank Phillips.

West Virginia did everything in its power to head off the impending trials of the Hatfields, even to the point of instituting legal proceedings, charging that they had been kidnapped. Eventually, the acrimonious arguments reached all the way to the United States Supreme Court, which in May 1888 ruled that there was no legal way to mandate the restoration of prisoners abducted from one state to another: the nine Hatfields would be tried in Pikeville.

This ruling and the posting of some sizable rewards rekindled the interest of numerous bounty hunters, all desperate to track down and either kill or capture the elusive Devil Anse. But when they arrived at the Hatfield homestead on Grapevine Creek, the old man was long gone.

In his rush to escape, Anse had sold off his land at ten cents on the dollar and headed east into the mountains. There, in a secluded valley near present-day Stirrat, he built a fortified cabin, with slots for rifles in case he and his men had to fight off intruders, and with doors twelve inches thick, enough to repel even a Winchester. There was enough food and water to withstand a siege, as Anse Hatfield swore he would never surrender to Kentucky.

In late August 1888, the trials began. Early on, the investigators had singled out Ellison "Cotton Top" Mounts as the weak link; under cross-examination he revealed what had happened on August 9, 1882, when the three McCoy brothers had been tied up and shot. He also described the 1886 shooting of Jeff McCoy, as told to him by Cap Hatfield. Besides Mounts's testimony, the prosecution produced nineteen witnesses, of whom almost half bore the name Hatfield, vivid evidence that the interclan division was not nearly so sharp as many have supposed.

In addition to the 1882 triple slaying, eight Hatfields were indicted for the murder of Alifair McCoy. Back when he was first interrogated, Mounts had confessed to this killing, under the impression that his testimony in the other cases would earn him a reduced sentence. It didn't happen. Alone among the defendants, Mounts was sentenced to death; all the rest received life imprisonment.

Ran'l McCoy's first reaction to the soft sentences was disbelief, then fury. But when he tried to raise a lynch mob, all he got was apathy. Folks in Pike County were just plain tired of the killing.

Across the border his hated rival was also striving manfully to put the past behind him. In November 1889, Anse Hatfield was summoned to appear in Charleston, West Virginia, on charges of moonshining. The old man had done a deal with federal marshals: surrender voluntarily on this charge and all other arrest warrants would be dropped. After one day in court, the trial was abandoned.

Back in Pike County, tension began to rise. With Mounts languishing in the death cell, many believed that the Hatfields would never allow him to hang. Of more concern to the jailers was Mounts's mental state, as he appeared to go soft in the head, though most suspected this was a ruse to avoid his fate. Governor Buckner set the execution date—February 18, 1890.

The first hanging in Pike County in forty years produced a carnival atmosphere. Sheriff Phillips, roaring drunk, entered into the festive mood, staggering with a revolver in each hand, yelling that he had dealt with the Hatfields and now he intended to clean up Pikeville. No one paid any attention. Thousands were on hand to witness the hanging, most in hopes that the Hatfields would sweep down and free their man at the last second.

In accordance with Kentucky law, which forbade public executions, Pike County authorities erected a fence around the gallows. However, they neatly circumvented the law by building the scaffold at the foot of a hill, thus providing an excellent vantage point for the massed throng. Clearly, the county wanted to send a message. There were no last-minute feats of derring-do, and Mounts went to the gallows unaided and unloved. He cried out as they pulled the black hood over his head: "They made me do it! The Hatfields made me do it!"[10] Seconds later, the only person legally executed in this long and bloody feud plunged to his death.

Ellison Mounts's execution signaled the end of the feud. It had lasted a dozen years and cost a dozen lives. By 1892, the railroad through the Tug Valley was completed and coal began to be shipped out, and as the railroads opened up more and more of these isolated valleys, internecine family feuds like that between the Hatfields and the McCoys withered away. There were new enemies to fight now, most notably the rascally coalmine owners. As the owners soon discovered to their cost, the bruising violence that had hallmarked the beginning of South Appalachian economic modernization was now aimed in their direction. Mountain men–turned-miners had lost none of their combative spirit, as they so ably demonstrated in a long conflict with owners that culminated in the bloody coal wars of the 1920s.

As for the two patriarchs who had instigated all this mayhem, they lived long lives. Ran'l McCoy operated a ferry in Pikeville until his death on March 28, 1914, from burns caused by his clothes catching fire. To the end he was consumed by bitterness, having never recovered from that dreadful New Year's Day of 1888.

Anse Hatfield moved his family away from the valleys to Main Island Creek, near Sarah Ann, West Virginia, where he got religion and started a lucrative logging operation. Unlike Ran'l, who never quit ranting against his hated enemies, in later years Anse refused to even mention the feud. Maybe it was conscience—after all, there was an awful lot of blood on Hatfield hands—more likely he was anxious just to bury the past and concentrate on his business dealings. Along with the money came respectability, since he lived to see his nephew Henry first become governor of West Virginia and then a United States Senator.

Anse's death on January 6, 1921, at the age of eighty-three, even made the *New York Times,* which reported that the old feud leader "died quietly in his bed last night of pneumonia." Hundreds attended his funeral, and later the family erected a $3,000 marble statue carved in Carrara, Italy, over the grave.

But anyone seeking a more appropriate epitaph to the bloodstained history of these two families need look no further than the account rendered by John Spears, an early historian of the feud, who in the late 1890s visited the long-abandoned cabin of Anse Hatfield on the east bank of the Tug Fork. Inside, so the story goes, he found hanging over a fireplace a gaudy lithograph that read THERE IS NO PLACE LIKE HOME, a homily lost on some other anonymous visitor who had scrawled in the margin, "Leastwise, not this side of hell!"[11]

CHAPTER 5

Stalin versus Trotsky

Years of feud:	1907–1940	
Names:	Joseph Stalin	Leon Trotsky
Strengths:	Infinite patience, ability to see the big picture, always one step ahead of his rivals	Magical orator, with an intellect to match
Weaknesses:	Psychopathic contempt for human life	Narcissistic and self-obsessed
At stake:	The legacy of Lenin and control of an empire that spanned half the globe	

No one in history has murdered so often or with such disdain as Joseph Stalin. The numbers beggar belief—some put the body count as high as twenty million—most either shot by firing squad, starved to death, dispatched to the front in some suicidal military disaster, or else worked beyond the limits of human endurance in the *gulags,* the network of labor camps that scarred the Soviet landscape like thousands of evil carbuncles.

Quite why this former theology student felt the need to slaughter on such scale is a mystery forever buried in the black morass of his psyche, but the fact remains that when it came to genocide, "Uncle Joe" acted with a murderous efficiency that made every other twentieth-century tyrant appear amateurish.

Wherever Stalin looked he saw, or imagined he saw, enemies, and he attempted to kill them all. But as we shall see, the one person whom he wished to eliminate above all others proved to be tantalizingly resilient.

Their paths first crossed at the 1907 London Congress, a grandiose title for a smallish symposium given over to Communist writers, thinkers, and activists who wished to exchange ideas and theories. At that time Stalin—then still using his real name, Joseph Dzhugashvili—was a thuggish, street-toughened revolutionary who had already packed a lifetime's experience into his twenty-eight years. He was born on December 21, 1879, the son of a drunken cobbler in Gori, Georgia. Growing up in Georgia, which had suffered centuries of tsarist oppression, meant that rebellion was in his genes; so it came as no surprise that while training for the clergy at a seminary in Tiflis (Tbilisi), he abandoned his Bible studies in favor of Marxism, with its heady promise of a fairer, more equitable society. So far as the priests were concerned, the youngster could keep such radical nonsense to himself, and at age twenty he was kicked out.

His only career option was that of professional revolutionary. After being elected to membership on the Tiflis Democratic Committee in 1901, he was arrested the following year and transported to eastern Siberia, where he languished for three years before escaping and returning to Tiflis, where he joined the Bolsheviks.*

In 1905, he traveled to Finland for a Bolshevik conference and there met Vladimir Lenin for the first time. Still only in his mid-thirties, Lenin was already the acknowledged icon of international communism, charismatic and pitiless, a zealot who preached an ironfisted revolutionary gospel, and in the young Georgian he recognized the same fire that burned in his own belly. Afterward Dzhugashvili returned to Georgia and organized bank robberies—so-called expropriations—to fund Lenin's cause. His reward was an invitation to the 1907 London Congress.

The undoubted star of the assembly was a silver-tongued firebrand named Lev Bronstein. Unlike Dzhugashvili, Bronstein was

*The Bolsheviks had come into existence in 1903, when the Central Committee of the Russian Social Democratic Labor Party (RSDLP) split. Lenin called his followers Bolsheviks (from the Russian word for "majority") and his opponents Mensheviks (from the word for "minority").

no peasant. His father had been that great rarity in Russia, a Jewish landowner, and on the family's Ukrainian estate, the young lad had enjoyed a life of privilege shared by few in the tsar's feudal empire. Yet he, too, had fallen victim to the seductive charms of Marx and Engels.

Bronstein was just six weeks older than Dzhugashvili, and his life had followed a similar course: arrest and imprisonment as a Communist agitator, exile to Siberia, escape from the frozen wastes, before fleeing to London in 1903 on a false passport that bore the name by which history would remember him—Leon Trotsky.

At that seminal London Congress, Trotsky had broken openly with Lenin's Bolsheviks, to side with the opposition Mensheviks, prophesying that Leninist theory would result in a one-man dictatorship. It was a courageous stance, one that would come back to haunt him decades later.

For now, however, Trotsky could take to the podium secure in the knowledge that no one in the revolutionary arena, not even Lenin himself, was his oratorical or academic equal. Like many extremely clever people, Trotsky was contemptuous of those whom he considered his cerebral inferiors, which perhaps explains why, when asked later, he had no recollection of the squat little bank robber from Georgia who had also attended the London conference.

But Dzhugashvili had most definitely noticed the bespectacled intellectual who could pluck honeyed phrases from the ether and whose brilliance and ambition shone beacon bright. There was danger here and Dzhugashvili knew it, and although he burned with jealousy, he consoled himself with the truism that revolutions are won with more than impassioned polemics; they need organizational skills and, above all, they need ruthlessness. Dzhugashvili suspected he had sufficient of the former; as for the latter, well, that went without saying.

After London the two men went their differing ways. Trotsky found work in Vienna as a journalist. A torrent of influential articles flowed from his pen, prompting many to mention his name in the same breath as Lenin's as a leader of world communism. With the outbreak of World War I, he moved to Zurich and then to Germany, where his opposition to the war brought a jail sentence. In 1915, he moved to Paris, only to be expelled as a result of his pacifist propaganda.

Back in Russia, Dzhugashvili's life had resumed its former path: a dreary succession of arrest, imprisonment, and escape. Being on the run so often required frequent aliases, and it was during this period that he adopted the name that he would use for the rest of his life—Stalin, or "man of steel." Yet another arrest, this time in St. Petersburg, brought him exile for four years to Turukhansk in western Siberia. Always planning ahead, throughout this incarceration he kept in constant touch with Lenin through a string of smuggled letters.

There was much to discuss. Increasing Russian dissatisfaction with the conduct of World War I, exacerbated by accusations of treason and horrendous food shortages, provided the catalyst for the apocalyptic events of March 1917, when the Romanov dynasty, which had ruled Russia for three hundred years, disappeared in a matter of days.

Trotsky was in the United States, editing a magazine called *Novy Mir (The New World),* when he learned of the upheaval in his homeland. Aware that the abdication of Tsar Nicholas II had left a nation rudderless and ripe for revolution, he hurried back to Moscow that May and threw in his lot with Lenin's Bolsheviks, determined to stake his claim in the political land rush that followed.

Stalin, too, had similar designs. Along with thousands of other political prisoners, he had been freed when the tsar fell, and now, like everyone else with a revolutionary ax to grind, he headed for Moscow. He found a city in chaos. By late fall the Bolsheviks, with Lenin at the helm, were strong enough to stage an armed coup. No one could have foreseen how those few bloody days—the October Revolution of 1917—would so profoundly shape the rest of the twentieth century.

Reign of Terror

No one disputed Lenin's role as godfather of the revolution, or his right to rule the Soviet Union as he saw fit. Terror, he decided, was the key; instill such fear into the population that submission to the state would be as natural as breathing. In order to give life to this malevolence, he established the Cheka, the dreaded secret police organization which, under a string of various names, would guarantee the authority of every Soviet dictator throughout the twentieth century.

Next, Lenin searched for a supporting cast. He needed strong men around him, men prepared to adopt his doctrine that the end justified the means, no matter how draconian those means might be. Trotsky was a natural: his role in the revolution had been second only to that of Lenin—as he never stopped reminding everyone—and he assumed the rank of Foreign Commissar.

Stalin was on far shakier ground. Ten years in prison and exile might have given him an ineradicable sense of having earned his place in the party hierarchy, but his own role in the revolution had been peripheral at best; indeed, in John Reed's exhaustive account of the Bolshevik coup, *Ten Days that Shook the World,* Stalin's name occurs just twice. (Later, Stalin banned the book. Mere possession of it meant exile to the gulag.) Eventually, Stalin was given the rank of Commissar for Nationalities, charged with preventing the old empire from coming apart at its ethnic seams, a task he pursued with unholy relish.

One month after the October Revolution, the newly formed Central Committee delegated the right to decide all emergency questions to a four-man team of Lenin, Stalin, Trotsky, and Lenin's close aide, Yakov Sverdlov. Together this quartet set about shaping a vast, amorphous nation that spanned eleven times zones and as many nationalities, 150 million people who spoke different languages, worshipped different gods, and had very different goals. Their only common ground was a passion to end Russian involvement in the war that was currently tearing Europe apart.

Trotsky's first duty was to implement the Bolsheviks' peace program—and buy time for the nascent Soviet Union—by calling for immediate armistice negotiations among the warring powers. Only Germany responded. At the resulting Brest-Litovsk conference (1918), Trotsky decided to turn the talks into a Marxist propaganda forum, with himself as the keynote speaker.

While he polemicized and coined phrases for the ages, shrewder heads met and negotiated, with the result that Germany got a great deal. Under the terms of the subsequent treaty, not only did Russia agree to pull out of World War I, but also ceded huge tracts of land to the jubilant Germans and their allies.

There was a frosty welcome for Trotsky when he returned to Moscow, for the reckless territorial concessions he had made. His first foray on the world diplomatic stage had been a dismal flop. Vain, prickly, unaccustomed to criticism of any kind, never mind the kind of mauling being dished up here, he sulkily resigned from the foreign commissariat to assume control of the Bolshevik Army.

There was much to do. Anti-Communist forces, the so-called White Army, had taken advantage of the internal bickering to strike back at the Bolsheviks, firing the first shots in what would be a two-year-long civil war that would leave millions dead, many through starvation, and make the specter of cannibalism a daily reality in Russian life.

Trotsky hurled himself bodily into his new job as he struggled to create a cohesive fighting force out of the disordered Bolshevik, or Red, Army. He led from the front, traveling the country in his personal train, always ready to place himself in positions of extreme jeopardy, reliant on sweeping rhetorical brilliance alone to save the day. He was a spellbinding orator and a magnificent sight as he stood draped in a long cloak, breath billowing on the frigid air, studious and demonic, looking for all the world as if he had just stepped from the pages of a Tolstoy novel. More organizer than military strategist, he was still a superb commander and, like all the Bolshevik leaders, utterly ruthless. The old order, he declared, had to be "swept away into the dustbin of history,"[1] and he suffered no sleepless nights about how best to achieve that goal.

With Lenin he devised the repugnant policy of civilian hostage taking. Another Trotsky invention was the so-called blocking unit, a fiendish ploy whereby hapless Red Army soldiers awaiting punishment in the military prison suddenly found themselves herded in behind advancing infantry with orders to stop, by any means, any Bolshevik troops who attempted to retreat. Failure to do so meant a bullet in the head. Trotsky's rationalization for the blocking units was airy and dismissive: "They provide the chance of dying with honor at the front or with shame at the rear."[2]

He was a merciless disciplinarian. On one occasion, when a Red Army regiment abandoned its position without orders, not only the commander, but every tenth soldier was shot dead—orders of Commissar Trotsky.

Stalin had also used the civil war to cement a reputation for ruthlessness. Like all the October Revolution leaders, he was committed unequivocally to the application of terror in all its guises. "I curse and persecute everyone I have to,"[3] he wrote proudly to Lenin. As if to demonstrate the point, on one occasion he had a band of troublesome military specialists rounded up and imprisoned in a prison barge on the river Volga. The barge then promptly sank for no apparent reason, drowning most of those on board. Problem solved.

Although Stalin lacked Trotsky's flair for military leadership, there was little to choose between them in cold-blooded callousness. Goaded on by Lenin, each was forced into ever more savage acts of brutality in order to advance their careers.

Their first open clash came in late 1918, when, on Lenin's orders, Stalin traveled south to the beleaguered city of Tsaritsyn to organize food supplies. Unable to curb his instinctive appetite for intrigue, Stalin got himself appointed to the local Revolutionary Military Council (RMC), and immediately began interfering with military operations, which were in the charge of onetime tsarist officer General Sytin, a Trotsky appointee.

Going behind Trotsky's back and bypassing the RMC, Stalin fired off a string of reports to Lenin, all of which vastly overstated his own role in the defense of Tsaritsyn. (Apart from the execution of several ex-tsarist officers whom he mistrusted, Stalin achieved little in Tsaritsyn.*) In early October, his patience exhausted, Trotsky demanded Stalin's recall on grounds of intolerable meddling and got his wish.

*Later, when he was revising the history of the civil war, Stalin claimed credit for the successful defense of Tsaritsyn and had the city named Stalingrad in his own honor. Nowadays it is called Volgograd.

Stalin was stung into action, and immediately began a slan-
derous whispering campaign against his rival and waited his
chance. Two months later, he and Feliks Dzerzhinsky, head of
the Cheka, were ordered by Lenin to investigate the causes of
the Red Army's crushing defeat at Perm, eight hundred miles
northeast of Moscow. Ordinarily such information, harmful to
the army's and Trotsky's reputation, would be buried in the
archives; in this instance, Stalin ordered its publication.

Infuriated by Stalin's treachery, Trotsky tendered his resignation to the Politburo, the policy-making body of the Central
Committee, only for it to be refused. Now it was Stalin's turn to
seethe, as Lenin, anxious to soothe Trotsky's injured pride, gave
him a signed carte blanche, to be used whenever his decisions
were questioned.

Trotsky rejoiced in his newfound status, and as the Red Army
gradually overwhelmed their anti-Communist opponents, his
star soared, leaving Kremlin power watchers with no doubt that,
temporarily at least, Stalin had been shouldered aside. In sheer
talent and administrative effectiveness, Trotsky had no peer,
but—and this was the great mistake of his life—he never grasped
the fact that vast intellectual capacity tends to intimidate, not
ingratiate. People tolerated him, but did not like him. He was
narcissistic, opinionated, and snobbish, unlike Stalin, who could
swap jokes and down vodka with the best of them. To Trotsky's
sophisticated eye, his main rival was an uncouth Georgian,
someone who spoke Russian with a comic foreign accent, "a gray
blur . . . the outstanding mediocrity of our party."[4]

What Stalin lacked in elegance was more than made up for in
persistence. Also, he was a matchless schemer, hardened by
years of seminary training, and he possessed reserves of mental toughness that Trotsky the highbrow could not even begin to
fathom.

One person who watched their feud with growing anxiety was
Lenin. Although he had frequently extolled Trotsky's role in the
revolution and civil war, and in all likelihood regarded him as his
natural successor, he was far from blind to the Ukrainian's defi-
ciencies. Yet these paled against the unease that Lenin felt when

confronted by evidence of Stalin's brutal suppression of his native Georgia. As someone who attached immense importance to the proper treatment of Russia's minorities, Lenin feared that Stalin's sledgehammer tactics would send the wrong signal, and yet he was strangely ambivalent about his protégé, defending him robustly against rivals' complaints that the Georgian held too many positions of authority.

As the scramble for power heated up, in the eyes of the party rank and file, Trotsky stood head and shoulders above all others. But those closer to the center of power had not forgiven the Ukrainian for his superciliousness, and inexorably they began to drift into Stalin's sphere of influence.

Stalin slowly wormed his way into the upper echelons of the Soviet hierarchy. While Trotsky wrestled in print with the arcane intricacies of Marxist theory, and began developing his theory of "permanent revolution," Stalin concentrated on the nuts and bolts of power. With Lenin's backing he assumed the new role of general secretary of the Communist party, a post that in effect gave him control over the most important party jobs. Able to dispense or withhold patronage at will, Stalin was now on the high road to omnipotence.

Lenin Cut Down

The timing could not have been more propitious, for just one month later, on May 25, 1922, Lenin, the godfather of the Soviet Union, was cut down by a serious stroke that left him partially paralyzed, weak, and ineffective.

As Lenin's natural heir, or so he thought, Trotsky readied himself for leadership, convinced his preeminence in the October Revolution would guarantee his succession. But he had reckoned without Stalin. Whereas Trotsky adopted an unctuous, high-handed attitude to events, refusing even to lobby other members, Stalin cut deals, cajoled and threatened, schemed his way into the heart of the party.

It was no contest.

Stalin, aided by two other veterans of the October Revolution,

Lev Kamenev and Grigori Zinoviev, broke out of the pack and together they formed a ruling *troika,* which left Trotsky blinking with disbelief behind his pince-nez at the way in which he had been outmaneuvered. Stalin became the puppetmaster, always hovering in the background, content to let others enjoy the limelight while he pulled the strings that made everything happen.

As Lenin struggled to regain his health, furious at the way in which Stalin had manipulated events, he was plagued by fears that he had created a monster. He summoned Trotsky to warn him of the dangers posed by Stalin, saying, "This cook can serve only peppery dishes."[5] He then offered Trotsky the position of deputy to himself, only for the haughty Ukrainian to reject the post as a meaningless sinecure, beneath his dignity to accept.

In short order, Stalin's baleful influence radiated out from the Kremlin to encompass all of the party apparatus, and soon he felt able to bully the ailing Lenin, especially after a second stroke in December 1922 further undermined the leader's health and influence.

Lenin used this recuperation period to dictate what became known as his "Testament," a revealing document that recorded his views of his two deputies. About the man who had duped him so thoroughly, he wrote, "[Stalin] has unlimited authority concentrated in his hands, and I am not sure he will always be capable of using that authority with sufficient caution," adding that he was "too coarse, and this shortcoming, fully tolerable within our midst and in our relations as Communists, becomes intolerable in the post of General Secretary. For this reason I suggest that the comrades consider how to transfer Stalin from this post and replace him."[6]

Trotsky also came in for a bruising. After describing him as the "most capable person in the current Central Committee," Lenin poured scorn on his excessive "self-confidence and a dis-position . . . too much attracted by the purely administrative aspect of affairs."[7]

Regretfully, Lenin concluded that neither could be trusted to rule alone, and for that reason he advocated a triumvirate of Trotsky, Stalin, and Zinoviev to succeed him.

Stalin, of course, had no intention of sharing power with Trotsky, or anyone else, for that matter. Stooges like Kamenev and Zinoviev were manageable, leaving Lenin to watch impotently as the troika embarked on a string of disastrous policy blunders. Fearing for the future of the nation he had created, Lenin again approached Trotsky, urging him to use the upcoming Twelfth Party Congress to expose Stalin's maltreatment of the Georgian minorities. At the same time, he offered to sever all relations with Stalin.

This was political dynamite. If Trotsky made public all of Lenin's concerns about Stalin and his henchmen, it was unthinkable that the general secretary could survive. However, Stalin's spies were everywhere and details of the Lenin-Trotsky meeting soon reached his ears, as did news that Lenin's health had gone into another serious decline. Facing political annihilation, Stalin staked his future, maybe even his life, on one reckless gamble. On March 7, 1923, he arranged for the upcoming congress to be deferred one month.

The gamble paid off. Just three days later, Lenin suffered the massive stroke that ruined him. Confined to a wheelchair, robbed of speech, he was helpless to assist Trotsky, who inexplicably chose not to denounce Stalin at the congress, confining himself to a lame speech on the future of Soviet industry.

What should have been Stalin's downfall became instead his coronation.

Later, Trotsky attempted to excuse his weakness. "I avoided entering into this fight as long as possible, since its nature was that of an unprincipled conspiracy directed against me personally. It was clear to me that such a fight . . . might . . . lead to dangerous consequences."[8]

Such passivity doomed Trotsky. The automatic transfer of leadership from Lenin to himself that he had expected was now an illusion. Stalin was reelected general secretary, and while Trotsky retained his seat on the Politburo, he held no formal position in the party. Yes, he still attended Politburo meetings, aloof as always, often reading French novels while others spoke, ostentatious with his silences, but nobody paid a scrap of attention to him.

For nine months Lenin lingered, finally dying on January 21, 1924. His funeral, held six days later, became the template for all Soviet funerals to come: rows of grim-faced mourners—Old Guard Bolsheviks to a man—each situated on the dais according to a sharply defined pecking order. All of the party hierarchy was present. Except Trotsky. While others braved the brutal Moscow winter, Trotsky lounged in the Black Sea sunshine, recovering, he said, from a minor ailment. He later claimed that Stalin had deliberately misinformed him of the date of Lenin's funeral, causing him to miss it and thus to weaken his standing, but documentary evidence does not support this claim. Trotsky had the time and the opportunity to return to Moscow for the funeral. For some reason he chose not to.

Not for the last time, Communist party hierarchical struggles would be decided on the funeral dais of departed leaders.

Stalin used the occasion to stake his claim as successor. Employing pseudo-biblical language gleaned from his seminary days, he initiated the cult of personality, which would elevate Lenin to near-godlike status in the Soviet Union while also evoking the image of himself as the reincarnation of the former icon. It was a master stroke. Stalin, the self-professed sole inheritor of Lenin's legacy, intended riding to absolute power on the coattails of a dead man.

With the keys of power now firmly in his grasp, Stalin set about finishing off his greatest rival. A wave of anti-Trotskyism swept through Moscow. As if by magic, dozens of damaging documents extracted from the archives of the tsarist secret police suddenly found their way into the public domain. In one, Lenin described Trotsky as "the basest careerist," an "adventurer,"[9] but most harmful of all was a letter written by Trotsky in 1913 in which he criticized Lenin, describing him in rude, unflattering terms. Hardly anyone noticed the date of the letter, just its combustible content.

Predictably, Trotsky launched into one of his high-and-mighty harangues, declaring it to be "one of the greatest frauds in world history,"[10] and comparing himself to Alfred Dreyfus as a victim of duplicity. But he could not deny its authorship, or its impact. In the minds of readers, as Trotsky ruefully admitted later, "Chronology was disregarded in the face of naked quotations."[11]

An avalanche of his past writings now came back to swamp

him: his early anti-Bolshevik speeches; the famous clash with Lenin in 1912. Almost in a daze, he attempted to curry favor at the Thirteenth Party Congress in a wheedling attempt at self-rehabilitation. Stalin just growled his derision. "A statement like Trotsky's is somewhat of a compliment with somewhat of an attempt at mockery—an attempt, of course, that failed."[12]

Stalin then twisted the knife with some acerbic taunts about his rival's much-vaunted part in the October Revolution, always a touchy subject with the general secretary. "This talk about Trotsky's special role is a legend being spread by obliging party gossips,"[13] he sneered.

Sensing blood, the jackals snapped at Trotsky's heels, demanding his removal from office and his expulsion from the party. The relentless criticism sapped his will to fight and his authority as war commissar became increasingly undermined as orders came back marked "Disregard," authority of Stalin.[14] Unable or unwilling to bear the humiliation any longer, he asked to be relieved of his duties as army leader and chairman of the Revolutionary Military Council of the Republic. Stalin tossed him a conciliatory bone: a seat on the Politburo, nothing more.

All through this silent coup, Stalin held his breath, fearing what might happen if Trotsky invoked the powers of the Red Army against him, a doomsday scenario that had also occurred to Trotsky's few remaining allies. They believed that with military backing Stalin could be destroyed, but the Red Army was already acutely sensitive to sudden shifts in power and Trotsky knew this. Skeptical that the army would support him in a revolt against the new Soviet strongman, he consequently ignored them.

Instead, Trotsky turned his asperity on Zinoviev and Kamenev, both of whom had opposed the armed insurrection in 1917, contrasting their lily-livered meekness with his own vigorous role in the revolution. Such harking back to 1917 only blackened Stalin's mood and he decided to administer the coup de grâce.

Stalin Scents Blood

All at once, Trotsky's theories and ideas were held up to the light and scrutinized mercilessly, in particular his controversial notion of "permanent revolution," which argued that it was impossible to build socialism just within the national boundaries of the Soviet Union, and that "a genuine upsurge of socialist economy in Russia will become possible only after the victory of the proletariat in the most important countries of Europe."[15]

Stalin retaliated with his own philosophical treatise, which took a diametrically opposed view to Trotsky's ideas, saying that socialism in one country *was* viable, even under conditions of capitalist encirclement. In this way, by cleverly polarizing the argument Stalin managed to portray Trotsky as a defeatist, almost a traitor to the revolution.

This latest humiliation drove Trotsky to the brink and sent his loathing for Stalin to near-psychotic levels. "The official sessions of the Central Committee became truly disgusting spectacles," he wrote. "The stage director of all this was Stalin . . . [through him] the habits of the Tiflis streets were transferred to the Central Committee of the Bolshevik Party."[16] Shaken out of his torpor at last, Trotsky threw down the gauntlet, proclaiming himself the true standard-bearer of Leninism.

It was now that his charmless personality made itself painfully evident. He had a close-knit circle of allies, mostly intellectuals, but had no power base within the Politburo, nothing with which to hurt Stalin, who had installed his minions in all the significant posts.

When Zinoviev and Kamenev wanted to expel Trotsky, Stalin adopted a paternal forbearance, arguing that such "bloodletting . . . is dangerous and contagious. Today one person is cut off, tomorrow another, the next day a third—but what will remain of the party?"[17] Such moderation—as phony as it was compelling—did much to impress those around him.

Friendless and alone, Trotsky countered in the only way he knew how, through the power of his pen. A flood of articles and tracts bombarded the party faithful as he struggled to regain his former authority. Extraordinarily for someone with his track record, he even had the temerity to suggest a greater democracy in party affairs. With Stalin's ostensible support, he sponsored a resolution urging that "the leading party bodies must heed the voices of the broad party ranks and must not regard criticism as a manifestation of factionalism."[18]

In putting his name to this resolution, Stalin, who had no intention of permitting any hint of democracy, was merely weaving the rope with which Trotsky would hang himself. He didn't have long to wait. Party apparatchiks exploded when Trotsky rashly urged a "new course," which "must begin by making everyone feel that from now on *nobody* will dare terrorize the party."[19]

Again Stalin seized on his enemy's blunder, twisting it skillfully to present himself in the best possible light. "They say that the Central Committee should have banned publication of Trotsky's article. That is wrong, comrades. . . . Just try to ban an article of Trotsky's that has already been read aloud in Moscow districts! The Central Committee could not take such a heedless step."[20] Politburo heads nodded sagely. Once again Comrade Stalin's statesmanlike tolerance toward his rival had won the day.

The noose was drawing tighter.

For all his cleverness, Trotsky was outmaneuvered every step of the way. He understood principles but not people, whereas Stalin was a master at trading on emotions. While Trotsky sulked, Stalin whispered in corners, making promises, extracting favors, forever scheming. A close observer recalled the secretary general's secretive tactics. "He tried to stay in the shadows . . . he was always wearing a mask. . . . He was a man whose wishes, whose aim was very clear, but you could never tell how he was going to accomplish it. He accomplished it in the most cunning way. And he allowed nothing to get in his way."[21]

Like a logger felling trees, Stalin whittled away at his enemies. In late 1925, it was the turn of Zinoviev and Kamenev, victims of their own increasing radicalism, to be ousted from power in one of Stalin's lightning purges. Like rats they ran to Trotsky's side. It gives some measure of his utter desperation that he welcomed these two Judases with open arms, and between them they went on the attack. Calling themselves the "United Opposition," they seized every opportunity to voice their criticisms before the party membership, despite the increasingly severe restrictions being placed on such debate. They stressed the importance of party democracy and economic planning, condemned the leadership's concession to bourgeois elements, and denounced Stalin's theory of "socialism in one country" as defeatist and cowardly.

Stalin merely yawned. It was all just empty posturing. Had this alliance taken place in 1923 or even 1924, he might have been doomed. By 1926, he was unassailable.

His only response was to mine the rich vein of anti-Semitism that permeated Russian life, with jeering references to the Jewishness of all three protagonists. The ensuing campaign of whispers and jibes was enough to drive Trotsky from the Politburo.

By 1927, Stalin's grip upon the party was sufficient to deliver him a majority no matter how eloquent or persuasive Trotsky's argument. A British Communist, Harry Young, present at the meeting when Trotsky was expelled from the Comintern, the organization that united foreign Communist parties around the world, wrote, "The meeting got very acrimonious. He defended the world revolution line and permanent revolution in the way that only Trotsky could. But of course it was all to no avail. The thing had been thrashed out in the Russian Communist Party Politburo and Central Committee."[22]

In October 1927, the Central Committee passed a resolution expelling Trotsky and Zinoviev while allowing them to remain party members. Trotsky's final speech to the Central Committee, a sharp-fanged attack on the party leadership, led to pandemonium on the conference floor. As Trotsky bellowed to make himself heard, chants of "liar . . . traitor . . . loudmouth . . . scum" drowned out his words.[23] The meeting ended in bedlam, with members filing out while Trotsky and Zinoviev floundered helplessly.

Most would have slunk away in defeat. Not Trotsky. Unable to comprehend the parlousness of his own position and displaying powers of self-deception that bordered on the deranged, he somehow convinced himself that the tide of opinion was moving in his favor. He even attempted to organize a comeback demonstration on the tenth anniversary of the revolution, but those few brave protesters who took to Moscow's streets on his behalf were soon rounded up by the secret police and their posters of Trotsky torn to shreds. Finally, on November 14, Stalin had had enough: Trotsky and Zinoviev were kicked out of the Communist party.

Worse was to come. On January 17, 1928, a gang of GPU*
agents barged into Trotsky's Moscow apartment and dragged
him off to the Yaroslavl Station, where he was shoved onto a
train bound for Alma-Ata, in Kazakhstan, in Central Asia. His
son, Leon Sedov, shouted to a gang of indifferent railroad workers: "Look who they are shipping off—Trotsky!"[24] Shoulders
shrugged, nothing more: no one cared about an out-of-favor revolutionary. Almost unnoticed, the train steamed out of Moscow
on its two-thousand-mile journey to the Chinese border.

Trotsky proved to be a restless exile, agitating all the while,
forever trying to rally followers to his cause. But he was fast running out of allies: in mid-1928, Zinoviev and Kamenev, after
promising to toe the party line, were restored to favor.

Embittered and alone, Trotsky immersed himself in his memoirs and published a string of inflammatory pamphlets, all
directed at Stalin. At long last, the fire and portent of Trotsky's
words struck a raw nerve in the Politburo, jolting members awake
to the dangers posed by Stalin's total domination. But they were
helpless. In just four years he had broken the back of organized
opposition and amassed more power than any tsar in history.

Trotsky's was a lone voice of dissent. In December 1928, the
GPU threatened reprisals if he continued his political activities,
but that did nothing to staunch the damaging flow of words, all
bearing the hallmark and magic of Trotsky's name.

Driven to distraction, in February 1929, Stalin took the step
that he would regret for a decade: he ordered Trotsky's expulsion from the Soviet Union.

After considerable international negotiation—few countries
wanted anything to do with such a troublemaker—Turkey agreed
to take Trotsky. Under great secrecy he and his family were
moved to Odessa and there placed aboard the steamer *Ilyich*.
As he sailed out of Odessa, Trotsky gazed back at the nation he

---

*The state security agency that succeeded the Cheka in 1924 and reorga-
nized as the NKVD in 1934. All these agencies were precursors of the KGB.

had helped fashion and build, little realizing that he would never see it again.

Home for the next four years was the island of Prinkip in the Sea of Marmara. It was a miserable exile, but at least he had his liberty and he intended to use it. Trotsky abroad was far more dangerous than Trotsky at home, as Stalin would find out.

Inside the Soviet Union, Stalin pulled down the blinds on the largest country on earth, shrouding it in a grim darkness that would last decades. All those lessons he had learned at Lenin's knee—the concentration camps, the summary executions, the deliberate use of terror to subjugate the population—were magnified as never before. First, he persecuted the *kulaks,* peasant landowners mostly. They were falsely branded capitalist exploiters, and millions were either executed or else starved to death, while their land was stolen by the state, all in the name of "collectivization."

Then Stalin went hunting other enemies.

At the top of the list was Leon Trotsky. Already Stalin regretted having banished his most vocal critic. Had Trotsky remained in Soviet custody, a simple bullet to the back of the neck would have finished the task. Instead, Trotsky unleashed a series of scathing books and articles, all designed to peel away the myth and reveal the devil that was Joseph Stalin.

Trotsky Declared "Non-Person"

On February 20, 1932, Stalin issued a decree stripping Trotsky of Soviet nationality. The following year, Trotsky left Turkey for France. There had been no letup in his attacks on the Soviet dictator, and there was certainly no reduction in Stalin's determination to silence forever the one man who dared defy him. He ordered all mention of Trotsky to be expunged from official records; his books disappeared from libraries, his face from photographs, paintings and films, his name from history books and memoirs. Terrified historians, aware that not only their careers but their very lives depended on their submissiveness, duly "forgot" Trotsky when writing accounts of the Soviet Union.

Stalin's paranoia took on even more frightening forms. In 1936, Zinoviev and Kamenev were put on trial on trumped-up charges of plotting the assassination of Politburo member Sergei Kirov, a murder that in all probability Stalin had arranged. They also faced charges of conspiring with the exiled Trotsky. Prosecutor Andrei Vyshinsky used their show trial to accuse Trotsky of having "rolled in the filth of the White Guard," of being the "organizing catalyst for the last remnants of the exploitative classes now annihilated in the USSR."[25]

Tortured repeatedly and deprived of sleep, Zinoviev and Kamenev shuffled like zombies into the dock, under a promise of leniency if they publicly confessed. Both duly did so. Both were shot immediately. At the same trial Trotsky was sentenced to death *in absentia*.

For Trotsky, now living in Norway, which had granted him asylum on condition that he refrain from political activity, no threat was enough to halt his criticism. Press releases, articles, letters to the League of Nations, all flowed from his pen at an astonishing rate as he peppered the world with reminders of Stalin's savagery. About his own fate, he was philosophical. "Stalin would pay dearly, at this moment, to repeal the decree that banished me: how pleased he would be to mount a show trial. But he cannot revoke the past; he will have to resort to using methods . . . other than a trial. And Stalin is obviously seeking these."[26]

He was right. NKVD agents who had kept a close watch on Trotsky's son, Leon Sedov, and through him, his father, discovered that after Norway had washed its hands of its vexatious guest and deported him, he had found passage on a tanker bound for Mexico. On January 9, 1937, Trotsky trudged wearily ashore in his latest refuge, aware that the apparatus of terror that he had so enthusiastically championed and helped to fashion would never let him rest.

Eventually, he settled in a large villa at Coyoacán, on the outskirts of Mexico City, where he continued to write, prophesying the downfall of his great enemy. "Stalin is drawing close to the termination of his tragic mission."[27] But there was more hope than expectation in his prose.

Back in Moscow, on Stalin's orders, a special unit of the NKVD was formed to deal with the Trotsky problem. In early 1938, his son, Leon Sedov, died under suspicious circumstances in a French hospital after a successful operation for appendicitis; then his second son, Sergei, who had been apolitical and had refused to go abroad with his parents, was arrested and died shortly thereafter. Other, more distant members of the Trotsky family simply disappeared.

Perhaps emboldened by distance, Trotsky decided to organize a "countertrial" to expose the judicial farce in his homeland. It was a half-baked idea, one that most intellectuals he got in touch with rejected out of hand, but eventually the veteran American educator John Dewey agreed to oversee a hearing held at Trotsky's heavily fortified house. In December of that year, the commission predictably "acquitted" Trotsky of the crimes with which he had been charged in the Soviet Union.

It was a meaningless gesture. By this time Stalin was the most powerful man on earth, sole ruler of a 200-million-strong empire that stretched from the Black Sea to the Bering Straits. No one had ever wielded so much executive authority over so many people, and he had no intention of being constrained by such irrelevancies as international boundaries.

On May 24, 1940, at four in the morning, armed commandos, dressed in police and army uniforms, staged a full-scale assault on Trotsky's villa. After overwhelming and tying up the guards, they slashed the telephone lines and the electric alarm system linking the house to the central police station in Coyoacán. Once inside, the attackers panicked, firing indiscriminately into two rooms where the Trotskys were thought to be sleeping. While Trotsky and his wife, Natalya, cowered under a bed, no less than seventy-six bullets riddled the walls above them. The whole house stank of cordite. Then the guns fell silent and the attackers ran off, hurling incendiary bombs as they fled.

Trotsky had survived, but not by much. On June 1, he called a press conference at which he denounced Stalin as the mastermind behind the attack. Others weren't so sure. At a subsequent inquiry, witnesses, egged on by the local Stalinist press, expressed the idea that Trotsky himself had staged the attack in a deliberate attempt to besmirch Stalin's name. How else, they argued, could so many rounds have been fired and yet no one was injured? Another puzzling aspect was how the attackers managed to gain access to the heavily guarded villa. Suspicion centered on a young American guard, Bob Sheldon Harte, who was keeping watch that night and had since disappeared. The investigators insisted that Harte must have opened the door for the assassins, sparking rumors that he was an NKVD agent. Trotsky refused to believe his bodyguard was a traitor and loyally defended him.

Gradually, as tongues loosened, details of the attack leaked out. It had been led by the Mexican artist and Communist party leader David Siquieros. A further revelation came on June 25 with the discovery of the mutilated body of Sheldon Harte, found at the bottom of a quicklime pit, near a house rented by Siquieros's brothers-in-law, Luis and Leopoldo Arenal.

Half a world away, in Moscow, the chain-smoking dictator sat stony-faced when told how Trotsky had escaped death by inches. The order went out: keep trying.

Friends urged Trotsky to leave Mexico, where he was too easy a target for the NKVD death squads. He shrugged off their concerns. "I know I am condemned. I am a soldier and I can see that all the cards are stacked against me. Stalin is enthroned in Moscow with more power and resources at his disposal than any of the tsars. I am alone with a few friends and almost no resources, against a powerful killing machine which has already eliminated the other opponents, Lenin's associates in the Politburo and the Soviet government. So what can I do?"[28]

One option was to transform the villa into a fortress, and this he did. Guards were tripled and huge new walls, eighteen feet high with electrically controlled steel doors, rose up from a sea of barbed wire that stretched in every direction, far enough to deter any grenade-throwing assailant. Suitably impressed by the fortifications, Trotsky hunkered down and waited.

An unreal air of calm settled over the villa. As Trotsky sloughed off his postattack depression, he took an interest in the work of a personable if somewhat enigmatic young Belgian left-wing writer named Frank Jacson, whom he had met just four days after the abortive command raid. Jacson was writing a thesis about Trotskyism and wanted the master's approval. At around twenty past five on the afternoon of August 20, 1940, he called at the villa and Trotsky received him.

Despite the sweltering afternoon heat, Jacson was carrying a rolled-up raincoat. Trotsky noticed the quirk, but said nothing as he led the young man into this office. He felt safest here. On the desk were two handguns; also within easy reach was a security alarm bell. After some small talk, Trotsky took the article from Jacson and bent over to critique it. As he did so, his guest lay his raincoat down on the table.

A few seconds later a terrible cry of pain echoed through the villa. Jacson had taken an ice pick, the kind used in mountaineering, from his rolled-up raincoat and buried it three inches deep in Trotsky's skull.

Guards rushed in and overpowered the assassin. His victim, still conscious, whispered in English, "It's the end . . . this time . . . they've succeeded."[29]

The next day Leon Trotsky died.

News of Trotsky's death was greeted deliriously in Moscow. According to *Pravda,* Trotsky had been murdered by "one of his own disciples,"[30] and for a while this appeared to be a distinct possibility as Jacson's real identity and motive remained in doubt. On April 16, 1943, after a trial lasting eight months, he was sentenced to twenty years in jail.

Ten years would pass before it became known that Jacson's real name was Ramón Mercader, a young Spanish Communist, handpicked and trained by the NKVD for the specific purpose of killing Trotsky.

Stalin had, of course, authorized the assassination. It emerged that L. Eitingen, the NKVD colonel who directed the operation, and the assassin's mother, Caridad Mercader, who also participated in the plot, were close enough to hear the commotion in the Trotsky house, though both had evaded capture. All the conspirators were lavishly decorated by Stalin. Mercader was made a Hero of the Soviet Union; his mother received the Order of Lenin.*

Stalin reserved his greatest honor for Colonel Eitingen. Not only was the assassination overlord promoted to the rank of NKVD general, but he received a personal assurance that as long as he, Stalin, remained alive, not a hair on Eitingen's head would be touched.† In making this promise, Stalin broke the habit of a lifetime. Always he had ruthlessly exterminated anyone who knew too much, but never before had he felt such a debt of gratitude. The death of Trotsky was almost cathartic in its effect on Stalin, allowing him to cast off those few flecks of doubt that had lingered since the October Revolution. With Lenin dead, and Trotsky too, who now would dare to dispute or correct the gospel according to Joseph Stalin?

*Mercader was released in 1960 and took up residence in Prague before later moving to Cuba, where he died on October 18, 1978. His body was returned to Moscow for burial.

†After Stalin's death, on March 5, 1953, Eitingen was arrested and demoted.

CHAPTER 6

Amundsen versus Scott

Years of feud:	1909–1912	
Names:	Roald Amundsen	Robert F. Scott
Strengths:	Attention to detail, physical fitness	Heroic courage, skilled communicator
Weaknesses:	Obsessively secretive	Amateurish planner, irritable, technically unqualified to command such a high-profile test of endurance
At stake:	The prestige of being the "First man to the South Pole"	

Ever since the dawn of time the urge to explore has been fundamental to mankind. The Phoenicians, the Romans, the Vikings, the Polynesians, just about every sizable civilization has gone in search of lands to conquer; and nothing in exploration—be it by land, sea, air, or space—holds the magical appeal of being *first*! At the start of the twentieth century, the number of available exploring "firsts" was shrinking fast. Most of Africa, South America, and Asia had been mapped, forcing explorers eager to carve their names in the record books to ever-greater extremes of latitude and altitude in order to satisfy that craving. The most physically brutal of these challenges lay among the ice and blizzards that guarded each Pole. Neither extremity was safe. In the Arctic the Americans Robert Peary and Frederick Cook waged a furious, often vitriolic, race to the North Pole that has left history puzzling over who (if either) won this battle; while at the opposite end of the earth's axis, the even more inhospitable Antarctic continued to repel all invaders. But the South Pole standoff couldn't last, all the world knew that. The only question was: who would get there first?

On the evening of October 12, 1910, a heavily laden three-masted whaler, the *Terra Nova,* docked in Melbourne, Australia, en route to Antarctica. That night the master of the vessel, a forty-two-year-old British naval officer, Captain Robert Falcon Scott, went ashore to collect his mail. Among the many letters was a terse telegram sent from Madeira in early October, when the *Terra Nova* had still been in the Indian Ocean. It read: BEG LEAVE TO INFORM YOU *FRAM* PROCEEDING ANTARCTIC. AMUNDSEN.[1]

Scott knitted his brow. *What the devil . . . ?*

Gradually, very gradually, mystification gave way to concern, then to a frigid, controlled fury. For years the stockily built Englishman had dreamed and schemed for this moment, when he could lead a successful expedition to the South Pole, the last great trophy in overland exploration. Fame, honors, not to mention considerable riches, awaited the first adventurer able to plant his nation's flag at the southernmost point of the world, and the ambitious Scott was convinced that Destiny had marked him out to be that man. Except that now the prize seemed about to be snatched from his grasp by some treacherous Norwegian! Scott set his jaw firmly. Such a disaster could not, would not be allowed to happen!

The greatest race in polar history was on.

Scott had cut his exploring teeth on the British Antarctic expedition of 1901–1904. His rousing account of hardship and bravery under the most arduous conditions, *The Voyage of the Discovery,* had thrilled a nation in sore need of heroes after the Boer War debacle, when a handful of farmers had bloodied the nose of the mightiest empire in history. The book had transformed a dreamy, balding naval officer into the leading light of British polar exploration. But it had also made enemies. Fellow *Discovery* expedition member Ernest Shackleton, in particular, resented the way in which his own role, and that of everyone else, had been relegated to that of a mere bit player while Scott hogged the limelight.

The rift between Scott and Shackleton demonstrated just how

bellicose turn-of-the-century polar exploration had become. This was an arena packed with bulging egos, and vicious clashes were commonplace. Some of the polar heavyweights, like Peary and Scott, carved out fiefdoms in the ice and expected others to yield exploring rights to them and them alone. Which is why the events of December 1908 had so unsettled the tetchy Scott. That was when Shackleton, having broken his promise not to use Scott's base at McMurdo Sound, had battled to within a hundred miles of the South Pole before being forced back.

The report jolted Scott into action. "I think we'd better have a shot next,"[2] he remarked to a colleague.

He envisaged an ambitious two-pronged expedition. On the one hand, there would be considerable scientific analysis, but the undoubted jewel in the crown was Scott's declared intention of reaching the South Pole. Capturing public imagination was one thing, raising funds another. Ministerial miserliness obliged Scott to trudge, begging bowl in hand, from corporate boardroom to lecture hall and back again, often enough for *The Times* of London to complain that it would be "deeply regrettable if, for want of either men or of money, the brilliant recent record of British exploration were at this point to be checked."[3] Eventually, the British government did cough up a grant, and slowly other funds trickled in from commercial enterprises, food companies mainly, anxious to have their brand names associated with such a high-profile venture.

Adding spice to an already highly seasoned dish, on February 3, 1910, the U.S. National Geographical Society announced that it intended launching an Antarctic expedition to begin in December 1911, with the goal of reaching the Pole one year later. Its leader would be Peary, fresh from his April 1909 triumph at the North Pole. Egged on by circulation-hungry newspaper editors keen to play up this challenge to British Antarctic exploring supremacy, Peary promised "the most exciting and nerve-wracking race the world has ever seen."[4]

However, the challenge would come, not from America, but from an obscure country whose independent existence could be measured in months, rather than centuries.

When Norway finally broke the shackles of Swedish domination in 1905, it marked the end of a two-hundred-year struggle for independence. Young, lusty, and eager to prove itself on the international stage, Norway might have been a minnow in geopolitical terms, but its nautical traditions, dating back a thousand years to the Vikings, were unrivaled; and in the specialized, often deadly field of polar exploration it had already shown itself to be world class. The great forerunner had been Fridtjof Nansen, who in the late nineteenth century had revolutionized Arctic exploration in his remarkable saucer-shaped ship, the *Fram,* with its reinforced sides specially designed to combat the crushing effects of the pack ice. Nansen's exploits had earned him national gratitude and the post of ambassador to Britain.

Now, though, the mantle of Norwegian explorer supreme had passed to a sailor who, more than anyone else, would come to embody the old Nordic tradition of fearless sea rover.

Roald Amundsen was born into a family of seamen and shipowners on July 16, 1872. In his early twenties he had abandoned a career in medicine in favor of adventure, and three years later gained his first polar experience as mate on the *Belgica,* Adrien de Gerlache's Belgian expedition to Antarctica. Upon his return to Norway, the studious Amundsen prepared for his first independent venture.

Polar immortality for the lanky explorer came in 1905, when, aboard his ship the *Gjøa,* he became the first person successfully to traverse the Northwest Passage from the Atlantic to the Pacific Ocean, a feat that had defied the greatest names in maritime history for over three hundred years.

Amundsen returned home to a hero's welcome, yearning to carve his name ever deeper into the annals of polar exploration. By instinct and geography, he was drawn to the Arctic and the hitherto unclaimed North Pole, which lay barely two thousand miles from the northernmost tip of his homeland. It became his obsession. The intention was to drift across the North Pole in Nansen's *Fram.* Then came the shattering news of Peary's triumph.

Writing later, Amundsen didn't mince words: "If I were to maintain my reputation as an explorer, I had to win a sensational victory one way or another. I decided on a coup."[5] And that, for an ice explorer like Amundsen, could mean just one thing—a full-court press on the South Pole.

Secret Plans

From the outset, Amundsen deliberately shrouded his plans in secrecy. Any leak, he reasoned, could only work to Scott's advantage. Newspaper reports hinted at the Englishman's fundraising difficulties, but all that might change overnight if rumors of a rival expedition began circulating. (After much initial hoopla, it had become apparent that Peary's South Pole ambitions were dead in the water.) For an established global superpower like Britain, the prospect of being upstaged by some lowly international newcomer such as Norway was unthinkable. Amundsen had no doubts: all those coffers and billfolds that Scott now found so difficult to access would open up like the Red Sea as outraged Brits rallied round to see off "Johnny Foreigner."

The astuteness, some might say duplicity, with which Amundsen proceeded revealed his single-minded nature. In public he maintained his pretense of going to the North Polar Basin to pursue scientific studies, an announcement that prompted Scott to contact him with a view to pooling scientific resources. Except that Amundsen proved curiously elusive. Letters went unacknowledged, phone calls unreturned. None of this seems to have aroused Scott's suspicion, nor was there any reason why it should. A product of the long and distinguished line of British "gentleman" explorers, where "a chap's word" was the litmus test of honor, it would never have crossed his mind that Amundsen intended traveling anywhere else except his avowed destination, the North Pole. Which is why he sent Amundsen a set of matched instruments so that comparative measurements could be taken of the North and South poles, gifts that the taciturn Norwegian accepted with acute embarrassment and continued silence.

Amundsen had other reasons for reticence. Had the newly formed Norwegian government—one of his principal backers— learned of his plans to scupper Scott's well-publicized attack on the South Pole, they might have panicked and pulled the financial plug. At this time few European nations, and certainly not Norway, wanted to ruffle British feathers, for fear of possible reprisals. Later, in defense of his much-condemned secrecy, Amundsen argued, with considerable justification, that had he made his plans public they would have been stifled at birth.

Quietly he set about piecing together the best organized expedition ever to venture to Antarctica. Food, clothing, equipment, schedules, he spent months checking and double-checking everything down to the very last detail; nothing was left to chance.

Scott, on the other hand, appeared to be improvising as he went along, almost caricaturing the traditional British disdain for professionalism, eschewing preparation in favor of inspiration. Sadly, there was just not enough of the latter on tap. On one point, though, he was adamant: Eskimo dogs would play a minor role in the expedition. Scott's mistrust of dogs stemmed from his *Discovery* days when, due to inexperience, he had suffered miserably with the ill-disciplined dog teams. This time around he intended pinning his faith on ponies, white preferably, apparently convinced that this coloring provided some kind of immunity against the frozen climate!

Amundsen was dumbfounded. "Scott . . . had come to the conclusion that Manchurian ponies were superior to dogs on the Barrier. Amongst those who were acquainted with the Eskimo dog, I do not suppose I was the only one who was startled on first hearing this."[6] Even so, ever suspicious and deeply protective of his own interests, Amundsen fretted over the possibility that Scott might yet change his mind and rely on dogs after all. With this in mind, Amundsen fired off a frosty memo to his own dog agent: "If you receive other orders for dogs, I hope you will remember that I was first."[7]

He needn't have worried. Scott had become obsessed with horsepower, at least for the first part of the journey. His plan called for ponies to haul the sledges across the Great Ice Barrier to the Beardmore Glacier, where they would then be slaughtered for food; thereafter, the expedition would rely on manpower to haul the sledges. Earlier, Scott had written: "No journey ever made with dogs can approach the height of that fine conception which is realized when a party of men go forth to face hardships, dangers and difficulties with their own unaided efforts."[8] Lofty sentiments maybe, but potential man killers on the terrifying Polar Plateau, where temperatures could plummet to -70°F. and unprotected flesh could freeze in seconds.

However, none of that mattered on June 15, 1910, when huge crowds lined the Welsh coastline to cheer wildly as the *Terra Nova,* minus Scott, who intended joining the ship later, slipped her moorings in Cardiff Docks and headed out into open water, carrying with her the hopes of a nation as she lumbered over the southern horizon.

It was a far more low-key affair a couple of months later, when the *Fram* slid almost unnoticed out of Norwegian waters on August 9, bound—so it was universally believed—for Cape Horn, then up the Americas to the Arctic Circle. Strange, though; a weird tension seemed to fill the air on board. Something was definitely not quite right. . . .

Scott joined the *Terra Nova* in Cape Town and took command for the long voyage across the Indian Ocean to Australia. The plan was to visit as many empire colonies as possible, waving the Union Jack, drumming up contributions, before proceeding sedately south to Antarctica.

But that telegram in Australia changed everything.

Amundsen had even kept his own team in the dark, waiting until the *Fram* reached Madeira on September 6 to take on fresh water and other provisions before gathering his men on deck to reveal their true destination. "It is my intention to sail Southwards, land a party on the Southern continent and try to reach the South Pole."[9]

This was jaw-dropping stuff. But before anyone had time to argue, Amundsen shrewdly appealed to his colleagues' patriotism, declaring it was now a question of racing the English. "Hurrah," shouted Olav Bjaaland, the expedition's ski expert. "That means we'll get there first!"[10]

Just before the *Fram* departed Madeira on September 9, Amundsen's brother, Leon, was handed the soon-to-be-infamous telegram, with strict instructions to delay its transmission until October, by which time, Amundsen calculated, his rival would be somewhere in the Indian Ocean and out of radio contact. Untroubled by any hint of scruple and with his conscience at least technically clear, Amundsen readied himself for the long voyage south, still checking those plans.

Half a world away, on board the *Terra Nova* the mood was somber. Lawrence Oates, sardonic and hardheaded and the only soldier among the mainly naval team, noted in his diary that from the moment Scott heard Amundsen was going south he was under pressure.

"Amundsen is acting suspiciously," Scott murmured one day. "In Norway he avoided me in every conceivable manner," adding savagely, "it's the Pole he is after, all right."[11] But how did he intend to get there? The general consensus on the *Terra Nova* was that Amundsen would attack the Pole from the Weddell Sea side, forgoing the Great Ice Barrier route, which had been traditionally British.

Back in London the mood was distinctly ugly. No country likes to be on the wrong side of a David and Goliath battle, with its concomitant loss of national prestige, and nervous glances were exchanged over the way that imperial Britain had been so comprehensively hoodwinked by a Scandinavian parvenu. Amundsen's revelation had come as a bolt from the blue. Longtime Scott patron Sir Clements Markham spluttered that Amundsen was a "blackguard," who had played a "dirty trick," and he forecast that "in any case, Scott will be on the ground and settled long before Amundsen turns up—if he ever does."[12]

Which turned out to be an accurate prediction.

When Amundsen finally made landfall in Antarctica on January 14, 1911, Scott had already been established at his McMurdo Sound base camp for nine days, using that time to begin the tedious but essential groundwork of laying depot stations across the Great Ice Barrier for the upcoming expedition. In the three months of Antarctic summer left to them, the British team forged their way to 79°30'S, where they stockpiled a huge food store, which they called One Ton Depot. Then came the wearisome trek back through storms and howling gales to McMurdo Sound and some astonishing news.

Far from being on the opposite side of the continent, in the Weddell Sea, Amundsen had established his headquarters—called Framheim, in honor of his ship—farther along the Great Ice Barrier, a distance of just four hundred miles.

Ice Confrontation

Amundsen's team had been spotted by the *Terra Nova* as it explored the Bay of Whales. After choking back their anger and some rather colorful curses, the British crew had found, to their considerable surprise, that they mingled easily with the Norwegians, with one crew member, Wilfred Bruce, going so far as to say, "Individually . . . all seemed charming men, even the perfidious Amundsen."[13]

Nothing, though, could disguise the underlying tension, and one-upmanship was rampant. Much of it hinged upon Scott's well-publicized decision to employ three untested motor sledges on his expedition. Amundsen, convinced that Scott was totally wrong about dogs, but far less confident about this newfangled technology, hemmed and hawed for a while before inquiring nervously about the motor sledges. A breezy response assured him that "one of them is already on *terra firma*,"[14] which Amundsen took to mean that the sledge had already crossed the Ice Barrier and reached the Beardmore Glacier.

Later, when the party broke up and the *Terra Nova* sailed out of the Bay of Whales, Amundsen wore a worried frown: a life's dream at jeopardy, all because of some infernal contraption. However, what the British had conveniently failed to disclose was that the motor sledge was actually *at the bottom of* McMurdo Sound, having accidentally sunk during disembarkation! Only later, when it no longer mattered, would Amundsen realize how thoroughly he had been duped.

For the time being, at least, he enjoyed one crucial advantage. Not only was the Bay of Whales easy to navigate and rich in fresh meat such as penguins and seals, but it lay a whole degree of latitude farther south than McMurdo Sound, putting him 60 miles closer to the Pole than his rival, a saving of 120 miles in a journey of 1,364 miles as the crow flies, or almost 9 percent. Only much later would the significance of this difference become so cruelly apparent.

Like Scott, Amundsen had deployed food supplies along his anticipated route. Unlike Scott, he had established not one but several major camps, at 80°S, 81°S, and 82°S. Altogether he had more than a ton and a half of supplies stored within 480 miles of the Pole. Now it was just a question of waiting, for on April 21, 1911, the Antarctic sun finally vanished from view, ushering in the long polar night.

This was a bad time for both men. Trapped in claustrophobic huts, their tempers wore thin and imaginations grew more fertile. Scott's anxiety was palpable. His overwrought response when told of the tense encounter at the Bay of Whales had alarmed those about him. According to Apsley Cherry-Garrard: "Scott jumped out of his bag . . . and said, 'By Jove, what a chance we have missed—we might have taken Amundsen and sent him back in the ship!'"[15]

Here were the first inklings of the irrationality that would increasingly mar Scott's role as expedition leader. His own previous exploits, and to a far lesser extent those of Shackleton, had instilled in him a conviction that the Great Ice Barrier was in some way an outpost of the British Empire that had come under attack from an invader. To even contemplate capturing Amundsen and shipping him off the continent was preposterous; to verbalize it bordered on the idiotic.

Amid the jingoistic rumblings in the British camp, Oates's diary entries retained their customary sense of proportion. "They say Amundsen has been underhand in the way he has gone about it, but I personally don't see it as underhand to keep your mouth shut . . . these Norskies are a very tough lot."[16]

They were also superbly equipped. Besides the all-important dogs, they had Eskimo fur clothing, specially lightened sledges, skis, and vast quantities of food and kerosene. Amundsen, the quintessential planner, was sanguine about his preparedness: had such supplies been available to Shackleton in 1908, "The South Pole would have been a closed chapter."[17]

Elsewhere, though, Amundsen's diary revealed a mind in torment. "Our plan is one . . . and . . . one alone—to reach the Pole. For that goal, I have decided to throw everything else aside."

On August 24, the sun reappeared for the first time in four months; even so, the temperatures remained dangerously low. Amundsen strained at the leash. Where were the British? What if they were already on their way? Two further weeks of delay curdled his already sour disposition. Finally, on September 8, his patience snapped. With the thermometer at -37°F., he left Framheim for the Pole.

This was a disastrous undertaking. To his astonishment the mercury kept falling, all the way to -70°F. Covered in sores, frost-bitten, and with dogs freezing to death at his feet, Amundsen finally accepted the folly of his decision and turned back, fighting through blizzards to refuge at Framheim.

His recklessness had nearly killed his team, and it had done nothing to improve his waspish mood. "The thought of the English gave him no peace," wrote Sverre Hassel, the team's expert dog driver. "For if we were not first at the Pole, we might just as well stay at home."[18]

Finally, the bad weather broke and on October 20, Amundsen, together with Bjaaland, Hassel, and two others, Oscar Wisting and Helmer Hanssen, departed on their historic journey into the unknown. Four sledges were used, each pulled by thirteen dogs. The first stages of the journey were almost effortless; at times it was even possible just to let the dogs pull the sledges while the men grabbed hold of the traces and were drawn along in comfort. Other than a little trouble with crevasses, they made excellent progress, and on October 24, the Norwegians reached the depot at 80°S.

Men and dogs glutted themselves in readiness for the struggle ahead. Having started two months and 6,000 miles behind, Amundsen was now 150 miles ahead of his rival.

It would be another week before Scott's party even left McMurdo Sound. Right from the outset the much-heralded motor sledges gave trouble in the subzero temperatures, and after five days they had to be abandoned. The ponies, too, with their sharp hooves were hopelessly ill-suited to polar travel, often plunging belly-deep into the snow, causing valuable time to be lost as they were dug out, their flanks encased in sheets of solid ice. At the end of each stage, the already exhausted men had to rub down and cover the ponies with blankets, then erect snow walls to protect them from the wind. Oates, the pony master, urged ruthlessness: drive the poor beasts till they drop, then slaughter them for food. Scott, an inveterate animal lover, would have none of it. Squeamish to the point of stupidity, he refused to submit the ponies to any more hardship than was necessary, oblivious to the deleterious effect this was having on his men.

By contrast, Amundsen's low-maintenance dogs darted lightly across the Great Ice Barrier, and at the end of each day burrowed into the snow to keep warm. Nor was there any trace of sentiment in Amundsen's plan. Even before the expedition began, he had calculated on what day each superfluous dog would be slaughtered to provide fresh meat for its companions.

All of which meant that while Amundsen regularly and without wasted effort notched up daily advances of twenty miles, Scott, even on a good day, rarely managed half that distance.

On November 7 Amundsen departed from his final depot at 82°S, carrying supplies for a hundred days, enough to last until February 6, 1912. As always, he erred on the side of safety, carrying ten times more food and fuel per man than his rival had budgeted, and in the next four days his team hauled a ton of supplies over the awesome ice ridges of the Axel Heiberg Glacier, up to the Polar Plateau itself, an incredible achievement. With this obstacle behind them, the five men pressed on toward their final goal. Not even a succession of blinding fogs was allowed to hamper their progress: with four skilled navigators in his team, Amundsen had no fears of getting lost.

Meanwhile, Scott crawled on at a treacle-slow pace. Unlike the Norwegians, he had only one trained navigator, himself, and his skills were rusty. Ponderous calculations and frequent mistakes made for lengthy delays. At the foot of the Beardmore Glacier, as arranged, Oates killed the last of the ponies. Henceforth, they would rely on manhauling their sledges, some weighing seven hundred pounds, all the way to the South Pole and back, a round trip of a thousand miles.

It was lunacy.

At ten thousand feet up on the Polar Plateau, tortured lungs struggled to grab sufficient oxygen from the thin air, dulling physical performance and mental acuity. Creeping past huge, gaping crevasses, large enough to swallow a skyscraper, the men dragged their sledges across the rippled pressure ridges, unaware that because of Scott's calamitous miscalculation of the number of calories necessary to carry out such inhuman physical effort, they were starving themselves to death with every step.

Malnourished and dispirited, Scott's team had no stomach to fight the raging blizzards that often trapped them for days in their tents, while Amundsen, on skis and with dogs, refused to yield to the elements and pressed on relentlessly. His determination to beat Scott was all-consuming. Every day the Norwegians pushed a bit farther ahead.

British Morale Sinks

As doubts began to sap British morale, Oates feared the worst. "If it comes to a race, Amundsen will have a great chance of getting there as he is a man who has been at this kind of game all his life, and he has a hard crowd behind him, while we are very young."[19]

His teammate, Henry Bowers, was equally concerned. "I must say that Amundsen's chance of having forestalled us with 120 dogs looks good,"[20] though in a later diary entry he vented his frustration, wondering how the "back-handed, sneaking ruffian"[21] was faring.

Very well, was the answer. On December 8, with the sun shining brightly, Amundsen passed Shackleton's Furthest South record of 88°23'S, and was within a hundred miles of the Pole. The dogs were ravenous and wearied, the men had many sores and frostbitten faces, yet still the party pushed on. Every step closer to the Pole multiplied Amundsen's foreboding that Scott had already beaten them. A collective panic began to jangle their nerves. Bjaaland summed up everyone's fears. "Shall we see the English flag? God have mercy on us. I don't believe it."[22]

The next day, December 15, 1911, at three o'clock in the afternoon, the sledgemeters told Amundsen that he had reached the southernmost point on earth. Cries of "Halt!" brought the team to a standstill. The bearded leader, swathed in reindeer skins, scanned every direction and saw nothing; no British flag, no British expedition, no signs of human habitation anywhere, just an endless white landscape of empty ice and snow.

His triumph was absolute.

Proudly, Amundsen placed the Norwegian tricolor at the geographical South Pole. Even at this, the greatest moment of his life, there was no room for complacency. Pragmatic to his bones, he knew that the winner was not necessarily he who won the race, but he who grabbed the headlines first. It was imperative that they return to Framheim as soon as possible.

On December 18, Amundsen left the South Pole with just one goal in mind—beat Scott back to the cablehead. He warned Hanssen, "If I know the British, they won't give up once they've started . . . [Scott] will arrive during the next day or two."[23]

For once Amundsen got it wrong. In fact, Scott was 360 miles behind, still crawling up the Beardmore Glacier.

By coincidence, on New Year's Day the two expeditions actually came within a hundred miles of each other, except that Scott was just emerging from the Beardmore Glacier, while Amundsen was descending from the plateau onto the barrier below, going flat out in the opposite direction. The contrast in attitude between the two teams could not have been more marked. So far as Amundsen was concerned, "The going was splendid,"[24] whereas Scott worried about his team's low morale. They had little to cheer about. Emaciated and frostbitten, half-blind from defective snow goggles, they now had to combat the insidious effects of scurvy, which had reduced their gums to mush.

January 3, 1912, brought the last division of the eight-man British team and Scott's biggest blunder to date. Astonishingly, he announced that contrary to expectations, he intended taking four men, not three, with him to the Pole. This appears to have been a sudden whim, perhaps born out of panic, because all the expedition's preparations and calculations, particularly for food and kerosene, had been predicated on just four men making the final polar assault. Scott's abrupt *volte-face* put an impossible strain on supplies already depleted to life-threatening levels. Watched by the displaced trio, who would return to base, Scott trudged off into the frozen wasteland. With him for the final stage were Oates, Bowers, a brawny seaman named Edgar Evans, and the expedition's sole medical practitioner, Dr. Edward Wilson.

And they were still 150 miles from their goal.

Day after day, Scott and his bedraggled team slogged onward. Deep down, all five men suspected that the race was lost; only national pride kept them going. On January 15, Scott injected a rare note of optimism into his diary entry: "It is wonderful to think that two long marches would land us at the Pole," only later to fall foul of his recurrent nightmare," . . . and the only appalling possibility the sight of the Norwegian flag forestalling ours."

The next day brought confirmation of all that Scott had dreaded: an abandoned sledge bearer with a black flag and many dog prints. His already fragile spirit disintegrated. "This told the whole story. The Norwegians have forestalled us and are first at the Pole. It is a terrible disappointment, and I am very sorry for my loyal companions."[25]

On January 17, more dead than alive, the British team duly reached the South Pole. A Norwegian flag tied to its makeshift pole, fluttering defiantly, mocked their final steps. Denied the elation of victory, Scott plunged into despair. "Great God! This is an awful place," he wrote in that day's diary.

Bowers struggled to salvage a crumb of comfort from the defeat. "I am glad that we have done it by good British man-haulage,"[26] he wrote to his mother. Oates, who by this time had come to despise Scott for his incompetence, tipped a nod of appreciation to Amundsen. "I must say that that man must have had his head screwed on right. The gear they left was in excellent shape and they seem to have had a comfortable trip with their dog teams, very different from our wretched man-hauling."[27]

Most humiliating of all, they found a tent pitched by Amundsen. Inside was some discarded equipment, a letter to King Haakon of Norway, and a covering note to Scott. It read:

Dear Captain Scott,

As you probably are the first to reach this area after us, I will ask you to kindly forward this letter to King Haakon VII. If you can use any of the articles left in the tent please do not hesitate to do so. With kind regards I wish you a safe return.

Yours truly

Roald Amundsen

Scott and his men stood motionless, utterly dejected. With spirits lower than the ambient temperature, they turned to face the way they had come. Ahead lay seven hundred miles of the toughest terrain on earth. Worse still, it was late in the season, and the brief Antarctic summer was fast drawing to a close.

Hundreds of miles ahead, Amundsen's expedition surged buoyantly onward. On January 26, he and his team skied into Framheim with all the zest of vacationers just back from an afternoon on the piste; indeed, he later characterized the expedition as little more than "a sporting stunt."[28] Four days later he loaded the thirty-nine surviving dogs onto the *Fram* and set sail for Australia.

Every mile of that journey was beset with anxiety for the Norwegian; even now, Scott might overtake him and claim all the glory. When just over one month later, on March 7, the *Fram* finally put into Hobart, Tasmania, Amundsen's first word was for news of the *Terra Nova*. Told there was none, he exhaled a silent sigh of relief.

He'd done it!

Amundsen's achievement burst onto newspapers around the globe. For days London had buzzed with rumors that Scott had won the great race; now it was time to face the truth. Sour grapes were the order of the day, with *The Times* grouching that Amundsen's sudden decision to go south and the secrecy that had surrounded it "were felt to be not quite in accordance with the spirit of fair and open competition which had hitherto marked Antarctic exploration."[29]

Accusations of "cheating" and—breathe the word quietly—"professionalism" abounded as the press derided Amundsen's meticulousness as somehow shameful, not fit to stand comparison with the "gentleman amateur" approach adopted by Scott. A rare British voice of unstinting praise came from Shackleton, delighted that his old rival had been so comprehensively routed. Shackleton's obvious glee drove Scott's wife, Kathleen, to seethe, "I would willingly assist at that man's annihilation!"[30]

It mattered not one jot; around the world, if not in Britain, Roald Amundsen was an exploring superstar, ready to reap the rewards of his labors. So while the Norwegian victor hit the lucrative lecture trail and began writing the book of his epic journey, the world waited for news of Scott and his team. . . .

Days stretched into weeks, then months; still the cables remained ominously silent. In April all optimism faded with the pale summer sun as winter's frigid shadow closed in once more.

It was the end of October before a search party was able to leave McMurdo Sound and set out across the blinding whiteness of the Great Ice Barrier. Prepared for a long haul up to the Polar Plateau, their rescue mission was heartbreakingly brief. On November 12, they discovered a single snow-covered tent. Inside, huddled together, lay the frozen bodies of Scott, Wilson, and Bowers. They had perished just eleven miles from One Ton Depot and the provisions that might have saved them.

Scott's agonizing return journey has quite rightly earned its place among the great epics of exploration. We can only guess at the full extent of the suffering because the primary record was kept by Scott himself, and it should be remembered that he was a fine writer whose words were ultimately intended for publication. He knew how to craft a tale guaranteed to make his countrymen's chests swell with pride, and he was eager to cast himself in the role of heroic leader, undone by factors beyond his control. Luck, or its absence, is a frequent theme, with every setback being laid at the door of Fate. Writing later, Amundsen dismissed such excuses. "Victory awaits him who has everything in order—luck people call it. Defeat is certain for him who has neglected to take the necessary precautions in time—this is called bad luck."[31]

No matter how self-serving, Scott's diary provides a moving testament to the strength of the human spirit under inhuman conditions as the five men battled blizzards, mountains and crevasses, walking to their doom. First to succumb was the bear-like Evans. Ironically, the sheer bulk that had so impressed Scott proved deadly in these conditions; Evans required vastly more fuel to keep going than his smaller-framed companions. While the others hauled their sledges across the murderous Beardmore Glacier, Evans shuffled along in confused, moody silence behind them. The end came on February 16, when he slipped into unconsciousness and never awoke.

For another month the four survivors stumbled blindly through mind-numbing blizzards across the Great Ice Barrier. Perhaps the defining moment of the expedition came on March 17. That was the day when Oates, limping in great pain from an old wound that had reopened and aware that he was hampering his companions' chances of survival, made the supreme sacrifice. Murmuring to the others, "I am just going outside and may be some time," he staggered out of the tent into the blinding snow, never to be seen again. "It was," Scott wrote, "the act of a brave man and an English gentleman."[32]

The last entry in Scott's diary was dated March 29, and read: "We shall stick it out to the end, but we are getting weaker, of course, and the end cannot be far. It seems a pity, but I do not think I can write more. R. Scott." There was a final, sad postcript, written in a shaky hand: "For God's sake look after our people."

The slow pace of communications meant that another three months passed before news of Scott's demise reached his homeland. The catastrophe struck a raw nerve. National pride had taken a hammering in April 1912 with the "unsinkable" *Titanic* tragedy. Now this. And yet the gloom was short-lived. In that curious way the British have of reworking failure into glory, the doomed expedition became a metaphor for heroic endeavor. Misty-eyed readers disregarded the bungled preparation, the almost criminal disregard for men's lives, the sheer stupidity, in favor of Scott's extraordinary physical courage and phenomenal stamina and that of his colleagues, particularly the gallant Oates, whose selfless bravery was thought to typify all that was best in British exploration. Had the team survived, in all likelihood history would scarcely recall them. Had they never been found, then the tragic circumstances of their deaths, so adroitly recorded by their leader, would remain a mystery. As it was, publication of Scott's narrative not only guaranteed immortality for himself and his team, it rallied a nation on the verge of war.

Ironically, the biggest loser in all this was Amundsen himself. Not only did Scott's tragedy tarnish the gloss of his fantastic achievement—as great as any in modern exploration—but it somehow succeeded in casting the stoical Norwegian, however unfairly, in the role of villain. Valiantly though he tried, his own book, *The South Pole,* did little to redress the distorted historical imbalance. Lacking Scott's literary flair, it was as lifeless and cold as the continent he had so recently conquered.

Amundsen never fully recovered from the tragedy. For the rest of his life* he was haunted by pangs of guilt: if only he had left more provisions at the Pole for his rival; if only he had been less secretive, not so competitive; if only . . . if only . . .

In the end he was undone by words, not deeds. For while Amundsen got the triumph, it was Scott, with his talented pen, who grabbed the glory,† a salutary reminder that contrary to what the hoary old maxim might proclaim, history isn't always written by the winners.

---

*In June 1928, Amundsen left Norway to fly to the aid of fellow explorer Umberto Nobile, whose dirigible had crashed on a second Arctic flight. Amundsen's plane vanished, though Nobile was later rescued. Months afterward, the discovery of floating wreckage told the tragic story of how Amundsen met his death.

†Joint recognition of their achievements came with the naming of the Amundsen-Scott South Pole Station.

CHAPTER 7

Duchess of Windsor versus Queen Mother

Years of feud:	1934–1986	
Names:	Wallis Simpson	Elizabeth Windsor
Strengths:	Iron-willed, ambitious, prepared to gamble all	Supportive of her husband in his hour of greatest need, the power behind the throne
Weaknesses:	See above	Overly protective of her royal status, flint-hearted toward those she deemed unacceptable
At stake:	A crown and an empire	

Feuds, particularly the great feuds of history, are usually rooted in a craving for power: one party wishes to gain ascendancy over another—even crush them—and nothing on earth will be allowed to deflect them from that goal. This is what makes the twentieth century's most notorious and enduring royal feud so extraordinary; for here, it was the sudden and wholly unwanted acquisition of power that caused all the trouble.

At the start of 1936, Elizabeth, the Duchess of York, was a lightly regarded member of the British royal family, a frothy confection of chiffon and silk, steadfast and caring as a wife, someone best known for having produced two highly photogenic daughters. True, she was married to the king's brother, but both she and her timid husband had grown used to living in the shadow of the popular, extroverted Edward VIII and neither had much appetite for the spotlight's harsh glare.

And yet, by the following December, this unassuming, almost nondescript woman found herself Queen of England, joint ruler of an empire that covered one-third of the globe, one of the world's most recognized celebrities. It was an elevation that left her physically ill and filled with loathing for the woman who had inspired this horrid transformation.

For Mrs. Wallis Simpson that same tumultuous year was no less life-changing. In a mere twelve months, this twice-divorced American socialite was catapulted from furtive mentions in newspaper gossip columns to international notoriety, the most hated woman on earth, an ogress to compare with the likes of Lucrezia Borgia or Marie de Brinvilliers. Such a savaging would have soured the sweetest disposition, and Wallis was no saint. Revenge was the order of the day as she set out on what would be an almost life-long mission to butcher the woman whom she believed had robbed her of her rightful role as Queen of England.

It was a battle waged in the drafty corridors of palaces and castles of England, and eventually across oceans, between two extraordinary characters. Between them, they changed not just the course of British history, but maybe that of the world as well.

They met on fewer than a handful of occasions, and each time the atmosphere crackled with tension. Observers cringed, waiting for the sparks to fly, but these women were old campaigners in the society stakes; each knew how the game was played. Overt displays of rancor were frowned upon. This was feuding at the first remove, filtered through stiff upper lips, cut-glass accents, and preternatural amounts of self-restraint.

For some the confrontation amounted to raw xenophobia—the snooty British aristocracy looking down its nose at the vulgar American upstart—but this is a gross oversimplification. Ever since the mid-nineteenth century, a steady stream of American heiresses had married successfully into British nobility; Winston Churchill's own mother, herself the daughter of a Wall Street speculator, is a case in point. No, the antipathy toward Wallis went far deeper than mere nationality. She was "a woman with a past," and in those more prudish times "a past," once acquired, was damnably difficult to shake off.

Appropriately enough for this most enigmatic of women, even her date of birth is shrouded in mystery. Most plump for June 19, 1896, though even Wallis herself was unsure. What we do know is that her father, T. Wallis Warfield, belonged to the unfashionable side of a wealthy Pennsylvania family, earned a pittance as a clerk, and died within six months of his daughter's birth. She was christened Bessie Wallis, Bessie after her mother's sister, Wallis after her father. Right from an early age she hated her name and called herself Wallis. While still young she went to live with relatives in Baltimore.

Even as a teenager she triggered criticism. Many thought her "fast," far too racy for the straitlaced Baltimore bluebloods. Although too angular and rawboned to be considered a classical beauty, she exuded a rare sexuality that inflamed hearts and loins alike, and she never could resist a handsome man in uniform.

On November 8, 1916, she married a naval pilot named Earl Winfield Spencer Jr. It was a romantic age and Spencer had dash and élan to spare; he also had problems with the bottle. Within days of the wedding Wallis realized her mistake: she had married a drunk, someone eaten up with jealousy, often violent. Despite this, she stayed with him and at the end of World War I, when Spencer was given command of the North Island air station near San Diego, Wallis went too.

Slowly the marriage withered. Despite this, Wallis was still playing the dutiful wife when, on April 7, 1920, the British cruiser HMS *Renown* put into San Diego. On board was the man widely regarded as the world's most eligible bachelor, the Prince of Wales. Golden-haired and youthfully handsome, the playboy heir to the British throne basked in the kind of adulation usually reserved for the likes of Douglas Fairbanks and Rudolph Valentino. As an unofficial ambassador for Britain, and more important for himself, he circled the globe, raising pulse rates and breaking hearts wherever he traveled, a regular Prince Charming.

Among those present at the official reception that evening were Lieutenant Commander Spencer and his wife, Wallis. Like dozens of others they had to content themselves with just a brief glimpse of the twenty-five-year-old prince before he disappeared, pressing the flesh and smiling nonstop, into the adoring throng.

While the prince resumed his world travels, Wallis took stock of her life. Marriage held fewer attractions than ever, and in

1924, after a string of unsuccessful affairs, she took off for China, still nursing fond memories of the prince. She wasn't alone in her admiration. Across the Atlantic an elfin young aristocrat named Elizabeth Bowes-Lyon was also rumored, if you believed the newspapers, to have fallen under the prince's hypnotic spell. In childhood this daughter of a Scottish earl had played often with the prince, but age only accentuated the differences between them. Whereas the prince was willfully self-indulgent, Elizabeth's sense of rectitude and duty came firmly out of the Victorian mold, and she had absolutely no intention of marrying any time-wasters.

Despite a lather of newspaper speculation linking her to the prodigal prince, the eminently sensible Elizabeth shrewdly looked elsewhere, and in 1923 it was announced that she had become engaged to Albert, Duke of York, the prince's younger brother.

Halting and hesitant and cursed with a paralyzing stammer that often rendered him literally speechless, Albert had little of his brother's flair and virtually none of his faults. He was dependable, dull, and thoroughly decent. Elizabeth had rejected his first proposal of marriage, but as his diffident appeal became more evident to her, the second time Albert asked she said yes.

They were married on April 26, 1923. At last, shy, timid Albert had the help and support he desperately needed. As for Elizabeth, she gained far more than a husband: after the ceremony she became Her Royal Highness and assumed a place right at the core of the British royal family, a position she would retain for the rest of the century.

Within two years, their first child, also named Elizabeth, was born, followed four years later by Margaret. Photograph-hungry newspapers wasted no time in turning the two little princesses into media favorites to rival Shirley Temple.

One of those transatlantic readers who regularly scoured newspapers for accounts of the British royals was Wallis. She had returned to Washington after a two-year stay in China and immediately sparked a family crisis by announcing that she intended divorcing her drunken husband. While relatives gasped and neighbors gossiped, Wallis pushed ahead and on December 10, 1927, the miserable marriage was officially ended. Wallis might be single again, but she had no intention of remaining that way.

One year earlier she had met Ernest Simpson, an affluent New Yorker and lifelong Anglophile. Like so many before him, the ship broker was completely bowled over by Wallis's uncanny allure. His wife, Dorothea, was less impressed. So far as she was concerned, Wallis was a common "man stealer," but Ernest was beyond reason. Biding his time, he waited until Dorothea was in the hospital, then ran off with his lover. The divorce came through in due course, clearing the way for his marriage to Wallis on July 21, 1928, in London.

The Simpsons slid easily into English society, where Wallis's throaty chuckle and frank worldliness marked her out as a curiosity on the starchy country house weekend circuit. In November 1930, they were invited to a gathering at Burrough Court, near Melton Mowbray in Leicestershire. Also on the guest list was the Prince of Wales.

The First Fateful Meeting

They were introduced upon arrival, and the next day Wallis boldly seated herself beside the prince at lunch, where her easy formality and lack of obsequiousness with the guest of honor startled other diners. Not that the prince minded; far from it. Wallis's forthright conversation refreshed a palate jaded from years of unswerving sycophancy. She was funny and she made him laugh, and he couldn't take his eyes off her.

Oddly enough, another six months would pass before they met again, this time at a fashionable soiree in London's Grosvenor Square. As the prince passed along the line of assembled guests, he suddenly halted before the slim, impeccably dressed brunette who was smiling so broadly. His blue eyes narrowed deep in thought. Moments later, after a hasty word with the hostess, he approached her. "How nice to see you again. I remember our meeting at Melton."[1] Once again, other guests were astonished by Wallis's confident air.

Signs of her increasing acceptance came six weeks later. On June 10, 1931, she was presented to King George V and Queen

Mary at Buckingham Palace. For the upwardly mobile and seriously snobbish, this bizarre ritual represented the pinnacle of social acceptance, an induction into the inner circle of London society, and Wallis was out to create a big impression. In a borrowed dress she curtseyed low before the monarch and his wife. To their side, resplendent in full dress uniform, stood the Prince of Wales, his face glowing with open approval.

Later that night at a private party, as the Simpsons prepared to leave, the prince offered them a ride home in his car. Wallis was ecstatic. Within months she and Ernest were fixtures on the prince's A-list of guests, regularly invited to all his private parties and functions.

All through 1933 and into the following year, the relationship strengthened and so did the gossip as Wallis's hold over the prince became the talk of London society.

Perhaps the defining moment in the relationship, the moment that would profoundly affect the future of so many lives, came on November 27, 1934, when Wallis was again invited to Buckingham Palace. Ernest also attended, but this time he was shunted off to one side and cut a rather sorry figure as his wife seized the spotlight. Wallis's eye-popping lamé dress—more Hollywood than Holyrood—drew gasps of astonishment, as did the prince's insistence on personally introducing her to everyone present.

Standing flinty-eyed among the onlookers were the Duke and Duchess of York. This was their first glimpse of the infamous Mrs. Simpson, the sultry temptress whose magnetic charms had so bewitched the prince and ignited so much delicious society gossip. Neither liked what they saw. Panting with adolescent excitement, the prince eagerly steered Wallis in the direction of his sister-in-law.

For the first time Wallis experienced what she later described as "the almost startling blueness"[2] of the Duchess of York's eyes as they raked her coolly from head to toe. Compared with Wallis, peacock brilliant in vivid violet, the duchess was a dull bird, indeed. She said nothing, of course, just inclined her head regally, but other guests, old hands in the cutthroat world of royal one-upmanship, recognized the warning signs. No words had been exchanged, but with that single look Elizabeth, Duchess of York, had registered her disapproval and laid the ground rules for the greatest of all modern royal feuds.

Like most at court, Elizabeth prayed that this flashy import would be just another of the prince's many flings, but his puppy-like attempts to accommodate Wallis's every whim, as embarrassing as they were frequent, soon banished that hope.

Inevitably, the rumor mill began to grind, with most of the gossip hinging upon the prince's rumored sexual inadequacies. Despite his playboy reputation, he had always been erratic with women. One jilted ex-lover, and therefore unlikely to be wholly impartial, grumbled that he was rotten in bed, prone to premature ejaculation; while other former girlfriends also hinted at a curious disinterest in the physical side of their relationships.

Had Wallis unlocked the sexual door to the prince's heart? And, if so, how? Suddenly, her visit to China, a stay that Wallis herself rarely mentioned, took on a far juicier significance. While there, breathed the scandalmongers, Wallis had visited the so-called singsong houses, or brothels, and acquired ancient Oriental techniques designed to cure male impotence and sexual dysfunction. The truth of these allegations is impossible to check nowadays, but most at the time were prepared to believe them; nothing else, it seemed, could explain her extraordinary hold over the prince.

With Ernest shoved unceremoniously into the background, Wallis often traveled alone to weekend parties at the prince's private residence, Fort Belvedere, many times acting as hostess. As her confidence and status grew, so did her recklessness. She was dangerously free with her opinions of other royals, in particular the Duchess of York, whom she considered to be phony. Her imitation of the duchess's high-pitched, rather affected manner of speech was merciless in its accuracy and always produced gales of laughter. Unfortunately for Wallis, during one particularly biting performance, the duchess herself chanced to enter the drawing room.

Everyone froze. Especially the duchess. One of those present recalled: "From the moment of overhearing [Wallis], the Duchess of York became her implacable enemy."[3] Wallis merely laughed off the gaffe, saying the duchess "had no sense of humor."[4]

All through 1935, the romance flourished. While papers

around the globe splashed stories and photographs about the lady from Baltimore who had stolen the prince's heart, British newspaper proprietors—entrenched establishment figures, for the most part—ganged up to hide all mention of the relationship from the very people who had the most right to know. But behind the scenes, many influential figures began casting fearful eyes at the palace.

In 1935, the reigning monarch, George V, was an old man in failing health. He had been on the throne for a quarter of a century, and for most of that time his eldest son had been a source of constant disappointment. Tradition dictated that by the age of forty, the Prince of Wales should have married and produced his own heir; instead, he was swanning around London like some giddy teenager in pursuit of a married woman, and one who had already been divorced! To the king's way of thinking, Wallis was "unsuitable as a friend, disreputable as a mistress, unthinkable as Queen of England."[5] Not for the first time, questions began to surface about the prince's fitness for the highest office of all.

Summoning Prime Minister Stanley Baldwin to the palace, the king ordered a full investigation into the mysterious *femme fatale* who was threatening to topple the House of Windsor. Reputedly, the resulting dossier, which concentrated on Wallis's Chinese adventures, was so explosive that the king ordered it sealed, more determined than ever that this Delilah should not become queen. But in the final weeks of his life, despair took over and he predicted to Baldwin: "After I am dead the boy will ruin himself in twelve months."[6]

At five minutes to midnight on January 20, 1936, the king died. One heartbeat later the Prince of Wales became the new sovereign, taking the title Edward VIII. His first task was to phone Wallis. This was the moment everyone had dreaded, none more so than the Duchess of York, whose hatred of Mrs. Simpson was now tinged by genuine anxiety.

Sadly, the new king fulfilled all the doomsayers' predictions: he was feeble, churlish, thoroughly incompetent. He had no concept of duty; appointments were delayed or missed altogether, and top-secret papers were left lying on desks where they might be read by any passerby. Eventually, Baldwin took the unprecedented step of withholding papers from the king, particularly in light of the new monarch's disturbing admiration of fascism in general and Adolf Hitler in particular.

Edward's childish reliance on Wallis meant that he consulted her on every detail, especially when it came to money. They were both greedy, and together they monitored the expenses of the royal household, ruthlessly firing several old family retainers in order to further line their own pockets, an act of treachery that other royals found repugnant beyond belief.

The Yorks retreated in disgust to Royal Lodge, their grace-and-favor residence on the grounds of Windsor Great Park. One day they had surprise visitors. Edward, who had just taken delivery of a new American station wagon, wanted to impress his brother, and while they put the car through its paces, the duchess was left to entertain Wallis.

"Her justly famous charm was highly evident,"[7] Wallis sourly remarked later. The already icy atmosphere dropped off the Kelvin scale when Wallis posed by the window and began airily suggesting how the gardens and landscaping might be improved. This was a brutal power play, Wallis's way of reminding her rival that the Yorks remained in this residence by favor of the king, and that at any moment that favor might be withdrawn.

The civilities were maintained for another hour before the meeting petered out in embarrassed silence. Wallis left in triumph, having gained the ascendancy she felt sure would endure forever.

Edward's bravado also gained weight. In May 1936, he began throwing out imperious hints that not only did he intend to marry Wallis, but she would be at his side when he was crowned. At this point, even the stuffy British press could no longer keep a lid on the scandal, and for the first time Mrs. Simpson became a national figure in the very land where she threatened to wreak such constitutional havoc.

The criticism reached the boiling point in August, when Edward and Wallis took a Mediterranean cruise aboard the *Nahlin*. Newspaper photographs of the besotted swimsuit-clad king gazing lovingly into Wallis's eyes caused outrage in his homeland. Call it naïveté, call it arrogance, the fact remains that Edward failed entirely to appreciate that monarchy without mystery is meaningless; and he was acting like the commonest of commoners.

Not that he gave a damn. Shortly afterward when they visited Balmoral, the royal residence in the Scottish Highlands, they again raised hackles. Dour locals, many of whom yearned for the taciturn days of Queen Victoria, could only gape in amazement as the king and his mistress, both dressed in shorts, strolled through the village.

A Royal Snub

News of this latest faux pas was still in the air when, on September 25, the king gave a dinner at Balmoral to which the Yorks were invited. As Elizabeth made her entrance, Wallis moved forward confidently to receive her. Without altering her fixed smile one jot, Elizabeth glided straight past Wallis, cooing silkily, "I came to dine with the king."[8]

The snub went in like a stiletto. As the Duke of York and the king lowered their heads in nervous embarrassment, Wallis, her face an imperturbable white mask, realized that at last she had overreached herself. That evening Elizabeth left early, smiling and radiant, with good reason: this round had definitely gone to her.

Just days later, Edward departed Balmoral for the last time. Few mourned his leaving. Once again, with Wallis pushing the buttons, he had gone on a slash-and-burn mission, cutting costs indiscriminately, summarily dismissing many old and loyal retainers.

This savage pruning yielded the king vastly more cash to lavish on his lover, which was just as well, for Wallis had some mighty expensive tastes. Having pushed Ernest to the verge of bankruptcy with her obsessive spending, she now had the virtually bottomless coffers of the crown to plunder. West End jewelers welcomed her with open arms as she snatched up diamonds, sapphires, rubies, and countless other prohibitively costly gems, forming the basis of a phenomenal collection that would become the passion of her life and the talk of London society.

As was news of her impending divorce. With Baldwin struggling to get the suit delayed, American newspapers predicted that "Wally" intended marrying the king the following June. In reality, the king was planning an even earlier wedding, so that she might be crowned with him in May 1937.

For the first time, the Yorks heard the dreaded word "abdication," whispered at first, then much louder. The duchess was incredulous, the duke aghast. One look at her husband's face, deathly pale, stoked Elizabeth's rage to apocalyptic levels. Hers had always been the strong hand in the marriage, and she was deeply protective of her husband, a subdued, sensitive man more at home by some trout stream than in the pomp of court. An accident of birth had made him royal; now an act of malice threatened to pitch him headlong into the biggest job of all. Surely, she prayed, surely her brother-in-law would come to his senses?

But the king was blind to all reason; nothing would deflect him from his pursuit. On October 27, 1936, Wallis was granted a divorce on grounds of her husband's alleged adultery, though few doubted that dear old loyal Ernest, the best-known cuckold on the planet, had tamely agreed to the separation in order to smooth Wallis's path to the throne.

Beleaguered at the palace he may have been, but Edward was not entirely friendless. Winston Churchill, an ardent "Simpsonist," enjoying lunch one day with playwright Noël Coward, grouchily demanded to know why the king shouldn't be allowed "to marry his cutie." Immediately Coward fired back: "Because England doesn't wish for a Queen Cutie."[9] And that summed up the general view: a queen with two ex-husbands, both alive and potentially dangerous, was unimaginable.

The crisis deepened. On November 13, the king was told that if he married Wallis, the government would resign. Three days later, Stanley Baldwin drove to the palace on a last-ditch mission, explaining to the king that his position was unacceptable. Edward had his response prepared: "I want you to be the first to know that I have made up my mind and nothing will alter it—I have looked at it from all sides—and I mean to abdicate to marry Mrs. Simpson."[10]

Utterly dejected, Baldwin left Buckingham Palace, returned to Downing Street, and went straight to bed, believing he had witnessed the end of the British monarchy.

When Edward broke the news to his brother, the impact was heartbreaking. Gaunt-faced and trembling with fear, the Duke of York beseeched Edward repeatedly to change his mind, but every plea fell on stony ground. There was a markedly different reaction when Edward went to tell his elderly mother, Queen Mary. He begged her to receive Wallis, but an imperious shake of the head and "she is an adventuress"[11] was all he got.

Edward's insensitivity toward his own family, particularly his mother, whose health since the death of her husband had been so fragile, incensed Elizabeth, who decided that blame for the whole grisly episode could be attributed to just one person— Mrs. Simpson.

She wasn't alone. Every outpost of the British Empire had been canvassed for its view. The result was unanimous: no one wanted Wallis at any price.

Deeply shocked by the scale and depth of animosity directed toward her, Wallis hastily decamped to France on December 3. From her self-imposed exile, she issued a statement saying she was "willing, if such action would solve the problem, to withdraw from a situation that has been rendered both unhappy and untenable."[12]

No one at court believed her. Wallis had her gaze firmly fixed on the throne, or so they thought; ever since childhood she had craved attention, and now she was at center stage in the biggest spotlight of all. Even if Edward abdicated, she was still determined to marry him, rather than face the ignominy of being discarded like so many of his previous lovers. For now, all she could do was wait.

On December 11, 1936, the abdication was formally ratified. Propped up in bed, suffering from the flu, Elizabeth became Queen of England. At least one close friend wondered if her sudden illness was more tactical than organic. "My reading of it," she said, "is that she knew her in-laws, and that there was going to be a welter of emotions which she didn't want to be part of."[13] Even Elizabeth later admitted, "I kept out of it all."[14]

Next day the HMS *Fury* moved out of Portsmouth Harbor, carrying the former king to exile in France, and from there to Austria.

Nine hours later, with tears streaming down his face, the Duke of York was sworn in as George VI. Never has anyone succeeded to the British crown so unwillingly or with such trepidation.

One of his first tasks was to confer on his brother the title Duke of Windsor. It was not a popular decision, especially among the upper classes, who rounded on the former king with breathtaking savagery. There were other casualties too. Like a pebble dropped in a pond, the ripples of disapproval spread outward, and soon anyone who had been close to the duke found themselves tarred with the abdication brush. As for Wallis, ensconced in Cannes, each day brought sackloads of hate mail from around the globe. Disgraceful in their intensity and deeply wounding to a woman who just weeks earlier had confidently expected to sit on the English throne, the hostile reactions drove her into paroxysms of rage. Each night she phoned Windsor in Austria and bawled him out. He in turn, unable to accept or even realize his diminished position, pestered his brother repeatedly by phone, offering unwanted advice, meddling, always meddling.

Suddenly and without warning, Windsor found his calls blocked or else unanswered. Frustration soon gave way to childish tantrums. He always believed it was Elizabeth who froze him out, a view later confirmed by a lady-in-waiting: "She [Elizabeth] helped put the bullets in the gun."[15]

By March the duke's letters to Wallis were tinged with hysteria. "God's curses on those English bitches who dare to insult you." She wrote back, "I blame it all on the wife—she hates us both."[16]

As a sop to propriety, the duke and Wallis had agreed not to meet until her decree was made absolute on May 3, 1937. The very next day Windsor rushed into her arms at a chateau in central France. It was not a joyous reunion, especially when the duke informed her that no royal family member would be attending their upcoming marriage.

Eight days later the Yorks were crowned king and queen. Isolated in France, Wallis listened to a radio broadcast of the ceremony, and later recorded her thoughts: "The words of the service rolled over me like an engulfing wave. I fought to suppress every thought, but all the while the mental image of what might have been and what should have been kept forming, disintegrating, and re-forming in my mind."[17]

Most were delighted at the outcome. During the glittering coronation, the king's simple dignity and that of his wife were hugely impressive. Even Churchill, Windsor's greatest supporter, was won over. At the moment Elizabeth was crowned, he turned to his wife, Clementine, and said, "You were right; I can see now that the 'other one' couldn't have done it."[18]

Marriage or Martyrdom?

Three weeks later in France, on June 3, with just a handful of guests looking on, the Duke of Windsor and Wallis Simpson became man and wife. The wedding itself was a somber, cheerless affair, more martyrdom than marriage. Looking like someone just minutes from the electric chair, Wallis posed for the photographs, horribly aware that by marrying her the duke had become a less important person.

Overshadowing the ceremony was yet more strife. In the midst of the abdication crisis, York had rashly agreed to his brother's demand that Wallis receive royal status, be accorded the title Her Royal Highness. Now, in what *Burke's Peerage* would later describe as "the last act of triumph of an outraged and hypocritical Establishment . . . the most flagrant act of discrimination in the whole history of our dynasty,"[19] Wallis was denied her rightful title. Henceforth she would be the Duchess of Windsor, but not Her Royal Highness.

Predictably, the opposition had been spearheaded by Elizabeth, on grounds that the royal family had already been damaged enough and that any further recognition of the Windsors' marriage would compromise the new reign. The reasoning, if not the legality, was sound. Most believed the marriage would fail—after all, Wallis was already twice-divorced and had enjoyed numerous affairs—and if she were given the title of Her Royal Highness, she would retain it for life. This snub, as petty as it was treacherous, more than anything else fueled the feud to come.

In the meantime the duke had more prosaic concerns. As king he had received an annual allowance, courtesy of the British taxpayer; now he was reduced to living on his own means and Wallis was still spending up a storm. He constantly badgered his brother for more money.

Once again, it was the new queen who cracked the whip. She had no intention of sponsoring Wallis's profligacy. A senior cleric who knew her well testified to her toughness. "I've always thought that [Elizabeth] was the real blocking mechanism behind resistance to the Windsors."[20]

Elizabeth was in no mood for forgiveness. Her husband had been sandbagged into a miserable situation not of his own making, one she feared might break him, and it was all the fault of that damned woman!

Wallis was equally unforgiving. Whereas the duke spread the blame for his wife's lack of royal status far and wide, she sharpened her focus to a short list of one—Elizabeth

Even more galling for the Windsors, the new queen—"that fat Scotch cook,"[21] as they termed her—was proving to be remarkably well suited to her unexpected role as a tower of strength for the fragile new monarch.

"I think she made the early years of his reign possible," Sir Edward Ford, the king's assistant private secretary, said later. "If he'd had to do it on his own, he might have been incapable of handling it. He was a highly strung, neurotic man who was not, by nature, self-confident, and he depended on her a great deal."[22]

Pretty soon all those skeptics who had greeted Edward's abdication with vast sighs of relief, doubting his fitness for the rigors of high office, could be seen sporting the smuggest of expressions. The duke had done it again. In September 1937, he and Wallis visited Germany and jumped right into the arms of a Nazi propaganda machine eager to wring out every last drop of advantage from this coup.

Photographs of the newlyweds fawning over a smirking Adolf Hitler sent shock waves of revulsion around the globe, nowhere more so than in Wallis's hometown of Baltimore, where her abominable lack of judgment surprised none and appalled many.

The Windsors' German jaunt became an unmitigated public relations disaster, both barrels right in the foot. In a foul mood they skulked back to France, only to be further tormented by glowing newspaper accounts of Elizabeth's soaring popularity. Even worse, so far as Wallis was concerned, the woman she had branded the "Dowdy Duchess" was actually making headlines as a fashion icon, territory that hitherto Wallis had regarded as very much her own.

The feud festered like an open sore and took on a crueler,

more vindictive edge. Each time the Windsors requested permission to return to Britain, they were denied entrance, and always their most vehement opponent was Elizabeth. On one occasion, asked whether Wallis would accompany the duke if he came to England, Elizabeth replied in the clipped verbal shorthand used by royals, "No, certainly not: wouldn't receive her if she did."[23]

The Windsors went hunting for revenge. A golden opportunity appeared to come in May 1939, when, with the storm clouds of war blackening the skies over Europe, the king and queen left for a state visit to America. Within hours the duke recorded an appeal for world peace, to be broadcast to the American people on NBC. It had all the appearance of deliberate sabotage.

If that was the intent, it failed miserably. The broadcast received scant coverage while, to the Windsors' fury, the king and queen received a rapturous welcome in New York, where an estimated four million crowded the streets of Manhattan to cheer as they drove to the World's Fair. It was an unprecedented triumph. At last they had emerged from the shadow thrown by the former king.

Soon, though, there were other far more important matters at hand. On September 1, German troops poured into Poland, and within days Europe was plunged into war. Immediately a ship was dispatched to collect the Windsors from their home in France, but when they returned to Portsmouth aboard the HMS *Kelly,* no member of the royal family was present to greet them, nor was any royal car sent. Indeed, had it not been for Churchill, who arranged for them to stay at Admiralty House in Portsmouth, the couple would have been reduced to finding rooms at a hotel.

Two days later the duke, *sans* Wallis, visited the king at Buckingham Palace. While the brothers patched up old wounds, Elizabeth, still unable to forgive the duke, remained conspicuously absent. During the brothers' brief conversation, neither wife was mentioned.

Finding something to do with the Windsors was a knotty problem. Elizabeth, apprehensive that their presence would deflect attention from the king, pressed for an overseas posting. The British government agreed to dispatch them back to Paris, where the duke was given a minor military role, which he performed with his habitual incompetence.

Wallis hated her new role as wife of a junior army officer and wrote bitterly to her aunt, "Even the war can't stop the family hatred of us."[24]

They didn't have long to languish in France. As the unstoppable Nazi panzer divisions thundered toward Paris at breakneck speed, scattering the government in every direction, the Windsors fled south and crossed into Spain on June 20, 1940, where, in a tokenly neutral country, they were courted assiduously by the Germans.

Churchill, by now prime minister, tried repeatedly to spirit the Windsors out of Spain and back to Britain, only to be balked by the duke's refusal to return unless Wallis was received by the king and queen. Such obduracy in time of war infuriated Churchill, who urged them to return and sort out the problems later, adding ominously that as the duke was now an army officer, he hoped it wouldn't be necessary for orders to be sent. Windsor gulped hard. Such thinly veiled threats of a court martial unhinged him completely and helped loosen his already irresponsible tongue to dangerous levels.

His blatantly pro-German stance mortified the American ambassador in Madrid, Alexander Wendell, who sent a secret memorandum to the State Department that detailed the duke's insultingly derisive comments about French preparedness for war and his opinion that a Nazi victory was inevitable. Such defeatist talk soon found its way to London and only hardened sentiment against the renegade couple.

Things got no better when the Windsors moved to Lisbon. Here, they openly mingled with German diplomats, contemptuously dismissing the king as a dunce, entirely under the sway of his scheming wife. Such was the vehemence and frequency of the attacks that many were forced to conclude that the Windsors had Nazi sympathies.

Certainly the Germans thought so. Already they had explored the possibility of reinstating the duke on the British throne, but when the Blitz, which began in August 1940, made it clear that Britain would not surrender, banishing the need for a quisling king, the Germans, too, washed their hands of the Windsors.

It is sobering to reflect that had it not been for Wallis, Britain might have had a Nazi sympathizer on the throne at the outbreak of World War II. How this would have affected the war's outcome remains a matter for speculation, but many in Whitehall were doubtless silently echoing Noël Coward's caustic suggestion at the time of the abdication that "a statue should be erected to Mrs. Simpson in every town in England for the blessing she has bestowed upon the country."[25]

The Royal Remittance Man

Eventually, Churchill, under pressure from the palace to get the duke and Wallis, "the lowest of the low,"[26] as far away as possible, devised a neat solution: governorship of the Bahamas.

The couple arrived in Nassau on August 17. Neither wanted to be there and it showed. The dripping heat and antiquated colonial atmosphere only added to their distress, which found expression in petulant outbursts over rank and etiquette. Wallis, in particular, found the experience grim. "One might as well be in London with all the bombs and excitement and not buried alive here,"[27] she wrote to a friend, before delighting a visiting journalist, Adela Rogers St. John, with her frankness about the duke's diminished role. "I do not believe that in Nassau he is serving the Empire as importantly as he might."[28] Such remarks, made from the sanctuary of a sun-soaked tropical paradise, did little to improve the Windsors' stock in bomb-devastated London.

Wallis's fuse got shorter with each passing day. Any mention of the royals was guaranteed to spark fireworks. She blamed their banishment on "a woman's jealousy and a country's fear his brother wouldn't shine if he was there!"[29] The duke, she said, had been "dumped here [Bahamas] solely by family jealousy . . . his own family . . . are against him."[30]

As the war reached its weary conclusion, the duke pleaded with the palace to relent and receive Wallis. When they refused, he petulantly resigned his post. On May 3, 1945, the Windsors' Bahamian exile came to an end when he and Wallis flew to the United States. Five days later the war in Europe officially ended.

Once in the States, the duke wasted no time in raising the diplomatic temperature. At a time when the full horrors of Bergen-

Belsen and Auschwitz were just being revealed to a sickened world, he astounded dinner guests with his assertion that if Hitler had been "differently handled,"[31] then war with Germany might have been avoided. To the end of his life the duke remained unrepentant, saying, "I never thought Hitler was such a bad chap."[32]*

Peacetime brought mixed blessings for the Windsors. As soon as Elizabeth made it clear that neither the duke nor his wife was welcome in Britain, the Windsors were reduced to roles as sybaritic Flying Dutchmen, endlessly circling the globe, seeking out the next cocktail party, the next fashion show. They were regulars at Palm Beach, although they soon outlived their welcome. "Just a couple of freeloaders" was the way one local dowager described them. "After a while, nobody wanted them around."[33]

Shopping, Wallis decided, was a way of fighting back: if she couldn't compete with her cursed sister-in-law at court, she could damn sure blow her away in the *haute couture* department. Her reward came in 1946, when she was voted the Best Dressed Woman in the World for the first of three consecutive years. It might not be Queen of England, but at least it gave her the ammunition to mock her less-stylish rival's "fourteen karat beauty," the woman the Duke of Windsor called "the Loch Ness monster."[34]

For a while the Windsors seemed on a slow road to social rehabilitation. Then came the disaster that so many in the British establishment had predicted and feared.

In 1950, rumors broke regarding Wallis and the outlandish Jimmy Donahue, one of the Woolworth heirs. Despite being flamboyantly homosexual, Donahue was seen alone with Wallis so often that tongues started wagging, though whether Donahue was pursuing the duchess or her androgynous husband never became clear. No doubt about it, a scandal was brewing, which is why the Windsors moved heaven and hell to sweep all mention of the affair under the carpet. Even so, the boozy Donahue continued to enjoy the couple's friendship and cause them plenty of embarrassment for many years to come.

---

*In 1945, Buckingham Palace took extraordinary steps to eliminate all documentary evidence of the Windsors' contacts with Nazi Germany. The prime mover in this subterfuge was the crown's most ferocious custodian, Elizabeth.

More problems followed. In 1951, *A King's Story,* the Duke of Windsor's own highly colored version of the abdication, became a best-seller. Once again there was an uproar, all the more so since its publication coincided with a marked deterioration in the king's health.

The timing could not have been more unfortunate. On February 3, 1952, George VI died. The official cause was cancer, but most believed that stress more than anything had foreshortened his life. Certainly his grieving widow thought so. Some weeks after the funeral—which the Duke of Windsor attended alone— the name of the Duchess of Windsor was raised in conversation. "Oh yes," replied Elizabeth, now known as the Queen Mother. "The woman who killed my husband."[35]

The acrimony continued to flare all through the fifties, snipe and countersnipe. When in the 1956 Grand National—Britain's premier horse race for steeplechasers—the Queen Mother's Devon Loch collapsed just fifty yards short of the winning line, while six lengths clear, Wallis's glee knew no bounds. "That poor, poor animal. To make all that effort and then to do a belly flop. How devastating!"[36]

"No, no, darling," interposed her husband. "You've got it wrong. It's his owner who has the belly flop." Overcome by such wit, both duke and duchess dissolved into fits of helpless giggles.

For the Queen Mother, this was a time of transition. Now that her daughter, Queen Elizabeth II, was on the throne, she was forced more into the background and with less at stake came the first signs of a crack in the feud. In March 1965, the duke traveled to London for an eye operation. He was accompanied by his wife who, elegant as ever, dropped a perfect curtsey when Queen Elizabeth II came to visit her ailing uncle. The duke, too, was conciliatory. He had just one request: that he and wife be allowed to be buried in St. George's Chapel within Windsor Castle. The request was granted.

Other members of the royal family were also keen to mend old broken bridges. In October 1970, Prince Charles visited the Windsors in Paris and delighted the duke by calling the duchess "Aunt Wallis." It was a special and rare moment, especially for the duke: his health was in sharp decline, and one year later the doctors diagnosed throat cancer.

The end came on May 28, 1972, when the man who sacrificed everything for the woman he loved died in her arms.

As promised, he was buried at Windsor Castle. Before the ceremony, the Duchess of Windsor had stayed at Buckingham Palace. It was the first time since the abdication, all those years before, that the woman who had so nearly toppled an empire had driven through those famous wrought-iron gates. Then she had been viewed as a manipulative monster, intent on destroying a thousand years of tradition; this time there was nothing menacing about her, just a shriveled little woman in black.

During the funeral service, the duchess was obviously distraught and heavily sedated. Her speech rambled, and several times she had to be shown the place in her hymnbook.

After the service came the most remarkable sight of all—the Queen Mother guiding the duchess to a settee and talking quietly with her. They had not spoken in thirty-six years, but the time for hatred was past. Besides, with the effect of the sedatives wearing off, the duchess was becoming visibly more emotional.

Later, her mind started wandering. "Where is the duke?" she suddenly cried. While other guests maintained a respectful distance, the Queen Mother, with an expression of great compassion on her face, again took her sister-in-law's arm and soothed her, saying, "I know how you feel. I've been through it myself."[37]

Then it was over. After the ceremony the duchess flew back to a life of almost total seclusion in France and an increasing reliance on alcohol. In October 1976, the Queen Mother traveled to Paris with the intention of visiting the duchess, only to hear that she was hallucinating and fast losing her grip on reality. Instead, she sent a bouquet of roses, one dozen white, one dozen red, with a card that read: "In friendship, Elizabeth."[38]

She took other steps to safeguard the well-being of her former rival, dispatching the dean of Windsor, Michael Mann, to Paris every six months to make sure that the duchess was being properly cared for.

After a long and painful illness, the Duchess of Windsor finally died on April 24, 1986. Sixteen members of the royal family attended St. George's Chapel when she was laid to rest next to her husband. Chief among the mourners was the Queen Mother, as poised and correct as ever, sphinxlike in her determination not to reveal the torrent of thoughts that must have flooded her mind as this final drama unfolded.

But the royal family still had one last barb up its sleeve—at no time during the service was the duchess's name mentioned, and nowhere on the plaque could be found the words "Her Royal Highness."

CHAPTER 8

Montgomery versus Patton

Years of feud:	1942–1945	
Names:	Bernard Law Montgomery	George Patton
Strengths:	Meticulous and methodical, a superb defensive tactician	Charismatic, matchless attacking brilliance on the battlefield
Weaknesses:	Impatient, arrogant, intolerant of opposing views, conceited	See Montgomery
At stake:	History's accolade as the greatest Allied general of World War II	

Of all the feuds covered in these pages, this was the most unnecessary and in many respects the most tragic. Who knows how many lives might have been saved had these two armor-plated egos not become embroiled in a trans-European chariot race, each spurred on by an implacable determination to efface the other from the history books? In the opinion of many—not least themselves—they were the two greatest Allied generals of the Second World War, and neither felt the slightest need or desire to share his triumphs with the other. Even amid the greatest carnage yet visited upon this earth, they demonstrated that no matter how dreadful the havoc, there is always room for a blood-curdling personality clash.

Let's begin this story in the deserts of North Africa. It is August 12, 1942, and a quirky London-born general named Bernard

Montgomery has just taken command of the Eighth Army. With his baggy corduroy trousers, huge beak of a nose, thin, reedy voice, and trademark beret, this sparrowlike Englishman fitted no one's picture of the archetypal military warrior, but beneath the meek exterior beat a heart of toughened steel. Which was just as well, for a bleaker situation was hard to imagine. In the past few months, General Erwin Rommel's all-conquering Afrika Korps had pushed the Allied forces back across Libya and into Egypt, almost to the gates of Cairo. If ever a savior were needed, now was definitely the hour.

Into the breach stepped Bernard Law Montgomery.

Truculent, abominable to subordinates, entirely disinterested in any opinion that differed from his own, Montgomery was all of these and more, but no matter. In his own mind he was the finest soldier on the face of the earth, and his first few months of command seemed to lend credence to this opinion as he first halted Rommel's forces, then routed them at El Alamein, the first great Allied success of World War II. We now know, of course, that British cryptanalysts had broken the German military code, and were thus able to feed Montgomery up-to-the-minute details of Rommel's every move; but at the time his seemingly supernatural battlefield prowess was sufficient to earn him favorable comparison with Caesar and Napoleon, an assessment with which Montgomery agreed wholeheartedly.

In February 1943, Britain's newfound Saint George decided to share his hard-won desert experience with other Allied commanders. He announced a Study Week in Tripoli, a kind of seminar in the sand. The turnout was disappointing, staff officers mostly. Montgomery grouched in a letter, "Only one American General has come (the Comd. of an Armored Corps; an old man of about 60)."[1]

In truth the "old man" was only a couple of years older than Montgomery himself, but there was a certain crankiness about him that gave the impression of testy dotage, made worse by Montgomery's ban on coughing and smoking while he spoke. A lifelong chainsmoker, the American was made to suffer in silence as Montgomery, hands clasped behind his back, feet spread, head tilted heavenward, expounded his long-winded theories of warfare, most of which hinged on the need for planning,

planning, and yet more planning. As the meeting broke up, the balding Californian made no attempt to conceal his skepticism. "I may be old, I may be slow, I may be stupid, and I know I'm deaf, but it just don't mean a thing to me."[2] With that, General Patton shouldered his way through the door, cigarette already in hand.

World War II came just in time for George Smith Patton Jr. All his life the Pasadena-born cavalryman had been searching for the "great conflict," the epochal event that would guarantee his place in history. A lowly colonel in the First World War, reduced to the rank of major in peacetime, the flamboyant Patton gave the impression of having sprung from the pages of antiquity. With his ivory-handled revolvers and highly polished boots, it was easy to imagine him exhorting his troops onward at Lexington or Concord—he had that kind of flourish—but by 1943 he was dangerously close to being an anachronism.

Montgomery represented the new face of warfare, planned with bureaucratic precision, logistics and supplies uppermost, nothing left to chance. Such sterility bored Patton. Even so, despite all his harrumphing, he was impressed with his prickly tutor, and that night in his notorious diary, he described Montgomery as "very alert, wonderfully conceited, and the best soldier—or so it seems—I have met in this war."[3]

It was not an opinion he would hold for long.

Ever since Operation Torch—the November 1942 U.S. invasion of North Africa—Patton had been pawing the ground like a maddened bull, desperate for action, and unremittingly critical of his transatlantic allies. So much so that General Dwight D. Eisenhower, overall commander of the Allies, had been forced to issue a warning. "George, you are my oldest friend, but if you or anyone else criticizes the British, by God, I will reduce him to his permanent grade and send him home."[4]

Patton reeled from the barb, and for the remainder of the war nothing would shift him from the view that Eisenhower was a political carpetbagger, intent on using this war as a stepping-stone to the White House.

Montgomery, too, was scornful of Eisenhower, and for much the same reason. Ike had more of the office than the officer about him and lacked combat experience, but where he did score was in conciliation. Nobody did it better. Just as well, really, because for the next two years it was Eisenhower's unenviable lot to mediate World War II's most spectacular sideshow—the malignant feud that raged between Patton and Montgomery.

At the root of Montgomery's resentment was an intense pique that after fighting unaided for three years, British and Commonwealth forces should suddenly be asked to play second fiddle to the "Johnny-come-lately" Americans. It might have been annoying, but it did accord with one of life's eternal verities— that he with the deepest pockets has the loudest voice. The United States was bankrolling the Allied war effort and, not unreasonably, expected to call the tune.

Montgomery got off to a bad start with the Americans when in February 1943 he had boasted to Eisenhower's chief of staff, General Walter Bedell Smith, that the Eighth Army would "finish it [the North African War] for them"[5] within the next six weeks. Confident that such bravado was windy nonsense, Bedell Smith casually offered to bet Montgomery anything that he liked. It was a rhetorical wager, the kind made in bars every night of the week, and yet Montgomery immediately pounced on it, suggesting "a Flying Fortress, complete with American crew . . . my personal property until the war ended"[6] as the prize.

Thinking no more of it, Bedell Smith agreed.

Sure enough, in April, at Wadi Akarit, Montgomery routed the Germans and immediately claimed his winnings. Such was his crass insensitivity that he entirely failed to understand how much this antagonized the Allies.* Patton, in particular, was incensed, mainly because it had been his rare timidity in pressing forward with U.S. forces that had allowed the British to claim the victory as their own.

Montgomery got his Fortress, the U.S. Army got hammered by the press back home, and Patton got busy. On April 16, 1943, he was ordered to begin planning the invasion of Sicily. For the first time the Californian cavalryman was about to command an army.

---

*Betting on the outcome of battles was a Montgomery trademark. Throughout the war he laid a string of substantial wagers with fellow officers, most of which he won.

Operation Husky

Sicily set the stage for everything that subsequently came between Patton and Montgomery. Initial plans for the island invasion proposed that Montgomery's Eighth would go ashore at the southeast corner of the island, while Patton's Seventh Army would target the region around Palermo, to the northwest. Montgomery, hungry for more glory for his Eighth Army and unconvinced of American battle readiness, thought the plan tactically unsound and said so.

Outrage in both the British and American camps forced Montgomery into a rare retreat. He wrote in explanation: "I know well I am regarded by many people as being a tiresome person. I think this is very probably true. I try hard not to be tiresome; but I have seen so many mistakes during this war, and so many disasters happen, that I am desperately anxious to try to see that we have no more; and this often means being very tiresome."[7]

As a result, Montgomery and Patton gave each other a wide berth during the latter stages of planning Husky, as the operation was called, which probably accounted for the scenes of general confusion when, on July 9, 1943, Allied airborne and seaborne forces began the largest landing of its type yet seen. Largely unopposed, Montgomery took Syracuse. His diary recorded his contempt for Patton's progress: "On my left the American 7th Army is not making very great progress at present; but as my left Corps pushes forward that will tend to loosen resistance in front of the Americans."[8]

With his self-confidence inflated to messianic levels, Montgomery rashly split his army into three and pushed on toward Messina. His audacious cable to the British commanding officer, Field Marshal Harold R. Alexander, suggesting that U.S. forces hold firm while he swung north "to cut off enemy completely,"[9] strained already fragile Allied tensions to the breaking point, as did his insistence that Sicily was not big enough to accommodate more than one offensive army.

Patton sneered his response. "If we wait for them [Eighth Army] to take this island while we twiddle our thumbs, we'll wait forever. There's plenty of room for both of us to fight."[10] His plan was to cut the island in two and head for Palermo. "Monty is trying to steal the show and with the assistance of Divine Destiny (Dwight

D. Eisenhower) he may do so."[11] Soon, Patton was able to indulge himself in a huge helping of *Schadenfreude* as Montgomery, weakened by splitting his army, crunched to a halt in the face of tenacious German resistance.

Champing at the bit, Patton complained to Alexander that as in North Africa, U.S. troops were being unfairly relegated to a subsidiary role. Alexander, keenly aware that Montgomery's assurances of a speedy victory would not be realized and not wishing to antagonize the Allies, gave permission for a reconnaissance in force northwestward. This was all Patton needed to press forward and to change the entire focus of the Sicily campaign.

Like Montgomery, he gambled and split his army, leaving General Omar Bradley to struggle through Sicily's mountainous interior while he scooted off to the west. His tactics were in striking contrast to those of the timid Montgomery. Patton drove his men onward regardless of ground conditions or artillery or aerial support, and showed scant concern for guarding his exposed flanks as he concentrated on forward movement, never indulging in Montgomery's penchant for regularly pausing to regroup.

In six days he took control of all the western part of the island and capped his advance by entering Palermo in triumph on July 22.

A century earlier, observing the futile British assault at Balaclava—the famed "Charge of the Light Brigade"—General Pierre Bosquet had remarked, *"C'est magnifique, mais ce n'est pas la guerre."* ("It is magnificent, but it is not war.")[12] Much the same could be said of Patton's march on Palermo. German commanders were baffled by it, with Field Marshal Kesselring professing himself delighted as Patton "just marched and captured unimportant terrain."[13] Even American commanders could see no strategic value in capturing Palermo, and the only reasonable assumption is that Patton, infuriated by Montgomery's arrogant assertion that the Eighth Army could win the Sicilian campaign single-handed, had decided to teach the bumptious Limey a lesson he wouldn't quickly forget.

Eisenhower, eager to damp down the feuding fires that were threatening to undermine staff morale, adopted his usual conciliatory manner. "Today the Seventh Army is worthy to fight alongside the Eighth. I can offer no higher praise."[14]

Montgomery gritted his teeth and sent Patton a goodwill message: "Many congratulations to you and your gallant soldiers on securing Palermo and clearing up the western half of Sicily."[15] In private he was far less charitable, expressing the hope that the glory-seeking general would now address himself to the primary task in Sicily—defeating the enemy.

He followed this up with a second cable to Patton: "Would like to visit you on Wednesday 28 July. Would arrive airfield 1200 hours in my Fortress. . . ."[16] The time had come for some serious points-scoring. Montgomery wanted to show off his new plane and put the upstart Patton in his place. Patton, mightily miffed, gave grudging assent, though he conspicuously skirted round Montgomery's query as to whether the airfield runway was big enough to accommodate a Flying Fortress.

It wasn't. Only skillful piloting prevented a disaster. Even so, the giant plane ended up on its side. Montgomery emerged from the wreck unscathed but deeply suspicious, as he made clear in a letter to a friend. "I very nearly got killed in my Fortress the other day trying to land at Palermo to see Patton. He said it was OK for a Fortress, but it was far too small."[17]

Also chafing Montgomery's notoriously thin skin was the fact that Patton had not bothered showing up to greet him at the airfield, a chore that he delegated to his ADC. Patton, meanwhile, determined not to be outdone by Montgomery's Fortress showboating, did lay on a full escort of scout cars and motorcycles to bring his guest to the palace of Palermo, where the all-conquering general had already established his headquarters. "We had a great reception," Montgomery recorded in his diary. ". . . I discussed plans for future operations with General Patton."[18]

Actually, Montgomery talked and Patton listened with mounting disgust as the Englishman outlined his strategy for Allied advances. The moment his guest left, Patton fired off a signal to General Troy Middleton to start pushing hard. "This is a horse race, in which the prestige of the U.S. Army is at stake. We must take Messina before the British!"[19]

Patton was off and running; except that now, instead of fighting Italians, he was facing battle-hardened Germans, a much tougher proposition, and indirectly it was their unexpected resistance that led to the notorious events that almost ruined his career.

Slapping Incidents

On August 3, 1943, frustrated by his inability to take the town of Troina, Patton visited a field hospital to boost morale among the injured men. As he made the rounds, he spoke to most of the soldiers in turn. All went well until he asked one private his reason for being hospitalized.

"I guess I can't take it, sir,"[20] the shell-shocked soldier replied.

Patton blew up like Mount Etna. Summoning up every curse in his colorful vocabulary, he lambasted the unfortunate soldier, called him a coward, slapped him across the face with his gloves, then kicked him out of the tent before storming off. And there the matter might have rested, except that just over one week later the general had cause to visit yet another field hospital.

Unbelievably, it happened again. One patient, still helmeted, sat huddled up and shivering. When asked about his illness, the man sobbed, "It's my nerves." Instinctively Patton lashed out with his hand. "Your nerves, hell; you are just a goddamn coward, you yellow son of a bitch!" A second blow sent the man's helmet flying. "You ought to be lined up against a wall and shot . . . in fact . . . ." Patton reached ominously for his pistol. "I ought to shoot you myself right now, goddamn you!"[21] Before the situation got completely out of hand, Patton stalked off, still yelling epithets.

Two such incidents, so close together, were impossible to keep under wraps, and news of Patton's astonishing outbursts reached the American High Command. On August 17, Eisenhower wrote to Patton: "I am well aware of the necessity for hardness and toughness on the battlefield. . . . But this does not excuse brutality, abuse of the sick, nor exhibition of uncontrollable temper in front of subordinates."[22]

Ike ordered Patton to apologize publicly to all parties concerned and to the two divisions from which the men came. Patton's reluctant speech, full of his usual rousing guff, went down badly with the troops, who stood in stony silence until he left.

Opinions were mixed about the incident. Bradley, never Patton's biggest fan, had no doubts what should happen. "If it had been up to me, I would have relieved him [Patton] instantly and would have had nothing more to do with him."[23]

Eisenhower took the more pragmatic view. "Patton is indispensable to the war effort—one of the guarantors of our victory."[24]

Significantly, one of Patton's stoutest defenders was Montgomery, who, although careful to distance himself publicly from what was an internal American problem, made no secret of his distaste for the humiliation that had been heaped upon Patton. Far better than most, certainly more than the office-bound Eisenhower, he appreciated the inhuman strains that combat could impose.

It was a rare moment of unanimity, and soon everything was back to normal, with Montgomery grumbling that Patton had been "nearly irrational"[25] in his determination to beat him to Messina. Bradley, too, was fast losing patience with Patton's grandstanding. "He steamed about with great convoys of cars. Great squads of cameramen. Became unpopular with the troops."[26]

In time Bradley, a fair-minded man, would come to loathe Montgomery with equal vehemence, but for now his distaste was reserved exclusively for Patton. On August 17, when Patton entered Messina in triumph, Bradley refused to attend, "sickened"[27] by Patton's mania for publicity. He missed a coronation. American reporters cabled home dazzling reports that shot Patton into the first rank of national heroes, a fighting general to fear and admire, someone with whom Montgomery, no matter how reluctantly, would have to share the limelight.

Then came disaster. Somehow, muckraking journalist Drew Pearson got hold of the "slapping incident" story, and it caused a sensation. Overnight, Patton, a walking propaganda machine, was undone by the very reporters he had so assiduously cultivated as they rounded on him like jackals. Senators and congressmen all lined up to take shots, demanding Patton's resignation, and for a while his career teetered on the brink of extinction.

But with Allied troops fighting their way bloodily up the Italian mainland, Eisenhower needed all of his best men, and that included Patton. To assuage public opinion, he did withdraw his controversial general from combat duty, softening the blow by telling Patton that he would command an army in Operation Overlord, the upcoming invasion of Europe.

Even in the tranquillity of rural England, controversy continued to haunt Patton. He had assumed command of the Third Army, and in between the endless training exercises he took time out to address a gathering at a women's club in Knutsford, Cheshire, on April 25, 1944. He made an impromptu speech in which he said, "It is undoubtedly our destiny to rule the world, we British, American, and, of course, Russian people, and the more we know each other the better it will be."[28]

Unlike their British counterparts, American newspapers maliciously omitted the all-important reference to Russia, leaving editors to gloat that "General Foot-in-Mouth" had done it again. Patton had discovered an indelible rule of self-aggrandizement—those that live by the PR sword, die by it also. The U.S. press murdered him. And this time Eisenhower joined in, publicly flaying his gaffe-prone general. Still, he refused to fire him, content to let the storm blow over, which it duly did.

Immobility gave Patton time to brood on what lay ahead, with most of his concerns centered on Montgomery, that "tired little fart,"[29] and his perceived battlefield timidity. Such views failed to prevent from him toasting "the health of General Montgomery" at a dinner one night, and declaring his "satisfaction in serving under him," although he did later write ruefully, "The lightning did not strike me."[30]

For his part, Montgomery was reluctant to antagonize Patton openly. Yes, he regarded him as a posturing braggart, untutored in the broader dimensions of warfare, but he recognized that behind the bluster lurked rare and inspirational gifts of leadership unmatched in the Allied camp—apart from Montgomery himself, of course!

As D Day neared, Patton fretted about his own seemingly limited role in the upcoming invasion and suspected the Brits of plotting against him. "If everything moves as planned there will be nothing left for me to do,"[31] he grumbled. Although much has been made of Patton's anti-Britishness, in truth his spleen was directed more against one man. "Monty does what he pleases and Ike says, 'Yes, Sir!'"[32]

Bradley, who toiled alongside these colossal egos, summed it up succinctly: "Patton didn't particularly like Monty. Too cocky for him. Possibly too much like Patton himself."[33]

Two such bloated egos in constant battle made for some tricky preinvasion conferences, as Eisenhower found out. Caught between Scylla and Charybdis, he ignored both and got on with the job in hand.

Patton's Great Speech

Patton continued to do what he did best: rallying the hearts and minds of those about to go into battle. He once remarked that eighty percent of being an officer consisted of morale-boosting, and nowhere was this better displayed than in the address he delivered to his men on the eve of D Day. It was colorful and profane, and while accounts vary as to exactly what Patton said—no two listeners seemed to recall the same words—most agree it ended something along these lines:

> . . . you may be thankful that twenty years from now when you are sitting by the fireplace with your grandson on your knee and he asks you what you did in the great World War II, you won't have to cough, shift him to the other knee and say, "Well, your granddaddy shoveled shit in Louisiana." No, Sir, you can look him straight in the eye and say, "Son, your granddaddy rode with the great Third Army and a son-of-a-goddamned-bitch named Georgie Patton!"

Such self-confidence was highly contagious, provided it was backed up by results, but for now Patton had to cool his heels and wait. When history's greatest combined air and sea invasion finally began on June 6, 1944, spewing thousands of Allied troops onto the Normandy beaches, Patton's Third Army languished across the Channel in England, much to the general's chagrin. As reports filtered back, he inveighed mightily against Monty for the apparent tardiness of the British advance, which was due in large part to a heavy concentration of German armor around Caen.

On July 7, the two rivals met for lunch. Impatient for action, Patton fumed while his hated foe delivered yet another of his interminable lectures on battle tactics. "Montgomery went to great length explaining why the British had done nothing," he recorded in his diary that night, but he was greatly excited by his own prospects. The intention was for his Third Army to surge into Brittany. The next day Patton wrote to his wife: "When I do start, I will, if current plans hold, have a swell chance."[34]

On Tuesday, August 1, the Third Army became operational, with orders to seal off the Brittany peninsula. Patton, typically gung ho, bet Montgomery that he would have the city of Brest "by Saturday night,"[35] just five days hence. He lost. Montgomery's assessment of battlefield logistics was as shrewd as ever, and it would be several more Saturdays before Brest fell to the Allies.

Undaunted, Patton swept inland, and in the weeks that followed, he gave perhaps the finest demonstration of rapid mobile warfare ever seen in military history. Disregarding his flanks, he set about surprising the enemy by sheer speed rather than by fighting, with stunning results. Back home, the fickle U.S. press once again took the renegade general to its bosom.

Montgomery was reduced to the role of astonished onlooker as Patton steamrollered across the French countryside with a verve that was entirely beyond the Englishman's compass. Even so, both generals managed to reach the outskirts of Falaise, forty miles south of Caen, at about the same time, closing the trap on vast numbers of German troops. With a great victory seemingly at hand, Bradley suddenly ordered Patton back, allowing a gap to appear, through which thousands of Germans were able to escape to fight another day.

Earlier Patton had implored Bradley, "Let me go on to Falaise and we'll drive the British back into the sea for another Dunkirk."[36] Now he was convinced that the Third Army had been halted in order to give all the kudos to Montgomery. In reality, Montgomery was as shocked by the decision as Patton had been, and it is as well to look higher up the command structure to explain this debacle. Once again, Eisenhower had betrayed his lack of battle experience. As Supreme Commander it was his job to oversee all major strategic decisions, but he was forever a hostage to caution, and on this occasion he failed completely to coordinate the movements of both armies.

Eventually, on August 20, the gap was closed and over ten thousand German troops lay dead, with a further fifty thousand taken prisoner. By this time Patton and his Third Army were long gone, surging east across the center of France, capturing territory at such a rate that it was impossible for supplies to keep up. Unconcerned by such trivia, Patton pushed ever farther.

Montgomery lamented his rival's success. "The general picture in this part of the front [Third Army] is that Patton is heading for Paris and is determined to get there and will probably do so."[37]

The statistics were incredible. When the Third Army crossed the Seine on August 25, it had advanced 400 miles in 26 days, accounted for 100,000 German troops, and suffered just 16,000 casualties. Patton, bedazzled war correspondents in tow, was writing headlines every day and rewriting the military textbooks. His army was, he bragged, advancing faster and farther than any in history—and then, quite literally, he ran out of gas.

While he waited impatiently for gasoline stocks to reach him, a bitter dispute broke out between himself and Montgomery over how best to prosecute the war. Each favored a single thrust into Germany: Patton wanted to surge through the Nancy Gap, while Montgomery favored swinging north through Belgium. Given the parlous state of German defenses at this time, either route would in all likelihood have succeeded, except that Eisenhower discarded both single-thrust plans in favor of a broad front.

Few doubt that this was a calamitous decision, but it had been forced upon Eisenhower by his generals' intractability. Had either Montgomery or Patton been prepared to swallow his pride and join the other in a single thrust, it is hard to imagine Eisenhower gainsaying their decision. Instead, unwilling to offend either side, he chose the soft option and probably extended the war by six months at least.

During this brief lull in action came a shocking announcement: Montgomery had been promoted to the rank of field marshal. In a glowing eulogy Eisenhower praised him as "the greatest living soldier"[38]—an accolade that made Patton retch—before adding in rather more subdued terms that Montgomery had been removed from the post of C-in-C Allied Ground Forces. Under pressure from Washington, with a presidential election on the horizon, Eisenhower had been ordered to assume direct command.

Montgomery didn't like it, of course, but the ultimate prize of Berlin still beckoned, and with Patton's hell-for-leather drive stalling south of the Ardennes, there was still time to restore his reputation as master of the battlefield.

On September 17, Operation Market Garden—Montgomery's

plan to attack Germany from the north—swung into action. Patton, disgruntled at being shunted onto the sidelines, wrote that day: "To hell with Monty. I must get so involved that they can't stop me." As it happened, Market Garden was a disaster. In the space of just seven days this combined air and ground attack through Holland cost seventeen thousand Allied casualties.

As predicted, Eisenhower's "broad front" was looking decidedly thin.

Patton didn't fare much better. Faced for the first time with genuine fortifications, he ground to a halt at the fortress stronghold at Metz. Despite a huge bombardment, Metz held and on October 13, the Third Army limped away, tail firmly between its legs. Defeat was a rarity for Patton, and it hurt; and although a second attack did eventually take Metz, his glittering reputation had suffered a big hit.

Then came the Battle of the Bulge.

Battle of the Bulge

Out of the blue, on December 16, German forces staged a stunning counterattack through the forests of the Ardennes in northern France and Belgium, designed to cut the Allied forces in two, the British to the north, the Americans to the south. Caught unaware by the counterattack's suddenness and ferocity, American troops were pushed back several miles to Bastogne.

An anxious Eisenhower asked Patton if he could hold Field Marshal von Runstedt, the panzer commander, in the south.

"*Hold* von Runstedt?" snorted Patton. "I'll take von Runstedt and shove him up Montgomery's ass!"[39]

Popular as this maneuver might have been—in all sectors of the Allied forces—Patton didn't quite manage it, but on December 26, after days of savage fighting, his divisions did relieve the besieged town of Bastogne, spelling out loud and clear that the German counteroffensive, or "Bulge," was doomed. Patton gloated, "The Kraut has stuck his head in the meat grinder and I've got the handle."[40]

To the north Montgomery had held firm, and in the press conference that followed, he indulged his irritating habit of grossly inflating his own contribution to the battle, making it appear as though once again he had saved America's bacon. Nothing could have been further from the truth. The Battle of the Bulge was emphatically an American victory, at enormous cost to American life, and for Montgomery to claim otherwise was almost criminally insensitive.

The furor reached Britain and forced Prime Minister Winston Churchill to address the House of Commons, where he repudiated Montgomery's vainglorious hyperbole, reminding everyone that for every British casualty during the Bulge there were fifty-five to sixty American casualties.

Others in the British High Command were also weary of Montgomery's constant glory seeking. Churchill's chief military adviser, General Hastings Ismay, summed up the prevailing mood with his wish that someone would "muzzle or better still chloroform Monty. I have come to the conclusion that his love of publicity is a disease, like alcoholism or taking drugs, and that it sends him equally mad."[41]

The Allied thrust was now irresistible. The only question was: who would reach Berlin first, Patton or Montgomery?

March 24, 1945, provided a big clue. That was the day when Patton phoned Bradley in high excitement. He had reached the Rhine! "For God's sake tell the world we're across . . . I want the world to know Third Army made it before Monty starts across."[42] As Patton and his officers crossed the bridge, he paused, unzipped his fly, and made a great display of urinating into the river before walking on, across the Rhine and into the heartland of Germany.

But Patton never did take Berlin, nor did Montgomery. Geopolitics won out over military strategy, with Eisenhower deciding that that plum should be left to the Soviet Army, a decision that nauseated Patton, who hated Communists even more than he loathed Nazis.

Events now raced by. On April 21, Soviet troops reached the outskirts of Berlin. Nine days later, trapped like a rat in his underground bunker, Adolf Hitler, the architect of all this madness, put a bullet into his brain.

All that remained was for the loose ends to be tied up. On May 4, Montgomery headed the Allied delegation at Lüneburg

Heath, where he received the formal German surrender. While Montgomery fussed over formalities—he refused to permit the surrendering generals to smoke and insisted that they salute him—Patton had continued fighting all the way to the Czech border, and was ready to push on to Moscow, if necessary, in order to thwart the massive land grab that Stalin's Red Army was engineering.

Suddenly, an order came through from on high—retreat.

To Eisenhower's eternal discredit, he had connived at the imposition of one dictator over another, meekly allowing Stalin to swallow up Czechoslovakia. For Patton it was the final betrayal, brutal evidence of Eisenhower's vaulting political ambition. With one eye on the White House, Eisenhower was unwilling to risk any American lives in a bruising showdown with the Red Army, an expediency that would condemn millions to the misery of Communist domination for decades. Patton had seen the warning signs and been rebuffed. Who knows how the postwar map of Europe might have looked had he been given his head?

On May 8, there came the unconditional surrender of all German forces. The war in Europe was over, and so was the feud between Patton and Montgomery.

While Montgomery busied himself with the problems of postwar European reunification, Patton continued to raise Washington's hackles. There was fury over his decision, as de facto governor of Bavaria, to appoint numerous lower-echelon ex-Nazis to key bureaucratic positions. There was logic to his method. Before and during the war, all of these jobs had been filled by Nazis; now, with the country in chaos, it made sense for them to help start rebuilding the shattered nation.

At a stormy press conference, Patton yelled at reporters who raised the question of denazification: "Do you want a lot of Communists [in power]? . . . The Nazi thing is just like a Democratic and Republican election fight."[43] Such ill-considered statements were too much for Eisenhower, who ordered Patton to apologize. The apology, halfhearted and unrepentant, destroyed Eisenhower's patience, and on September 28, 1945, George Patton was relieved of command of the Third Army and put out to pasture.

It was a sad end to a brilliant career. Patton was a colossus, self-made and self-perpetuating. To the troops who worshipped him he was larger than life, but his death, when it came, could hardly have been more humdrum. On December 9, 1945, while driving in Germany, the warrior who had dodged a thousand battlefield bullets was pitched headlong into the windshield. A seemingly minor collision, it broke his neck and left him paralyzed. On December 21, an embolism killed him.

As for Montgomery, after the war he was instrumental in the creation of NATO, and in later years he wrote his memoirs, which demonstrated that he had lost none of his contentiousness or vanity. He died on March 24, 1976.

Assessing these two men is difficult. Most observers regarded Montgomery as an insufferable prig, bursting with his own self-importance, someone of whom Churchill once famously said, "In defeat unbeatable, in victory unbearable."[44]

By the same token Patton's bombastic grandstanding led many to question his sanity, as witnessed by the delusional ramblings that laced his posthumously published diary. "When I think of the greatness of my job . . . I am amazed. But, on reflection, who is as good as I am? I know of no one"[45] runs one typical entry.

So, just how good was he?

In attack he was unsurpassed, incisive, inspired, and above all lightning fast. Set-piece confrontations were a different matter. "To George, tactics was simply a process of bulling ahead," wrote Bradley. "Never seemed to think out a campaign. Seldom made a careful estimate of the situation. I thought him a rather shallow commander."[46]

By contrast, Montgomery was the forerunner of the modern military planner, cautious, always weighing the risks, obsessed with detail. It is easy to picture him fitting seamlessly into an operation such as Desert Storm. He was a master tactician in defense who took command at a time when defense was the only Allied option. Unfortunately, having peaked early in the war, he struggled thereafter to maintain his reputation and influence, and in comparison with the dashing Patton, he often appeared unimaginative and overly watchful.

So who was the greater general? The arguments rage to the

present day. Each has his legions of hagiographers and detractors, and sadly most of the skirmishing has been waged on that most odious of battlefields, xenophobia. Setting individual characters aside, it should be remembered that World War II was an *Allied* victory: without early British Commonwealth resilience, the war would have been lost; without American resources and resourcefulness, it would never have been won.

CHAPTER 9

Johnson versus Kennedy

Years of feud:	1955–1968	
Names:	Lyndon Baines Johnson	Robert F. Kennedy
Strengths:	The ultimate political wheeler-dealer, flexible, pragmatic	Single-minded in pursuit of a goal
Weaknesses:	Vacillating paranoiac, capable of making Rabelais blush	Snobbish, cold-hearted, incapable of forgiveness
At stake:	The legacy of Camelot	

It was the blackest day in America since Pearl Harbor. At Andrews Air Force Base, just outside Washington, DC, a pall of disbelief hung over the small crowd that had gathered in the cool evening air to watch the blue and white jetliner as it taxied to a halt on the runway. Suddenly, a lone figure rushed out across the tarmac and boarded the plane even before the gangway was firmly secured. No one tried to stop him. Once inside, the newcomer elbowed his way through the ashen-faced passengers, muttering, "I want to see Jackie."[1] The throng parted to let him through.

Only one man held his ground. He was a large, imposing individual, and the harrowing events of the past few hours were etched deep into every crevice of his rumpled face. Even so, he had expected some acknowledgment of his newfound authority. But the younger man was having none of it. Attorney General Robert F. Kennedy brushed past Lyndon Baines Johnson as if he didn't exist, intent only on reaching his newly widowed sister-in-law as she mourned beside the casket that contained her murdered husband's body.

"[Bobby] ran," said Johnson later, "so that he would not have to pause and recognize the new president."[2]

In all honesty, no one was surprised.

For seven years the two men had fought the nastiest turf war that anyone in Washington could remember. "There was something about the personality of Bobby that irritated the devil out of Johnson, and something about Johnson's personality that obviously irritated Bobby,"[3] recalled LBJ's press secretary, George Reedy.

In every respect save one—ambition—they were polar opposites. Robert Fitzgerald Kennedy, the austere Ivy League multimillionaire who frowned on ostentation, a poetry buff weighed down by a sense of noblesse oblige, groomed to perpetuate and extend the family's influence into every corner of public life. Contrast that with Johnson's dust bowl background: the southwest Texas farm boy who never forgot the numbing poverty of his childhood, yet grew into a regular hill country dandy with a hankering for fine suits and chunky diamond rings, the good ol' boy who could turn the air blue with his locker room ribaldry.

Only politics could have brought together two such disparate personalities. Each had been weaned on the stuff. Johnson's father had served five terms in the Texas Legislature, while Joseph Kennedy, former bootlegger and failed movie mogul, had been ambassador to Britain under Franklin Roosevelt.

And unintentionally it was Joe Kennedy who sparked all the trouble. It began in the fall of 1955, when the Democratic party was scrambling for a candidate to field against President Eisenhower the following year. Among those sniffing the political wind was John F. Kennedy, senator from Massachusetts, oldest surviving Kennedy son and America's first made-for-TV politician. With his youthful vigor and dazzling smile, Kennedy could light up those television pixels in a way that made his rivals appear comatose, as if they had been dipped in formaldehyde. But there were drawbacks. First, his age: he was just thirty-eight. And there was his religion: no Catholic had ever been president.

Neither handicap was insurmountable, reasoned Joe, but, pragmatic as always, he deemed it best if this time around John positioned himself for a tilt at the vice presidency. That way he could make the transition from regional to national figure, while any damage incurred in the anticipated November massacre could be mended in time for the 1960 election. Such a strategy required a sacrificial lamb, someone prepared to tackle Eisenhower for the presidency. Given the incumbent's enormous popularity, the field of potential Democratic candidates was not exactly overstocked, but Joe, a keen spotter of political horseflesh, had isolated one possibility from the herd—Senate Majority Leader Lyndon Johnson.

Nobody knew Washington better than the big guy from Texas, and with his broad power base among southern Dixiecrats and matchless negotiating skills, he was, Joe figured, sure to give a good account of himself.

After enlisting the assistance of his favorite son, Bobby, who was running JFK's campaign, Joe huddled with Johnson's close friend Tommy Corcoran. Joe offered a deal: if Johnson would announce his candidacy for president and privately pledge to take John as his running mate, Joe promised to bankroll the ticket. Corcoran relayed the offer to the LBJ Ranch, on the Pedernales River in Texas. Johnson turned him down flat, fobbing him off with the excuse that he had no interest in pursuing the Oval Office. In reality, he, too, had his eye firmly fixed on 1960, and he wasn't about to be Eisenhower's punching bag for Joe Kennedy or anyone else, no matter how well stuffed the campaign war chest.

Reaction among the Kennedys was mixed: Joe was disappointed, John was unsurprised, Bobby was livid. Inexplicably, he took Johnson's refusal—as understandable as it was predictable—as a grievous personal insult to his father, whom he thought had made a generous offer. As a result, Bobby turned on Johnson with the ferocity of a Rottweiler.

"When Bobby hates you, you stay hated,"[4] Joe Kennedy once proudly boasted.

Sure enough, Johnson stayed hated.

The feeling was entirely mutual. To Johnson's way of thinking,

Bobby was "a grandstanding little runt"[5] who was riding the family coattails to fame. Neither could stand to be in the same room as the other.

But for now there was an election to fight. As in 1952, Adlai Stevenson led the Democratic ticket, this time with Estes Kefauver as running mate, and as expected, they were buried. Eisenhower returned to the White House just long enough to pick up his golf clubs, allowing Johnson to continue his majestic domination of the Senate and to ready himself for the real fight in 1960.

Nursing a sorely bruised ego, Bobby was left to brood and hone his prodigious feuding skills at the Justice Department, taking on Teamsters boss Jimmy Hoffa while laying the groundwork for his brother's second campaign, this time for the number-one slot on the ticket.

Johnson, meanwhile, could afford to chuckle. The "snot-nosed kid,"[6] as he termed Bobby Kennedy, had been well and truly trounced by a recognized Washington giant, probably the toughest political infighter America has produced. For more than two decades Lyndon Johnson had been playing the Washington game, and nobody did it better.

New Deal Rookie

He had arrived in town in the early thirties, a New Deal Democrat burning with zeal and ambition, and right from the outset his career was meteoric. During his four years as a congressional secretary he met and married Claudia Alta Taylor, a young woman from Texas known to her family and friends as "Lady Bird," and so began the cult of LBJ, from their shared initials. It was a handy abbreviation that stuck in voters' minds, and helped propel the ambitious Texan from political secretary to congressman, all the way to senator in 1948.

Helping him every step of the journey was his mentor and longtime family friend, Sam Rayburn. By 1955, Johnson was majority leader in the Senate, while Rayburn was Speaker of the House. Taking advantage of Eisenhower's increasing lethargy, these two Texans virtually ran the country, advancing or blocking legislation at will.

Johnson was a peerless political operator, a kind of Capitol Hill bookmaker, extending credit where necessary, ruthless about calling in markers, always shaving the odds in his favor. No one could cajole or browbeat quite like him. On the phone he was merely intimidating; in the flesh he could scare the pants off the toughest campaigner. His tactics became known as "The Treatment," a virtuoso performance in the black arts of persuasion. The craggy face would loom in until there was less than one inch of breathing space for the quaking victim; one bearlike paw would encircle the victim's shoulder, the other would reach metaphorically for other, more sensitive, anatomical regions. Which got squeezed the most depended entirely on the answers that Johnson received. He could be lovable and loathsome, generous and brutally unforgiving, often within the same breath.

Not everyone was terrified. As the campaign for the 1960 Democratic nomination heated up, Robert Kennedy was in Washington one night at a stage premiere when he introduced his showbiz friends to LBJ's longtime associate, Bobby Baker. "This is Little Lyndon Johnson," jeered Kennedy. "You should ask him why Big Lyndon won't risk running in the primaries against my brother. They're supposed to make 'em tough down in Texas, but Big Lyndon doesn't look so tough to me."[7]

Bobby had good reason for his cockiness. Johnson was floundering from a rare political miscalculation, stemming from his underestimation of JFK. In 1958, he told fellow Democrat Tip O'Neill "You and I know the boy can't win. He's just a flash in the pan."[8]

As a consequence, early on Johnson had thrown his weight behind Hubert Humphrey, while at the same time bad-mouthing Kennedy to anyone who would listen. Protestant West Virginia would, he crowed, stop the Catholic Kennedy bandwagon cold when the primary circus pulled into town on May 10, 1960. It didn't work out that way. The margin of Kennedy's emphatic victory was enough to drive Humphrey out of the race.

Which left Johnson as the only possible obstacle between JFK and his party's nomination. But Johnson was playing a cagey hand. He and his advisers, headed by Sam Rayburn, were betting on a deadlocked convention. At that point Johnson would start calling in his markers, a crude reminder to party leaders of his heavyweight political acumen, leaving them no alternative but to nominate him for the presidency. That was the plan, and that was why Johnson held off publicly declaring his candidacy until July.

While their leader vacillated with the bouts of Hamletlike indecisiveness that would plague his career, Johnson's team played hardball, resurrecting old smears centered on Joe Kennedy's prewar ambivalence about the rise of Nazi Germany. Simultaneously, long-suppressed stories about JFK's struggles with Addison's disease, a wasting condition of the adrenal cortex, suddenly leaked into the press, and although JFK refused to implicate Johnson personally in the slur, blaming the latter's aides, Bobby had absolutely no doubts about where to direct his outrage. He took dead aim at Johnson.

Suddenly the campaign trail turned even uglier, when the youngest Kennedy scion, Ted, mused publicly on the possibility that Lyndon might not have fully recovered from the mild heart attack he suffered back in 1955. This led to a fierce confrontation between the two Bobbies, Kennedy and Baker. Bobby swept aside Baker's complaint about the comment, snarling, "You've got your nerve. Lyndon Johnson has compared my father to the Nazis and [your side] lied in saying my brother is dying of Addison's disease. You Johnson people are running a stinking damned campaign and you're going to get yours when the time comes!"[9]

Payback time came on July 13 at the Los Angeles Democratic convention. Once again Johnson misjudged the party's mood as John Kennedy beamed his way to an overwhelming victory. Now it was just a question of picking a running mate, oddly enough not something that the Kennedy clan had considered. When they did, one name leaped out of the pack—Lyndon Johnson.

They needed him. Only Johnson could deliver the electorally decisive southern vote, where Kennedy's Catholicism was bound to be a negative factor. Offsetting this Johnson plus was the antipathy of northern liberals, who despised the Senate leader as a bullying redneck whose civil rights record was murky, to say the least. But votes were votes and, grudgingly, Johnson was offered second place on the ticket.

To the shock of many and the horror of some—himself included—Johnson accepted.

Bobby, furious at this latest turn of events, fought like a demon to reverse the decision, even to the point of personally visiting Johnson and offering him any job he wanted in the Democratic machine if he backed off. Every approach was rebuffed. At first hand Bobby got an Oscar-worthy demonstration of the Texan's extraordinary acting ability. Johnson was, he said, "one of the greatest sad-looking people in the world. You know, he can just turn it on . . . I thought he'd burst into tears. . . . He just shook, and tears came into his eyes, and he said, 'I want to be vice president, and if the president [JFK] will have me, I'll join him in making a fight for it.'"[10]

Not knowing whether to puke or cry, Bobby crawled from the meeting like a whipped dog.

In his wake he left behind an implacable enemy. For the rest of his life, nothing would deflect Lyndon Johnson from the conviction that Bobby, unilaterally and with premeditated spite, had attempted to destroy his political future.

The feud continued right through to election night. It was at the time the biggest nail-biter in American history as Richard Nixon fought to keep the White House for the Republicans. When the dust settled and the votes were counted—some of them twice in parts of Illinois, if you can believe the rumors—Kennedy squeaked past Nixon to become president of the United States.

Later that same night Johnson drank coffee in an Austin diner, gloomy and discontented. Not only had he surrendered the most powerful legislative job in America for the impotence of the vice presidency, a traditionally thankless post; even worse, Bobby had been made attorney general.

While Johnson continued to fume about that "snot-nosed little sonofabitch,"[11] Bobby wasted no time in carving out his fiefdom. Only six months into JFK's presidency, *U.S. News & World Report* proclaimed him the "number two man in Washington . . . second only to the president in power and influence . . . the Assistant President."[12]

It was a shameful humiliation for Johnson, and his role as a bit player was soon cruelly evident. Early in his presidency, Kennedy was in the cabinet room surrounded by advisers discussing a message to Congress. The meeting had barely begun when Kennedy paused, glanced around the table, and barked, "Where is the vice president?" All he got was a row of blank faces: no one had remembered to notify Johnson of the meeting. Kennedy bawled them out. "Don't ever let this happen again. You know what my rules are, and we will not conduct meetings without the vice president being present."[13]

There was a strange kinship between the hillbilly Johnson and the urbane president. Although Kennedy had frequent and good cause to doubt Johnson's truthfulness on all occasions, he was also an admirer of Johnson's raw political skill. Each recognized the other's qualities and was prepared to turn a blind eye to their shortcomings. Johnson appreciated the consideration. "President Kennedy was very good to me," he later wrote, "and tried his best to elevate the office [of the vice presidency] in any way he could."[14]

The reverence for the office of president that had hallmarked Johnson's time as Senate leader spilled over into the Oval Office. Whatever he might think in private, at no time was he ever less than exemplary in his public support for the president. Once, when a guest at the LBJ ranch disparaged JFK, Johnson nearly threw him out.

Bobby felt no such duty. Every chance he got he humiliated Johnson, often darting past him into the Oval Office without a word or nod. During one White House meeting, which the president had asked Johnson to close, Bobby listened in obviously bored silence for a while, then summoned a minor official and whispered, "I've got a date, and I've got to get on this boat in a few minutes. Can't you tell the vice president to cut it short."[15]

Understandably reluctant to halt the vice president in midflow, the official opted to do nothing and returned to his seat, only to be motioned back. "Didn't I tell you to tell the vice president to shut up?"[16] snapped Bobby, red-faced. This time the official crept slowly around the table and mumbled in Johnson's ear. Without missing a beat, Johnson glared at the messenger and continued talking, and ended the meeting only when he was good and ready. All the while Bobby boiled, furious at being defied. At the meeting's end he stamped childishly from the room.

This was a rare victory for Johnson as he found himself pushed ever nearer to the margins of power. Almost puppylike in his determination to please, he once cornered Bobby and pleaded, "Why? Why don't you like me?"[17]

Bobby unleashed one of his patented glares, icy blue and cold enough to freeze mercury, before stalking off in silence, leaving Johnson to wallow in the self-pity that was always his closest ally.

Further clashes came as Bobby, head of the Justice Department, planned strategy for the looming civil rights battle. Johnson's schizophrenic track record in this area was always a bone of contention between the two men. In 1948, he had strenuously denounced Harry Truman's civil rights program and had voted against such legislation, although he had notably refused to join with other southerners in their manifesto protesting the 1954 U.S. Supreme Court decision on segregation in public schools. For the ex-schoolteacher, that was one discriminatory bridge too far.

What Bobby utterly failed to comprehend was Johnson's compulsive pragmatism. For a hard-core idealist like Bobby Kennedy, the world was starkly black and white, whereas Lyndon Baines Johnson couldn't even begin to count the shades of gray that populated his universe. It was all about getting along. As a young man he had mingled with blacks and poor Mexicans in Texas, gained their support, and fought their cause in the House. But the Senate was a whole different ballgame. Radicalism was a rare visitor to this august chamber, and Johnson had a career to build. Admittedly, in 1957 and 1960 he did ensure the passage of two moderate civil rights acts, and he accepted special assignments, such as the chairmanship of the President's Committee on Equal Employment Opportunity, an agency that enlarged job opportunities for blacks, but on the whole Johnson was an unreliable quantity in the thorny area of civil rights.

Or so Bobby thought. "We're having a difficult time with Johnson,"[18] he grumbled as the battles in the diners and the buses down south began appearing on the nightly news with damaging regularity.

Jackie and "The Colonel"

Nor was Bobby the only Kennedy scornful of the vice president: Jacqueline, too, had a mean line in the verbal barbecue when it came to the Texan element at the White House. It was she who dubbed the Johnsons "Colonel Cornpone and his Little Porkchop,"[19] a pejorative eagerly latched onto by the clique that gathered regularly at Bobby's Hickory Hill estate in McLean, Virginia. Bad-mouthing Colonel Cornpone was a favorite sport among the Hickory Hill gang, a pastime that reached its nadir when they presented Bobby with an LBJ voodoo doll to hoots of merriment.

Given the continual baiting he suffered, it is hardly surprising that Johnson's hatred and fear of Bobby reached maniacal proportions. Every slight, both real and imagined, was blamed on "that little shitass,"[20] and he deeply resented the influence that Bobby exerted over his brother. When it came to Oval Office briefings, Johnson moaned, Bobby was always "first in, last out."[21]

That didn't stop him trying to mend bridges. Not that it made the slightest bit of difference. Bobby had nothing but contempt for him. One White House insider recalled, "If Bobby had treated him with respect, instead of going around calling him Colonel Cornpone, it would have been entirely different."[22]

Johnson fared better abroad. His tour of Southeast Asia in May 1961, designed to assure pro-Western Asian nations that the United States had no intention of withdrawing, was counted a success. And later that year he journeyed to Berlin after the building of the Wall, once again to reassure anxious West Berliners of the strength of the American commitment.

But these were rare successes. Foreign policy would always be Johnson's blind spot, and never was this more apparent than during the Cuban missile crisis, when his vacillating conduct earned him no friends at all. At first, he advocated moderation, but as the crisis deepened his resolve began to buckle, until he slid weakly into the arms of the hawks, who counseled belligerence. Fortunately for mankind, cooler heads prevailed, but thereafter Bobby Kennedy would remain convinced that Lyndon Johnson was a coward under pressure.

Johnson's sense of insecurity worsened. Despite public assurances from the president that he would be on the ticket in 1964, he continued to fret about "these kids from the White House,"[23] convinced they were conspiring to ruin him. In reality, Kennedy never wholly trusted his deputy. Talking to Jackie one late fall day in 1963, he described Johnson as "incapable of telling the truth."[24]

Next morning President Kennedy flew to Dallas.

The Secret Service agents who shepherded the new president off Air Force One on that grim Washington evening of November 22 were guarding one mighty scared man. During the flight Lyndon Johnson had babbled incoherently about all kinds of global plots and conspiracies; indeed, some reports claim that one aide had to actually slap Johnson's face in order to get some sense out of him. Again word got around that Johnson's nerve had buckled in a crisis.

For one person such conduct was unforgivable.

Not only did Bobby believe that Johnson had botched the chaotic departure arrangements in Dallas, and added to his sister-in-law's torment with his bizarre insistence that the plane delay its takeoff until he had been officially sworn in as president, but he was convinced that the country was now saddled with a reactionary weakling. "People just don't realize how conservative Lyndon really is," said Bobby. "There are going to be a lot of changes."[25]

In a masterpiece of twisted logic, Bobby and his supporters even contrived to lay blame for the Dallas tragedy at Johnson's door. Their president had been strong-armed into visiting Texas by the Texan Johnson, they reasoned, and now Texas had killed him. The absurdity of such thinking seems obvious now, but these were overwrought times, and it was an allegation vehemently rejected by Johnson, who denied ever putting pressure on Kennedy to visit his home state.

Equally fatuous was Johnson's attempt to tar Bobby with his brother's death, which he always believed had been ordered by Cuban leader Fidel Castro. Ever since the Bay of Pigs fiasco, Johnson had blamed Bobby for American policy excesses in Cuba. Now the chickens had come home to roost. According to Johnson, Bobby "had been operating a damned Murder Incorporated in the Caribbean. . . . President Kennedy tried to get Castro first, but Castro got Kennedy first."[26]

Johnson's paranoia showed no signs of abating. Within hours of entering the White House, he ordered that a Dictaphone be placed in the Oval Office so that he might record phone calls. On November 27, he summoned Bobby for a meeting in an attempt to clear the air. All it succeeded in doing was in widening the gulf between them. "Your people are talking about me," complained Johnson. "You can't let your people talk about me and I won't talk about you."[27]

He blustered for a few minutes about the changes that were necessary until, inevitably, the subject turned to Dallas. Right away Johnson blundered by claiming that Air Force One had taken off as soon as Jackie Kennedy had arrived. It was a foolish and unnecessary falsehood, one that allowed Bobby to leave the meeting with all his prejudices confirmed: Lyndon Johnson was a liar.

He carried that animosity into the first cabinet meeting. One observer recalled Bobby's expression of contempt, saying it was "quite clear that he could hardly countenance Lyndon Johnson sitting in his brother's seat."[28]

There was another ominous sign that Johnson's vendetta against Bobby was about to be raised a notch: he started getting regular deliveries of top-secret files from a longtime ally.

If there was anybody in the world who hated the Kennedys more than Lyndon Johnson, it was J. Edgar Hoover, the tyrannical boss of the FBI whose secret files had terrified generations of American politicians into cringing obsequiousness. Hoover had the goods on just about everybody in Washington, all neatly recorded in his secret files, and those same files now wound up on Johnson's bedside table, where they made for some tantalizing reading. He scoured them, according to his personal secretary, Marie Fehmer, so as to "have a little more information on his enemies."[29]

Rumors that Hoover was spoon-feeding Johnson tidbits of scandal hit Bobby Kennedy like an avalanche. Aside from any concerns about his own private life—and there was a mountain of these—as attorney general and head of the Justice Department, he was technically Hoover's boss, but it was position without power. Hoover was untouchable. "I have no dealings with the FBI anymore," Bobby whined to Johnson in June 1964. "I understand that . . . he [Hoover] sends all kinds of reports over to you about the Department of Justice."[30]

With quite magnificent hypocrisy Johnson innocently denied all knowledge of such subterfuge and directed his attention elsewhere. He was on the brink of his finest hour. One week later, on July 2, he signed the 1964 Civil Rights Act into law. At last he had stepped out from JFK's shadow with a momentous piece of legislation all his own. And he wanted everyone to know it. People at the signing ceremony noted the iciness with which Johnson treated Bobby.

It was astonishing; in just a few short months the roles had been entirely reversed. Now Johnson was calling the shots. His allies urged him to go for the jugular. "You're going to have trouble with Bobby," Tommy Corcoran told Lady Bird. "We all know how an attorney general can screw everything up. He can indict anybody, he can investigate anybody."[31]

But Johnson wouldn't listen. For all his paranoid hatred for Bobby, he felt duty bound to extend to Bobby the courtesies that JFK had extended to himself, nor was he about to invite accusations that he was trying to ease the younger brother out of power.

Bobby took his reduced role badly, convinced that Johnson was out to destroy him in public life. The rift became wider, the insults even more vindictive. "Our president was a gentleman and a human being . . . this man is not. He's mean, bitter, vicious—an animal in many ways,"[32] he said in an archive interview taped for posterity. Then he attempted to draw further distinctions between the two men by claiming, "What does Johnson know [about poverty]?"[33] which was a tad rich coming from someone whose only financial concern since the cradle had been wondering just where to invest those trust-fund dividend checks.

"Don't get mad, get even," old man Kennedy had preached, and none of his offspring had followed that dictum with greater vigor than Bobby, which is what made his next move so surprising—a blatant pitch for the role of vice president in the upcoming election of November 1964. Cunning as ever, Bobby explained his reasoning to a friend: "If there's one thing Lyndon Johnson doesn't want, it's me as vice president."[34]

Bobby Miscues

A significant development came on July 4, 1964. After phoning Johnson to offer his Independence Day congratulations, Bobby hurriedly put Jackie on the line, hoping her saccharine sweet talk might improve his chances for the VP slot. Johnson could scarcely conceal his contempt, appalled that anyone would use a grieving widow as leverage for personal advancement. Spluttering with rage, he immediately called Secretary of State Dean Rusk, and between them they spent a splenetic few minutes trashing Bobby's naked ambition and ruthlessness.

The absurdity of a Johnson-Kennedy axis was soon highlighted by an Oval Office dispute in which LBJ ordered Bobby to fire one of his aides from the Democratic National Committee. When Bobby refused, Johnson let him have both barrels. "President Kennedy isn't president anymore. I am!" To which Bobby replied, "I know you're president, and don't you ever talk to me like that again."[35] Then he stormed from the White House in a cold rage.

The fight resumed that evening over the telephone and ended with Bobby slamming down the receiver and growling to an aide, "I'll tell you one thing: this relationship can't last much longer."[36]

Nor would it. Johnson was getting meaner by the minute. "If they try to push Bobby Kennedy down my throat for vice president, I'll tell them to nominate him for the Presidency and leave me out of it,"[37] he threatened. But when press speculation about a possible running mate in the upcoming election reached fever pitch, Johnson struck like a diamondback rattler.

He summoned Bobby to the Oval Office and, after a customary round of good ol' boy platitudes, he dropped the guillotine. "I have concluded . . . that it would be inadvisable for you to be the Democratic candidate for vice president in this year's election."[38]

All the blood drained from Bobby's bony face. Convinced the conversation was being taped, he refused to be baited and remained civil. He was offered, and refused, his pick of the plum jobs, saying that he preferred to stay at the Justice Department. Then he left.

In his glee, Johnson almost two-stepped his way around the Oval Office desk, chortling, "That damn albatross is off my neck," and immediately summoned a select group of White House reporters to share his triumph. He didn't spare any detail. "When I got [Kennedy] in the Oval Office and told him it would be 'inadvisable' for him to be on the ticket as the vice president nominee, his face changed, and he started to swallow. He looked sick. His Adam's apple bounded up and down like a yo-yo."[39]

Everyone laughed, because Johnson was the "Prez" and always told a good story, but the level of gloating cruelty sickened many of those present. Of course, that didn't prevent the story from finding its way into the press, much to Bobby's fury and embarrassment. Naturally, when asked, Johnson assumed his best Huck Finn air of injured innocence and disclaimed all knowledge of the source for the story.

"He tells so many lies," said Bobby. "I think he actually believes his own bullshit. At least when I tell a lie, I know I'm lying."[40]

The Hickory Hill gang fought back, planting stories in the press about the manner in which their hero had been mistreated. "If they just keep on," Johnson warned, "I'm gonna sock him right in the puss and I don't want to do that."[41]

As the level of acrimony rose ever higher, Johnson's mood swings began to deepen and darken. All his life he had suffered crippling bouts of self-doubt, but nobody expected him to pull a stunt like the one he engineered on August 25, 1964, slap in the middle of the Democratic convention in Atlantic City. Convinced that the people of America were ganging up on him, Johnson phoned George Reedy and told him that he intended to withdraw from the nomination race.

Reedy gulped hard as his senses reeled. This was insane, Johnson's approval ratings were stratospheric; no way could he lose in November. Johnson was deaf to all reason. Later that day Lady Bird wrote her husband a rare letter, urging him to reconsider, but as evening crept on and Reedy walked with Johnson on the White House lawns, the president was still determined to quit.

And yet somewhere in the darkness of that long, troubled night, Lady Bird's plea reached deep into the Johnson psyche and hauled him back from the brink. Come morning, the doubts were gone, replaced by his old swaggering feeling of omnipotence. He flew to Atlantic City, revived and resurgent. When, to wild cheers, he accepted the nomination of his party, his uncharacteristically shrill speech was the only outward sign of the inner turmoil he had endured. To accompany him on the ticket he chose Hubert H. Humphrey, a popular liberal from Minnesota with many supporters.

Two weeks later, on September 3, 1964, Bobby resigned as attorney general. The pressures had finally overwhelmed him: it was time to move on. "It is with regret that I receive your resignation,"[42] Johnson wrote, but there was no masking the relief. So what if Bobby intended running as senator from New York; for now at least, the heir to Camelot was out of the presidential loop.

Johnson yearned for an electoral victory of epic proportions. Back in 1948, he had scraped through the runoff Democratic primary election in Texas by the razor-thin margin of 87 votes out of nearly 900,000, and ever since then he had been saddled with the derisive nickname "Landslide Lyndon."

Now he wanted to bury that reputation for good. It has to be said that the Republicans made it easy for him. Barry Goldwater's brand of conservative zealotry, particularly in foreign policy, appeared to have been fashioned by Doctor Strangelove, and given a choice between Armageddon and Avalon, even once removed, the American voters decided it was no contest.

On November 3, 1964, Johnson coasted to the biggest presidential victory in history, winning 486 electoral votes to Goldwater's 52, and bagging all but 6 states.

Lyndon had his landslide at last. The Democratic tidal wave swamped the House and the Senate, gaining a big majority in each. Among the freshman senators was Bobby Kennedy, who romped home in New York, securing the widest margin of victory by any Democrat in that state since 1938.

With his confidence sky-high, Johnson embarked on building the "Great Society," the most ambitious plan of social change in the United States since the New Deal. Drawing unashamedly on the work initiated by his immediate Oval Office predecessor, Johnson shoehorned a prodigious raft of bills through Congress: Medicare; the Voting Rights Act of 1965, which outlawed illiteracy tests and other obstacles designed to disenfranchise African Americans; federal aid to primary and secondary schools increased substantially. Two new federal departments—Housing and Urban Development, and Transportation—were set up, and responding to Johnson's call for an "unconditional war on poverty," Congress liberalized unemployment compensation, expanded the food stamp program, and enlarged opportunities for youth employment. No session of Congress since 1935 had attacked social and economic problems on such a scale, and no U.S. president had ever been in such control of his country.

But it wasn't all honey and roses. While Johnson had done more to advance the cause of social justice than any other president—certainly more than John Kennedy—still he was mocked by the eastern establishment. "I always knew the greatest bigots in the world lived in the East, not the South,"[43] he concluded grimly.

And he had troubles elsewhere: less than one month after his inauguration, American bombs began to rain on Vietnam.

The Curse of Vietnam

It was an inherited problem. Under President Kennedy, U.S. soldiers, officially advisers, had trained South Vietnamese forces to combat aggression from the Communist North. Johnson pursued the same path, steadily expanding the U.S. military presence in 1964 from 16,000 to nearly 25,000 men.

Almost without anyone noticing, he "Americanized" the war. Beginning in February 1965, U.S. planes bombed North Vietnam, gradually increasing the scale of the attacks and the importance of the targets. In July a rapid expansion of American ground forces got under way. By year's end, some 180,000 American troops were in Vietnam, and the number doubled during 1966, a move that Johnson hoped would force the North Vietnamese to the bargaining table. But, like most of his military advisers, he had gravely underestimated the Communist resolve.

Among the first to voice doubts about the military buildup had been Bobby Kennedy, but in early 1965 Vietnam was still a popular cause and his comments had prompted stinging newspaper accusations of antipatriotism, enough to drive the freshman senator into his shell.

Smarting from the first public setback of his new career, Bobby licked his wounds and sharpened his focus. With one eye fixed firmly on the election of 1968, he embarked on an ambitious plan to convince the American public—and history—that Vietnam was no longer his brother's folly but the Johnson War, and in this he was largely successful.

As Vietnam soured, Johnson was trapped. At a time when ghettoes across the nation were convulsed by riots, the spiraling costs of the war, both economic and emotional, cut deep into his domestic agenda as he struggled to convince an increasingly skeptical nation that it could afford both "guns and butter." The fight against poverty, the civil rights campaign, both were relegated to the back burner as Vietnam came to dominate Johnson's thinking. The 1966 congressional elections were brutal evidence of just how far he had fallen, with the Republicans gaining forty-seven seats in the House and three in the Senate.

Nothing, it seemed, could quell the unrest. Antiwar demonstrations became a daily event, university campuses degenerated into battlefields, and inexorably American support for the war waned. Each night the TV news broadcasts were littered with body bags and everyone seemed to be telling Johnson, "This is your fault."

In less than nine months his approval ratings plunged from 63 percent in January 1966 to just 44 percent in October. In his fury he lashed out at opponents of his Vietnam policies as disloyal to him and the country. Vietnam was a war he believed in; it was nothing he wanted to do, but he felt he had no choice, it was vital to the country's self-interest.

And, of course, he knew where to place the blame. "We've got Bobby . . . and this crowd hitting us every day from the inside so our party's just split wide open."[44]

Kennedy was rebuilding his reputation fast. In January 1967, he took off for a well-publicized fact-finding mission to Europe that was long on style and short on substance, but it kept his name in the headlines and needled the hell out of Johnson. "I never saw such an arrogant fella,"[45] he complained.

With the war's body count soaring daily, Johnson couldn't appear in public without risk of protests, and he became even more emotionally distraught. Vietnam brought out the worst in him: ranting rages closely pursued by trench-mentality depressions that were bad enough for aides to fear for his sanity. Georgia Senator Richard Russell, a close friend and mentor, couldn't bear to see Johnson alone at the White House, because the president would cry uncontrollably.

Withdrawal and defeat became unthinkable, and when Bobby's

opposition to the war became more public, more virulent, Johnson summoned him to the White House. It would be their toughest encounter yet. Johnson accused his old enemy of meddling in foreign affairs, an accusation that Bobby refuted entirely, provoking the president into a monumental tirade. "I'll destroy you and every one of your dove friends," he roared. "You'll be dead politically in six months!"[46]

Ordinarily, Bobby would have launched his own verbal counterattack, and yet, a short time after this meeting, he was uncharacteristically fulsome in a speech praising the president's considerable domestic achievements. "If I hadn't said all those things," he explained to mystified Hickory Hill gang members, "that would have given Lyndon Johnson the opportunity to blame everything that was going wrong . . . Vietnam, the cities, the race question . . . on that sonofabitch Bobby Kennedy."[47]

His genuine views were revealed just two weeks before the speech, when he had conferred with longtime ally Arthur Schlesinger. "How can we possibly survive five more years of Lyndon Johnson? Five more years of a crazy man?"[48]

America was also wondering.

A string of disappointing results in early primaries raised serious doubts about LBJ's chances of renomination. And then, despite the fact that U.S. troop levels had reached almost 500,000, came the Tet offensive on January 31, 1968. As Communist troops swarmed south, seemingly irresistible, LBJ's approval ratings plummeted. On March 31, looking haggard and frazzled to the point of distraction, he appeared on national TV to announce a partial pause in the bombing of North Vietnam. Near the end of the broadcast, he added an almost throwaway footnote that stunned the world—he would not run for the presidency in November 1968.

Into the vacuum stepped two of his most voluble Democratic critics: Senator Eugene McCarthy and, inevitably, Robert Kennedy. Those expecting the customary Kennedy victory juggernaut were sorely disappointed. Bobby could smile like John, he even sounded like him on occasion, but he lacked his brother's indefinable charisma, and when it came to ideas and beliefs, he was all over the map. Betrayal was an oft-heard criticism. At one time or another, misguidedly or not,

Bobby was perceived as having trampled underfoot his brother's beliefs.

And he still feared Lyndon Johnson. On April 3, the two men talked at the White House. Bobby wanted to know if Johnson intended throwing his weight behind any candidate in particular. Johnson wasted little time on his hated foe, piously declaring that he was no kingmaker. At meeting's end the two shook hands. It would be the last time they ever met.

Despite suspicions that Johnson was secretly canvassing for his deputy, Hubert Humphrey, Bobby slowly gained ground. But the California primary would be critical.

When the votes were counted on June 4, 1968, Bobby had topped the poll with a big majority. Together with his entourage and several reporters he retreated to the Ambassador Hotel in Los Angeles for a celebratory party. At fifteen minutes past midnight, as Kennedy was making his way through the hotel, a Jordanian immigrant named Sirhan Sirhan raised a .22-caliber Iver-Johnson Cadet revolver to the back of Bobby's head and opened fire. Apart from Bobby, five people were wounded, none fatally.

For over twenty-five hours Bobby Kennedy lingered in intensive care. On June 6, at 1:44 A.M., the life support machine was turned off and he was pronounced dead. Next day, Johnson, declaring the news "too horrible for words,"[49] signed into law immediate legislation authorizing Secret Service protection for major presidential candidates. Not that it would have saved Bobby Kennedy. A lifelong hater of personal weakness, he had earlier refused to beef up his personal security and became furious at suggestions that he should.

For the remaining few months of his presidency, Johnson was mired in Vietnam. On election night America gave its verdict on the Johnson years when Richard Nixon swept to victory over Hubert Humphrey.

Broken in spirit and body, Johnson limped from office on January 20, 1969, with nothing left except to retire to his Texas ranch and write his memoirs,* in which, predictably, Bobby

---

*LBJ suffered recurring heart trouble, and he died at his ranch near Johnson City, Texas, on January 22, 1973.

Kennedy cropped up often. And in that rosy hue that invariably tinges political hindsight, Johnson judged that it had all been the other guy's fault. "Perhaps his political ambitions were part of the problem,"[50] he mused, unwilling as always to admit his own role in the feud.

Johnson craved power, but not the absolute power that the presidency bestowed. He had prospered in a back-slapping world of back-room deals, promises, threats, and guile, a million light years removed from the awesome responsibilities of the Oval Office. Twice he resolved to walk away from it all; second time around he did. Assessing his role in history is complex: for many he is a failure, forever tarnished by Vietnam; on the other hand, numerous allies cite his enormous civil rights achievements, undeniably superior to those of his predecessor.

On the civil rights front, it should be remembered that Johnson enjoyed two distinct advantages over JFK: first, he had a huge congressional majority and, more significantly, he was the beneficiary of a vast amount of goodwill from the American people. After the disaster in Dallas they desperately wanted him to succeed, and for the first couple of years he delivered in spades. But the crucible of Vietnam was deadly for a mind crippled by indecision, a hesitancy that contrasted so vividly with JFK's courageous handling of the Cuban crisis. And always he was haunted by the specter of Bobby lurking in the shadows.

No one will never know if Bobby Kennedy would have won the presidency or even the Democratic nomination in 1968, and opinions are naturally divided as to what kind of president he would have made. One thing is certain: he was every bit as much a victim of his brother's legacy as was Johnson. And therein lay the problem. Bobby Kennedy and Lyndon Johnson were two men fighting to fill the same pair of shoes; and if history has tended to make those shoes just a smidgen bigger than they really were, well, that's just human nature, and nobody's big enough to fight that.

CHAPTER 10

Hoover versus King

Years of feud:	1961–1968	
Names:	J. Edgar Hoover	Martin Luther King Jr.
Strengths:	Cleaned up a corrupt investigative unit and turned it into one of the world's finest crime-fighting agencies	Inspirational orator and leader, with bottomless reserves of bravery
Weaknesses:	Dictatorial blackmailer who failed to maintain the standards he demanded of others	Sexually indiscreet
At stake:	Civil rights in America	

On the morning of January 5, 1965, a young Atlanta woman opened a package that had been forwarded from her husband's workplace. As president of the Southern Christian Leadership Conference (SCLC) and its chief spokesman, her husband spent large chunks of each month on the road campaigning, and at times like these his secretary knew to forward his mail to his home address. Inside the flat package the woman found a folded letter and a reel of tape. Her first reaction was that the tape contained a recording of one of her husband's speeches. Then she read the letter. Semiliterate and unsigned, it didn't pull any punches:

> King, look into your heart. You know you are a complete fraud and a great liability to all of us Negroes. White people in this country have enough frauds of their own but I am sure that they don't have one at this time that is anywhere near your equal. You are no clergyman and you know it. I repeat you are a colossal fraud and an evil, vicious one at that. . . .

So far, just another crank letter, but soon it lurched into something far more sinister:

> King, there is only one thing left for you to do. You know what it is. You have just 34 days in which to do [sic] (this exact number has been selected for a specific reason, it has definite practical significance). You are done. There is but one way out for you. You better take it before your filthy, abnormal fraudulent self is bared to the nation.[1]

The message was unequivocal—kill yourself, or else.

Obviously, there was a very sick mind at work here. And it got worse. The tape made for some spicy listening. Carefully edited—only to be expected, considering the source—it had been cobbled together from numerous liaisons in hotel rooms across America and left nothing to the imagination. Every sigh, every moan, every orgasm was clearly discernible, as were the voices.

The absent husband had clearly enjoyed himself on those long road trips.

Not unreasonably, the wife grabbed the phone and gave her husband hell. When Martin Luther King Jr. did finally return home to confront the evidence of the tape, he and his close friend Ralph Abernathy, whose own indiscretions had also been captured by the eavesdroppers, listened in grim silence. When the tape clicked off, Abernathy glanced across at his shaken colleague and said simply, "J. Edgar Hoover."[2]

For close to five decades, American national security and J. Edgar Hoover were synonymous. As director of the Federal Bureau of Investigation from 1924 to 1972, this complex character, who doted on gossip and horse racing and not much else, and who lived with his mom until he was in his mid-forties, wielded more raw power than anyone else in America, a modern-day Torquemada. Reds, hoodlums, Nazis, subversives of every shade, the director tackled them all on behalf of a grateful nation, most of which swallowed the bromide that without Hoover at the helm, America was headed for hell in a handcart.

It was a magnificent propaganda coup.

Some of it was even true. Mostly, though, it was all due to timing. Hoover was just plain lucky. His rise to power coincided with an explosion in broadcast media; radio was still in its infancy, and like those other remorseless self-aggrandizers of the period, Hitler and Stalin, the FBI boss was quick to harness the new technology for personal motives. In under a decade he rose from obscurity to the most famous true-life cop the world has seen.

He achieved this extraordinary metamorphosis by placing himself at the epicenter of every potentially profitable crisis. After scoring some big propaganda brownie points on the Red Scare in the twenties, Hoover exploited the ballyhoo that enveloped the 1932 Lindbergh kidnapping and Roosevelt's New Deal crime-fighting initiatives, to vastly increase the bureau's investigative horizons and, more important, to beef up his all-important public profile.

Reporters loved him because he made for dynamite copy. Walter Winchell, a longtime FBI stoolie, was merely the most famous of the string of tame journalists who daily inflated the Hoover myth. In homes across the land, it became a family tradition to huddle around the radio and marvel at Winchell's fantastically embroidered accounts of the director and his heroic G-men. Books, movies, magazines, newspapers, all jumped on the bandwagon, boosting the fast-talking pudgy bureaucrat into a folk hero to rival anything that Hollywood could manufacture.

Congress bought the entire package. Hoover's annual begging trips to the Hill were masterpieces of hype and inventiveness. Bug-eyed congressmen quaked in the face of Hoover's apocalyptic predictions of what might befall Western civilization if the FBI were not given every last cent he asked for. "I have never cut his budget," boasted Congressman John Rooney, chairman of the subcommittee that oversaw FBI funding. "And I never expect to."[3] With buddies like that, Hoover had it made. Key to his success as law-enforcement superhero was selectivity: he always chose the soft target. In the 1930s, while Mafia kingpins Lucky Luciano and Meyer Lansky were slicing up America's gangland pie, unhindered and unacknowledged, Hoover squandered vast amounts of time and tax dollars chasing a bunch of two-bit hoods that nowadays would scarcely rate a mention on the eleven o'clock news.

George "Machine Gun" Kelly had never raised a machine gun in anger in his life—or any other type of gun, for that matter—but one pass through the FBI propaganda mill transformed this henpecked bungler into a murderous criminal genius whose existence threatened the very fabric of American life. Dozens of other mediocrities achieved similar notoriety.

But nobody got more famous than Hoover. His absurd speeches—tommy-gun fast, stuffed with unverifiable "facts," and ALWAYS IN UPPERCASE!—bulldozed critics and doubters aside. By 1935, he was impregnable. Even Franklin Roosevelt, who early on realized that he had sanctioned the creation of a monster, preferred to look the other way. There just weren't any votes in knocking America's favorite lawman.

World War II only burnished the director's luster. Even before Pearl Harbor, the FBI was monitoring German spies and compiling a list of foreign nationals and citizens for possible detention. At the outbreak of hostilities all suspected dangerous aliens were quickly rounded up. The well-publicized apprehension and subsequent execution of several Nazi agents also demonstrated that Hoover was on the ball, although in reality the arrests owed more to acts of betrayal than any great FBI detection skills.

Peacetime brought a serious problem: how to maintain FBI funding levels. Hoover needed a new bogeyman; after the horrors of Auschwitz and Belsen, his favored prewar fund-raisers—bank robbers and inept kidnappers—held all the menace of recalcitrant Girl Scouts. And tackling organized crime wasn't an option, since, according to J. Edgar Hoover, the Mafia did not exist. Which left just one promising area to explore.

Both during the war and shortly thereafter, FBI agents had uncovered evidence of Communist subversion within the United States. Hoover shrieked that if the FBI and the American people relaxed their guard, the Reds would take over, as they had in Eastern Europe. It is easy now, with the benefit of hindsight, to dismiss his fears as tendentious garbage; in the context of the times, with the Cold War getting icier by the hour, he had a point.

Until the day he died, Hoover never quit railing against the threat of communism; and under his watch the FBI did pull off some notable counterespionage coups. His big flaw was that he saw Reds everywhere: in the government, in the armed forces, in the movies, and especially in the newly emerging civil rights movement. And it was here that he collided headlong with the man whom he would grow to hate more than anyone alive, someone just as skilled in media manipulation as himself, an idol to millions and a bone-fide twentieth-century icon.

The Struggle Begins

The Reverend Martin Luther King Jr. first flashed onto the national scene during the 1955 Montgomery bus boycott, begun in the aftermath of Rosa Parks's refusal to give up her bus seat to a white man. As the highly articulate president of the Montgomery Improvement Association, the twenty-six-year-old Baptist minister became a lightning rod for redneck bigotry and white supremacists. They bombed his house and whooped with joy when he was convicted of trying to interfere with bus company operations, but they couldn't stifle his message. No violence, no surrender, preached King, and his followers took him at his word. For a year blacks in Montgomery held firm; no one rode the bus: people walked, car-pooled, or else hitched rides, until eventually the Supreme Court declared Alabama's segregation laws unconstitutional.

It was a stunning victory.

Buoyed up by this success, King and other black ministers formed the SCLC in Atlanta on January 11, 1957, with King as president. The stated objective was to fight for black voting rights across the rural South and to do away with segregation; modest goals, ostensibly, but enough to set FBI alarm bells ringing at the bureau's Atlanta office, which began investigating the SCLC for possible Communist connections.

All campaigns need a mouthpiece, and King's intoxicating blend of high-octane oratory and passive nonviolence was a headline grabber, even north of the Mason-Dixon line. On February 18, King got his first *Time* cover. The following May he pushed his way into the major leagues when he addressed 35,000 demonstrators at a rally in Washington, DC, roaring over and over again, "Give us the ballot!"[4]

Ever since the birth of mankind, established authority has feared the great public speaker, and King was unbeatable. With his glorious, soaring voice and powerful imagery, he could transport the fervor of a Baptist church service to any venue and any size audience, a rare gift that soon earmarked him as the most potent symbol of the struggle for black civil rights.

For a privileged conservative like Hoover, raised in an era and a household where blacks were servants and expected always to remain so, King's rise amounted to a direct assault on the American way of life, one that needed neutralizing, by any means possible.

Immediately after King's inaugural Washington speech, Hoover opened a file under "racial matters." By September 1958, King merited a file all to himself, after he was spotted being approached on the steps of a Harlem church, in which he'd delivered a guest sermon, by black Communist party member Benjamin J. Davis.

Insidiously, the FBI rumor mill began to grind.

In January 1959, Hoover raised the ante, ordering FBI agents to burglarize the SCLC's offices, just the first of twenty known break-ins between that date and January 1964. Gathering information on King became priority one, and it was later admitted by FBI Assistant Director William Sullivan that King's telephone had been tapped "since the late 1950s."[5] Simultaneously, bureau agents began infiltrating organizational meetings and conferences.

Evidence of King's increasing stature came during the 1960 presidential contest. He was in jail at the time, serving four months hard labor in his hometown of Atlanta for parading without a permit, when, at the urging of campaign strategists, Democratic hopeful John F. Kennedy telephoned King's wife, Coretta, to sympathize with her and to affirm the goals of her husband's movement. Some analysts have claimed that this well-publicized call clinched Kennedy's razor-thin victory.

Whatever its effect on the ballot, the phone call had one undeniable outcome: after Kennedy's election and the appointment of his brother Robert as attorney general, true or not the impression gained strength in Washington that King had the inside track at the White House and the Justice Department.

Hoover smelled danger. The troublemaker he loathed most was apparently in tight with his bosses.

In May 1961, an FBI report again circulated scurrilous suggestions regarding King's supposed links to the American Communist party (CPUSA). In 1948, it said, while still a student, King had been affiliated with the Progressive party. Furthermore, his fellow SCLC executive, Wyatt Tee Walker, had once subscribed to *The Worker,* a Communist newspaper. The report also revealed that King had not been investigated yet.

In the margin Hoover scrawled "Why not?"[6]—two words that triggered the start of a vitriolic feud that rolled and pitched for seven tempestuous years.

King was no Caspar Milquetoast. Nowadays it is often forgotten just how tough this Baptist minister could be. Look beyond the dewy-eyed remembrances and we find a hardened political infighter who could kick butt with the very best. On January 8, 1962, the SCLC bravely released a special report attacking Hoover's FBI.

Hoover took up the challenge. That same day a report of his own winged its way to Attorney General Robert Kennedy. It amounted to smear by association. Having failed to uncover a shred of proof to corroborate earlier suspicions that King had Marxist leanings, Hoover had targeted the preacher's associates, in particular Stanley Levison, a rich, white socialist and longtime civil rights activist. The report contended that Levison, "a secret member of the Communist Party, USA," enjoyed a "close relationship" with King.[7]

After studying the report, Robert Kennedy gave Hoover the nod. On the night of March 15, 1962, FBI agents secretly broke into Levison's New York office and planted a bug; five days later they did it again, this time installing a wiretap in his office phone. Among other tidbits harvested by this electronic surveillance (ELSUR) was news that Jack O'Dell, who also had alleged ties to the Communist party, had been recommended by both King and Levison to serve as an assistant to Wyatt Tee Walker.

This was all Hoover needed. Martin Luther King's name went right into Section A of the FBI Reserve Index, just one step below those individuals registered in the Security Index and scheduled to be rounded up and "preventively detained"[8] in the event of a declared national emergency. Robert Kennedy also authorized round-the-clock ELSUR of all SCLC offices, as well as King's home.

As rumors of the covert FBI operation filtered back to the civil rights campaign, King realized he was up against an enemy prepared to stop at nothing. His colleague and later mayor of Atlanta, Andrew Young, remembered the sense of betrayal. "In the late fifties, early sixties, we thought of the FBI as our friends . . . the only hope we had."[9]

Now the actual extent of that "friendship" had been cruelly revealed.

King vented his outrage in an interview that appeared in the *New York Times* on November 18, 1962, fulminating about a desegregation march in Albany, Georgia, in which hundreds of demonstrators, black and white, had been jailed. "Every time I saw FBI men in Albany, they were with the local police force . . . one of the great problems we face with the FBI in the South is that the agents are white Southerners who have been influenced by the mores of the community . . . to maintain their status, they have to be friendly with the local police and people who are promoting segregation."

Hoover read the article and turned puce. King's previous accusations of discriminatory FBI hiring policies toward blacks and other minorities had left a bad taste in Hoover's mouth—no matter how justified—and now he was hinting at collusion and dereliction of duty!

Such blatant criticism of his beloved FBI was unheard of, and it spurred Hoover into action. Over many weeks, while he softened up President Kennedy, repeatedly whispering in his ear that King was consorting with active Communists, a concerted crusade was mounted to destabilize the highly strung activist. On one occasion, waiting proudly to step into a secret luncheon with JFK at the White House, King was taken to one side by some Justice Department officials and warned about Levison's Communist sympathies. It was a psychological master stroke. King's euphoria vanished as if punctured like a balloon. In an instant the high honor he was about to receive felt tainted and cheapened.

Hoover's relentless brainwashing finally did the trick. JFK capitulated, convinced at last that King posed a risk. He was an uneasy convert, though. At a subsequent meeting with King, he led him out to the Rose Garden and murmured, "I assume you know you're under close surveillance." Then, steering the conversation toward Levison and O'Dell, he patted King on the shoulder and said, "They're Communists." After reeling off the same alarmist claptrap that Hoover had drip-fed him, he added an ominous rider: "If they shoot you down, they'll shoot us down, too."[10]

King left the White House, anxious and angry. Hoover's clammy tentacles appeared to reach into every corner of power, even the Oval Office. King revealed his suspicions to a friend. "The President is afraid of Hoover himself, because he wouldn't even talk to me in his own office. I guess Hoover must be bugging him, too."[11]

Despite thousands of man-hours, the FBI failed utterly to establish any connection between Martin Luther King and the

CPUSA. But all that ferreting did uncover one rich vein of investigative ore.

Caught Between the Sheets

Martin Luther King liked women. And they adored him. As a powerful, charismatic leader, he found no shortage of willing partners ready to ease the stress of those long road trips. "I'm away from home twenty-five to twenty-seven days a month," he said once. "Fucking's a form of anxiety reduction."[12] Besides a trio of regular mistresses, he occasionally used prostitutes, as did many of his retinue. FBI wiretaps picked up all the lurid details.

Hoover's lizard eyes glinted.

Forget crime, forget the Commies, Hoover's extraordinary grip on power could be explained in one word: sex! It did for them all! The boss of the FBI knew exactly who was doing what to whom, and how often. Bedroom antics were his obsession. He had the dirt on everyone: presidents, politicians of every hue, the judiciary, movie stars, sports figures, rock 'n' roll icons, business tycoons, luminaries of the arts world, any public figure. Every indiscretion, every sexual preference, every scrap of gossip, all found their way into the secret files that Hoover kept under lock and key in his office. Whether these files were as explosive or as revealing as rumor claimed is academic: all that mattered is that people feared they were.

Hoover's files were a Washington legend. So what if his own private life was considered scandalous by the standards of the times—for decades, he and Associate FBI Director Clyde Tolson were far more than just close friends—none of that mattered. Hoover made the rules. He could ruin careers with a word or a call. He could also salvage them as well by suppressing unwanted publicity, always making sure, of course, that the quaking beneficiary realized his indebtedness to the FBI. Even the Kennedys, John and Robert, were terrified of what the old man knew. It was awesome power.

By the same token, presidents shamelessly used Hoover's files in their search for dirt on their political rivals, critics, or other government officials. (Lyndon Johnson was especially fond of browsing them at bedtime.) Every request was eagerly met, with each one adding to the director's aura of omniscience.

Now Hoover, the self-appointed guardian of public morals, was preparing to turn all his vast blackmailing heat on the man he dubbed an "alley cat."[13]

In 1963, King turned in a backbreaking workload, traveling 275,000 miles and making more than 350 speeches. April found him in Birmingham, Alabama, where the commissioner for public safety, a lumpen demagogue named Eugene "Bull" Connor, boasted that "blood would run in the streets"[14] of the city before it allowed desegregation. So, when King and his followers came to march, Connor sicced his baton-swinging goons on them. They cracked heads and mowed down demonstrators with water cannons, dumbly unaware that every atrocity was being captured by TV cameras that gave the rest of the world its first glimpse of Dixie-style apartheid. Each night the civil rights movement got hundreds of thousands of dollars worth of free TV advertising, courtesy of Bull Connor.

Like hundreds of other demonstrators, King was thrown into jail, but this was a defining moment in the civil rights battle as Connor's swaggering braggadocio boomeranged in the worst way possible. Martin Luther King entered his cell a troublesome preacher; he emerged, eight days later, a world figure.

He parlayed that international fame into a seminal moment in history. On August 28, 1963, an estimated quarter of a million Americans assembled at the Lincoln Memorial, in Washington, DC, to hear King deliver arguably the greatest speech of the twentieth century.

"I have a dream . . . I have a dream" thundered out across America and into the national psyche. Just up the road at the White House, President Kennedy, watching the historic event on TV, nodded his approval. "He's damn good."[15]

Hoover's FBI sidekick, William Sullivan, also caught King's *tour de force* and immediately noted in a memo, "We must mark him now, if we have not done so before, as the most dangerous

Negro of the future in this nation from the standpoint of Communism, the Negro and national security . . . it may be unrealistic to limit [our actions against King] to legalistic proofs that would stand up in court or before Congressional Committees."[16]

Tragically, within hours of his greatest triumph, King nearly threw it all away. That night, still pumped full of adrenaline, he retired to the Willard Hotel in Washington, where FBI wiretaps caught him and several friends engaging in a sexual free-for-all.

"This will destroy the burrhead,"[17] gloated Hoover next day as he salivated over the tape. Soon, recordings of the assignation were doing the rounds of Washington newspaper offices, but in that more tactful age, nobody would touch them. For a while, a disappointed Hoover even toyed with the idea of taking the tapes directly to RFK, but his courage failed him.

Meanwhile, the Martin Luther King bandwagon gained steam.

When, in late 1963, *Time* magazine named King its "Man of the Year," Hoover's famously short fuse just blew. "They had to dig deep in the garbage, to come up with this one,"[18] he scrawled angrily across the wire copy of the announcement. However, cooler heads at the FBI scoured the entire *Time* article, and, lurking in the biographical background, they found an interesting item: twice in his early teens, King had attempted suicide. Maybe here was an opportunity. . . ?

Before long, FBI analysts had unearthed an even bigger nugget of blackmailing gold. On February 22, 1964, King and some colleagues checked into the Hyatt House Motel in Los Angeles and started kicking back in private. As the locker room humor got rougher, King took center stage. Recalling TV coverage of JFK's funeral, during which his widow bent and kissed the middle of the casket, King guffawed, "That's what she's going to miss the most."[19]

Every word was captured on tape.

Hoover's joy was boundless. At last he had him! Previously, worried that Robert Kennedy would alert King, Hoover had withheld full details of the surveillance from the attorney general. Now the gloves were off. Hoover made sure that a full transcript of King's "vilification of the late President and his wife"[20] landed on his brother's desk.

Robert Kennedy was appalled. Whether for personal or political reasons he began to back away from King. His eyes had been opened to the danger—and how to combat it. Hoover let him simmer awhile, allowing the famed Kennedy revenge instinct to take hold before asking permission to instigate more taps. He got it, of course.

After such a promising start, 1964 spiraled downhill fast for Hoover. In spring came news that Marquette University, in Milwaukee, intended giving King an honorary degree. This was especially shocking news: back in 1950 the university had given Hoover the selfsame honor. In a fit of pique, Hoover dispatched an agent posthaste to persuade Marquette to change its mind, which obligingly it did. The agent who pulled off this coup received a personal commendation from the delighted director and a few extra bucks in his paycheck.

Hoover left no stone unturned. Alarmed by news that the National Council of Churches (NCC) was pouring cash into King's campaign, he saw to it that they were briefed about King's personal conduct. As a result, the NCC immediately withdrew all funding.

A rare beacon of light in an otherwise gloomy year for the director came on May 8, 1964, when it was announced that, despite reaching the mandatory retirement age of seventy, Hoover would be allowed to continue as FBI director, courtesy of a special executive order signed by longtime crony President Lyndon Johnson.

Superficially, Hoover was untouchable, but events continued to spin out of his control. In September, when King was scheduled to visit the Vatican, Hoover's friend the archconservative Cardinal Spellman was leaned on by the FBI to persuade Pope Paul VI not to grant King an audience. To Hoover's dismay and considerable disgust, the pope chose to ignore the advice.

King Wins Nobel Peace Prize

Then, in October, came the worst news yet, a real stunner. From Sweden it was announced that Martin Luther King had been awarded the 1964 Nobel Peace Prize. Hoover reeled as if he'd been punched in the gut. For years he had craved this award, shamelessly lobbying many influential Americans to write the committee, and every time he had been cold-shouldered. Now his *Private Enemy Number One* was getting the world's most coveted honor!

Hoover's bitchiness got the better of him.

On November 18, 1964, the director unexpectedly summoned eighteen female members of the National Press Club over to his office for coffee and a rare interview. During the three-hour meeting he rambled and fumed, eventually turning the subject to King. With his aides looking on in horror, Hoover, recalling King's earlier criticisms in Albany, Georgia, barked in typically bombastic style, "I asked [for an appointment] with Dr. King, but he would not make the appointment, so I have characterized him as the most notorious liar in the country. That is on the record!"[21]

Cartha "Deke" DeLoach, FBI liaison officer with the White House, blanched and passed Hoover no less than three notes pleading for him to take the remark off the record, but the old man was adamant. Later, this time off the record, he went even further. "[King] is one of the lowest characters in the country."[22]

The next day Hoover's tirade lit up the nation's front pages. King, fast learning the art of statesmanship, reacted coolly, delivering a piquantly double-edged response. "I cannot conceive of Mr. Hoover making a statement like this without being under extreme pressure. He has apparently faltered under the awesome burden, complexities, and responsibilities of his office."[23] In a public telegram to the director, he said he would be happy to meet with him and had "sought in vain" for any record of his request for an appointment.

As FBI eavesdroppers discovered, privately King was far more trenchant. Hoover was, he ranted, ". . . old and broken down . . . senile," someone who "should be hit from all sides"[24] until President Johnson brought him to heel.

Hoover's opinion of King was already well known: "King is a tom cat . . . with obsessive, degenerate sexual urges."[25] And now the time had come to neuter this troublesome feline, once and for all.

One week later FBI officials began shopping the X-rated tape around the nation's top newspapers. Again there were no takers. That same month an FBI agent was dispatched to Florida, where he mailed the infamous package to Atlanta. Although it was addressed to King, the FBI knew perfectly well that he was on the road, and that in his absence Coretta King would open her husband's mail for him. The intent was clear: if they couldn't destroy the man, they damn sure would destroy his marriage.

Somehow the package languished, unregarded and unopened, in the Atlanta office all through December. During this hiatus, news reached Lyndon Johnson that DeLoach was hawking the tape all over Washington. In a fury, Johnson contacted Hoover and ordered him to meet with King and patch things up. Hoover had no choice but to obey, and on December 1 a summit meeting was held in his office.

Although accounts of what happened during the meeting differ widely, most agree that Hoover and King were polite to each other and that the director used the occasion to deliver a fifty-minute monologue praising the FBI's accomplishments. According to Ralph Abernathy, "Mr. Hoover gave Martin a lecture, reminding him he was a man of the cloth. . . . He said, 'You boys, if you're doing nothing wrong, you don't have to worry about anything. But if you're doing something wrong, we know about it.'"[26]

Veiled, maybe, but the threat was unmistakable and dagger sharp. Hoover had come within an inch of revealing just how much dirt he had on King, and the impact was painfully apparent. Abernathy saw his friend quake. "Martin responded by becoming nervous and eating his nails. He was troubled."[27]

"Quite amicable"[28] was all a grim-faced King would say to curious reporters when he emerged from the showdown.

By comparison, Hoover's postmeeting demeanor could not have been more triumphant. He believed he "had captivated King, really charmed him." An FBI wiretap told otherwise. "The old man talks too much" was King's private verdict. According to Sullivan, "There was no hope for [King] after that."[29]

Covert Subversion Campaign

Immediately the FBI began plotting how to usurp King and replace him as a black leader with someone more malleable. Their favored option was Samuel Pierce, a conservative Manhattan lawyer who would later serve in the Reagan administration. William Sullivan decided that the FBI should help Pierce "to be in the position to assume the role of the leadership of the Negro people when King has been completely discredited."[30]

The war of attrition took its toll. By the time King flew off to Sweden, a heavy cloud of depression had settled over him, inspired by a dread of Hoover going public with the tapes. When King was awarded the Nobel Peace Prize on December 10, his acceptance speech, weary and uninspired, revealed a mind in torment. "Those who pioneer in the struggle for peace and freedom will still be battered by the storms of persecution, leading them to nagging feelings that they can no longer bear such a heavy burden."[31]

Hoover, asked later about the Nobel Peace Prize, snorted his disdain. "[King] was the last one in the world who should have received it. . . . I held him in complete contempt because of the things he said and because of his conduct."[32]

The following month Coretta Scott King found a package in her mailbox.

It took this incident to make King realize just how virulent, just how wide-ranging was the FBI campaign to discredit him. Less than twenty-four hours after hearing the tapes, his reaction was caught on a wiretap. "They are out to break me."[33] He was right. Hoover called in every marker and enlisted every ally he could find. Suddenly, the IRS started jumping all over King's tax returns. At the same time, those lucrative speaking engagements began to dry up as the hosts wilted under FBI pressure and withdrew invitations. Everywhere he looked, King sensed some arm of government reaching out to club him down.

But there were others, too, far closer to home, who wanted to see the back of Martin Luther King.

By the mid-1960s King's role as undisputed leader of the civil rights movement had come under threat. Younger, more militant campaigners such as Stokely Carmichael and H. Rap Brown were picking up support from coast to coast as they expounded a vision of "Black Power" in direct contradiction to King's brand of nonviolence.

Not that it mattered to J. Edgar Hoover. When it came to civil rights, he was color-blind; all black activists were agents of subversion. Years earlier, over lunch with then Senator Lyndon Johnson, Hoover had lumped King in the same category as the openly combative Malcolm X. "We wouldn't have any problem," he rasped, "if we could get those two guys fighting, if we could get them to kill one another off. . . ."[34]

Under siege from all sides, King refused to abandon the principle of nonviolence. In early February 1965, he was imprisoned at a voter-registration march, this time in Selma, Alabama; then, three weeks later, on February 21, Malcolm X was shot dead at a rally in Harlem.

This assassination marked a turning point in the civil rights battle. Frustrations that had been repressed for decades suddenly boiled over. The dignified, peaceful demonstration—so long the bulwark of King's crusade—got rudely shoved backstage by some ugly riots. The Los Angeles suburb of Watts exploded in August, and again the following year. By 1967 many of America's largest inner cities toppled on the brink of anarchy. President Johnson publicly announced, in the wake of violent uprisings in Detroit and Newark, that he had issued standing instructions that the FBI should bring the agitators to heel, by any means at its disposal.

Hoover needed no second bidding.

Secret COINTELPRO Begins

On August 25, 1967, a secret memorandum was issued to all FBI offices. It came from the office of J. Edgar Hoover and was headed:

COUNTERINTELLIGENCE PROGRAM BLACK NATIONALIST—HATE GROUPS
INTERNAL SECURITY

. . . The purpose of this new counterintelligence endeavor is to
expose, disrupt, misdirect, discredit, or otherwise neutralize the
activities of black nationalist hate-type organizations and group-
ings, their leadership, spokesmen, membership, and supporters,
and to counter their propensity for violence and civil disorder. . . .
No opportunity should be missed to exploit through counterintelligence techniques the organizational and personal conflicts of the
leaderships of the groups and where possible an effort should be
made to capitalize upon existing conflicts between competing
black nationalist organizations. . . . You are also cautioned that
the nature of this new endeavor is such that *under no circumstances should the existence of the program be made known outside the bureau.* [Emphasis added.][35]

These secret FBI Counterintelligence Programs, or COINTEL-
PROS, were nothing new. The first one had been created in 1956
to investigate the CPUSA, and had already been invoked to jus-
tify the persecution of King and the SCLC. But now the "Black
Nationalist Hate Groups" had a COINTELPRO all to themselves.*

FBI field offices were urged to work closely with local police
and prosecutors. First, however, before any scheme could be
initiated, it had to be cleared with the top FBI brass in Washington, who demanded assurances of anonymity for the bureau.
Records show that upward of two thousand individual actions
were officially approved.

The tactics were sledgehammer tough: agents and informers
were expected not just to spy on political activists, but to discredit and distort their lives. Anyone whose political bias was
deemed even slightly left of center could expect harassment. This
was achieved through a variety of means: break-ins, vandalism,
grand jury subpoenas, false arrests, frame-ups, and physical vio-

*Ultimately the FBI disclosed the existence of six different COINTELPROS.
Besides those mentioned here, these were: "Groups Seeking Independence
for Puerto Rico" (1960–1971); Socialist Workers party (1961–1971); "White
Hate Groups" (1964–1971); and "New Left" (1968–1971). The latter operations hit antiwar, student, and feminist groups.

lence were threatened, instigated, or directly employed. All at once, political activists found themselves facing eviction or job loss. It was state-sponsored terrorism, nothing less.

At times, the cruelty was bone chilling. When Jean Seberg, a white actress prominent in the civil rights movement, became pregnant, the FBI planted scurrilous stories in the press that the father was a Black Panther. The psychological fallout from this wholly untrue propaganda resulted in the child being stillborn and ultimately drove Seberg to suicide.

Nothing was off-limits. One COINTELPRO communiqué urged that "the Negro youths and moderates must be made to understand that if they succumb to revolutionary teaching, they will be dead revolutionaries." Elsewhere the FBI routinely put out phony leaflets, posters, pamphlets, newspapers, and other publications in the name of movement groups, mailed out anonymous letters, and made anonymous telephone calls.

Documents show that the FBI had "between 5,000 and 10,000 active cases on matters of race at any given time nationwide. In 1967 some 1,246 FBI agents received . . . racial intelligence assignments each month. By [1968] the number had jumped to 1,678."[36]

Hoover was playing Big Brother, and he was playing for keeps.

And yet, oddly enough, the figurehead who more than anyone else had prompted Hoover's imposition of the Black Nationalist COINTELPRO remained largely unaffected by it.

By late 1967, after a long, hot summer of trouble on the streets of America's major cities, King was struggling to maintain his influence, especially with liberal Americans, many of whom appeared to hold him personally responsible for the riots and the burning ghettoes.The criticism just spurred him to greater efforts. In the spring of 1968, he journeyed to Memphis to lend his support to a garbage workers' strike. On April 3, he addressed a meeting. He wasn't scheduled to speak long, his throat was sore, and he used a speech that he'd given before. Tonight, though, it seemed to contain a rare thunder, enough to rival the storm that lashed the streets outside. "He's allowed me to go up to the mountaintop and I've looked over. I've *seen* the promised land. I may not get there with you. But I want you to know tonight, that we as a people *will* get to the promised land. . . . I'm not fearing any man. Mine eyes have *seen* the glory of the coming of the Lord!"

The next evening, while standing on the balcony of his Memphis hotel room, Martin Luther King was cut down by an assassin's bullet. He was just thirty-nine years old.

"THEY FINALLY GOT THE SONOFABITCH!"[37] The shout echoed through the FBI's Atlanta field office when news first came over the radio that King had been shot. Confirmation a few minutes later that the minister was dead was enough to get one agent literally jumping up and down with joy.

The assassination sparked a firestorm of protest across the country. Two days after the murder, as rioters tore up the capital's neighborhoods, the director of the FBI was nowhere to be found. It was Saturday. Hoover had gone to the track.

Anyone expecting that King's assassination would draw a line through this feud grievously underestimated J. Edgar Hoover. Even death provided no sanctuary from the director's wrath. Hot on the heels of King's murder, FBI agents peppered newspaper columnist Jack Anderson with rumors that King had been fooling around with a dentist's wife in Los Angeles, only to get himself shot by a vengeful husband. It was one hell of a story, if true. But as Anderson soon discovered, the dentist had neither the desire nor the opportunity to murder King and the FBI knew this. It had been just another shoddy FBI stunt to discredit King's image.

One year later, the FBI was still hard at furnishing defamatory material to conservative lapdogs, fighting to block efforts to honor the slain leader. Hoover lobbied like crazy to prevent King's birthday from being declared a national holiday and sanctioned a scheme to persuade members of Congress that King had been a "scoundrel." Such briefings, he stressed, should be conducted "very cautiously."[38] It worked. No politician was prepared to run the risk of antagonizing the director.*

But all that was about to change.

*Martin Luther King Jr.'s birthday was eventually declared a national holiday in 1983.

Plot Revealed

On the night of March 8, 1971, a group of political activists raided the offices of the FBI resident agency in Media, Pennsylvania. Among the hundreds of documents taken was a single page headed COINTELPRO.

Three weeks later, Majority Leader Hale Boggs stood up in the House of Representatives to say the unthinkable: "The time has come for the Attorney General of the United States to ask for the resignation of Mr. Hoover."[39]

A collective intake of air seemed to suck all the oxygen from the room. Every eye swiveled in Boggs's direction. Drunk again? His problems with the bottle were notorious, but no, he seemed sober enough. In stunned silence the assembly listened as Boggs reeled off a list of Hoover's "Gestapo" tactics—the phone tappings, the bugs, the surveillance, the harassment, the bullying. It was a damning litany. In the past, critics who'd claimed that the FBI carried out covert operations on its own citizens had been branded Commie cranks, agitators; now it was transparently clear that many of the accusations had been justified all along. J. Edgar Hoover, the boyhood idol of millions, had used his secret police just like Soviet dictators had used the KGB.

Hoover had been caught red-handed. Public outrage and the Freedom of Information Act did the rest. Overnight, all of COINTELPRO operations were shut down.

For the last shaky year of his reign, Hoover hunkered down as the fire came in from all sides, much of it from former close allies within the FBI itself. But while President Nixon—who'd also featured prominently in those infamous secret files—wrestled with the sticky dilemma of how best to ease the fractious director quietly out the door, Hoover solved the problem for him. On May 2, 1972, he died.

A grateful nation accorded Hoover the rare privilege for a private citizen of a state funeral. Nixon read the eulogy. "For nearly one fourth of the whole history of this Republic," he intoned, "Edgar Hoover has exerted a force for good in our national life. . . ."[40]

Nobody batted an eyelid.

For all his faults, Hoover left a remarkable legacy. When he took over as director of the Bureau of Investigation in 1924,* he inherited an outfit riddled with scandal and corruption, a public disgrace. Outgoing boss William Burns had been notorious for cronyism, as well as a general disregard for irrelevancies such as qualifications. Hoover changed all that. In just a matter of months he cleaned house ruthlessly, firing incompetent and undereducated agents, instituting rigorous background checks on all job applicants, creating a climate of investigative integrity that remains the envy of every other police force on earth. Sadly, the director failed to live up to the kind of standards he demanded from his employees.

He served under eight presidents. Most were terrified of him; only Harry Truman ignored him. Theoretically, any attorney general could have fired him, but none dared. And yet, for all his vast power, his thousands of field agents, he was curiously ineffectual. Of the more than 500,000 investigations carried out by the FBI on so-called subversives, not one resulted in a court conviction.

And when it came to Martin Luther King and communism, Hoover really was off base. Recently disclosed KGB archives have shown that far from being a pawn of the Kremlin, King was a source of constant irritation to the gray men in Moscow who, like their FBI counterparts, were cock-a-hoop when the Reverend was shot. They didn't want an advocate of peace and tolerance in the United States, they wanted racial strife, lots of it. And after failing miserably in their attempts to get the CPUSA to influence King, the KGB set out to nullify him by planting disinformation in black newspapers claiming that King was an "Uncle Tom."

This meant that for several years the FBI and the KGB were united in a common goal—destroy Martin Luther King. Ironies don't come any more exquisite.

In the final analysis, King proved too big for all of them. Although no saint, he was heroic. The risks he took on behalf of others, awesome and ultimately catastrophic, have guaranteed

*"Federal" was not added to the name until 1935; only then did it become the FBI.

his place on history's A-list, and in terms of personal bravery, he outfought Hoover at every turn. On the eve of yet another dangerous march, King once told fellow demonstrators: "I would rather die on the highways of Alabama than make a butchery of my conscience."[41]

Nobody knows when, where, or if J. Edgar Hoover butchered his conscience. That was not the kind of question the director cared to answer.

NOTES

Chapter 1: Elizabeth I v. Mary

1. Wright, p. 245
2. Weir, p. 14
3. Laing, II, p. 275
4. Klarwill, p. 193
5. Pollen, *Letter*, p. 41
6. *Melville*, p. 94
7. Pollen, *Letter*, pp. 38–43
8. Ibid., p. 43
9. Weir, p. 129
10. Klarwill, p. 215
11. *Cal. Scot.*, p. 666
12. Weir, p. 133
13. *Melville*, p. 89–99
14. Ibid.
15. Ibid.
16. Tytler, VII, p. 115
17. Anderson, pp. 54–55
18. Harrison, p. 53
19. Weir, p. 199
20. Ibid., p. 201
21. *Cal. Scot.*, p. 97
22. Plowden, p. 162
23. Murdin, p. 559
24. Weir, p. 277
25. Hartley, I, p. 418
26. Weir, p. 295
27. *Cal. Spain*, II, p. 581
28. Weir, p. 345
29. Somerset, p. 405
30. Ibid.
31. Weir, p. 361
32. Pollen, *Babington Plot*, pp. 21–22

33. Morris, p. 286
34. Harrison, p. 181
35. Neale, p. 149

Chapter 2: Parliament v. Charles I

1. Gardiner, p. 58
2. Gregg, *Cromwell,* p. 27
3. Notestein & Relf, p. 104
4. Gregg, *Charles,* p. 186
5. Ashworth, p. 5
6. Gregg, *Cromwell,* p. 17
7. Carlton, p. 235
8. Ibid.
9. Ibid.
10. Wedgwood, p. 335
11. Bruce, p. 93
12. Ibid.
13. Roots, p. 98
14. Carlyle, I, p. 173
15. *Mercurius Civicus,* April 30, 1646
16. Warwick, p. 331
17. Carlyle, I, p. 295
18. *Mercurius Elenctius,* December 6, 1648
19. Ibid.
20. Walker, p. 49
21. Blencoe, p. 237
22. Carlton, p. 350
23. Gregg, *Charles,* p. 439
24. Ibid.
25. Gregg, *Cromwell,* p. 156
26. Ibid.
27. Rushworth, p. 1429
28. Spence, p. 286
29. Hill, p. 155

Chapter 3: Burr v. Hamilton

1. Hendrickson, p. 418
2. Ibid., p. 9
3. Wilson, *Princeton Review,* 1896
4. Jenkinson, p. 22

5. Ibid., p. 33
6. Davis, II, p. 20
7. Burr, letter to Peter Van Gaasbeek, April 9, 1796
8. Lomask, p. 205
9. Hamilton, letter to Gouverneur Morris, December 24, 1800
10. Mitchell, p. 354
11. Jenkinson, p. 81
12. Mitchell, p. 244
13. Syrett, XXI, p. 312n
14. Mitchell, p. 367
15. Ibid., p. 345
16. Ibid., p. 368
17. Lomask, p. 347
18. Account of duel taken from Syrett, Vol. 26
19. Ibid., p. 355

Chapter 4: Hatfields v. McCoys

1. Simmons, p. 1
2. Carrington Jones, p. 272
3. McCoy, p. 169
4. Carrington Jones, p. 59
5. Letter printed in *Wheeling Intelligencer,* April 24, 1888
6. Rice, p. 60
7. Ibid., p. 63
8. *Pittsburgh Times,* February 1, 1888
9. Waller, p. 232
10. *Cincinnati Enquirer,* February 20, 1890
11. Spears, *Mumsey's Magazine 24* (June 1901), pp. 494–509

Chapter 5: Stalin v. Trotsky

1. Volgonov, p. 3
2. Ibid., p. 119
3. Medvedev, p. 56
4. Ward, p. 20
5. Lewis & Whitehead, p. 52
6. Ibid., p. 54
7. De Jonge, p. 172
8. Medvedev, p. 115
9. Ibid., p. 99
10. Trotsky, *My Life,* p. 516

11. Ibid.
12. Medvedev, p. 128
13. Ibid,. p. 132
14. Voroshilov, p. 103
15. Medvedev, p. 129
16. Trotsky, *Stalin,* pp. 413–414
17. Medvedev, p. 145
18. Ibid., p. 122
19. Ibid., p. 124
20. Ibid.
21. Lewis & Whitehead, p. 56
22. Ibid., p. 57
23. *Pravda,* November 2, 1927
24. Medvedev, p. 176
25. Dugrand, p. 127
26. Ibid., p. 40
27. Trotsky, *Writings,* pp. 331–332
28. Dugrand, p. 49
29. Ibid., p. 51
30. Ibid., p. 128

Chapter 6: Amundsen v. Scott

1. Preston, p. 127
2. Memo from papers of British Antarctic Expedition 1910–1913
3. Preston, p. 115
4. *Daily Mail,* February 12, 1910
5. Amundsen, I, p. 138
6. Ibid., p. 158
7. Letter dated October 5, 1909
8. Scott, Vol. 1, p. 467
9. Huntford, p. 299
10. Ibid.
11. Ibid., p. 322
12. Undated letter to Scott Keltie
13. Letter to Kathleen Scott, February 27, 1911
14. Memo from papers of British Antarctic Expedition 1910–1913
15. Cherry-Garrard diary, February 24, 1911
16. Oates letter to his mother, November 23, 1910
17. Amundsen diary, July 1911
18. Hassel diary, August 13, 1911
19. Oates letter to his mother, January, 24, 1911

20. Preston, p. 166
21. Ibid., p. 168
22. Bjaaland diary, December 14, 1911
23. Huntford, p. 495
24. Amundsen, Vol. 2, p. 135
25. Scott diary, January 16, 1917
26. Letter dated December 17, 1912
27. Preston, p. 185
28. Ibid., p. 5
29. Ibid., p. 200
30. Kathleen Scott diary, March 12, 1912
31. Thomas, p. 233
32. Scott diary, March 17, 1912

Chapter 7: Duchess of Windsor v. Queen Mother

1. Thornton, p. 60
2. Duchess of Windsor, p. 225
3. Thornton, p. 75
4. Ibid., p. 75
5. Channon, p. 35
6. Middlemass & Barnes, p. 976
7. Duchess of Windsor, p. 225
8. Thornton, p. 113
9. Lesley, p. 187
10. Middlemass & Barnes, p. 995
11. Bryan III & Murphy, p. 220
12. Duchess of Windsor, p. 273
13. *Daily Telegraph,* July 6, 1999
14. Ibid.
15. Ibid.
16. Letter from Duke to Wallis, March 1937
17. Thornton, p. 144
18. Soames, p. 274
19. *Burke's Peerage 1967*, pp. xxi–xxii
20. *Daily Telegraph,* July 6, 1999
21. Thornton, p. 259
22. *Daily Telegraph,* July 6, 1999
23. Bruce Lockhart, p. 413
24. Bloch, pp. 52–53
25. Lesley, p. 183
26. Queen Mother, letter to Sir Walter Monckton, July 1940

27. Thornton, p. 217
28. Rogers St. John, p. 527
29. Letter to Mrs. Bessie Merryman, March 31, 1941
30. Bloch, p. 334
31. Donaldson, p. 337
32. *Daily Mail,* November 24, 1982
33. Private conversation with author
34. Thornton, p. 280
35. Ibid., p. 259
36. Ibid., p. 276
37. Ibid., p. 330
38. Ibid., p. 354

Chapter 8: Montgomery v. Patton

1. Hamilton, p. 143
2. Ibid., p. 142
3. Gelb, p. 196
4. Patton diary, February 3, 1943
5. Hamilton, p. 151
6. Letter to Sir Alan Brooke, April 12, 1943
7. Hamilton, p. 219
8. Ibid., p. 300
9. Alexander papers (WO 214/22), PRO
10. Hamilton, p. 314
11. Patton diary, July 17, 1943
12. *Oxford,* p. 136
13. Ambrose, p. 227
14. Davis, p. 436
15. Gelb, p. 324
16. Eighth Army war diary (WO 169/8494), PRO
17. Letter to Brooke, August 14, 1943
18. Gelb, p. 334
19. Hamilton, p. 334
20. Ibid., p. 358
21. Ibid., p. 359
22. Gelb, p. 369
23. Hamilton, p. 338
24. Miller, p. 532
25. Gelb, p. 242
26. Hamilton, p. 336
27. Gelb, p. 369

28. Hamilton, p. 568
29. Irving, p. 362
30. Hamilton, p. 602
31. Ibid., p. 601
32. Gelb, p. 362
33. Ibid., p. 338
34. Hamilton, p. 723
35. Hogg, p. 104
36. Bradley, p. 377
37. Hamilton, p. 792
38. Patton diary, September 1, 1944
39. Brendon, p. 173
40. Office of the Chief of Military History Collections, PA
41. Brendon, p. 117
42. Gelb, p. 408
43. Lyon, p. 361
44. *Oxford,* p. 203
45. Horne, p. 74
46. Gelb, p. 338

Chapter 9: Johnson v. Kennedy

1. Schlesinger, p. 675
2. Ibid.
3. *The White House Tapes,* TV interview, 1999
4. Heymann, p. 364
5. Schlesinger, p. 933
6. Henggler, p. 62
7. Shesol, p. 33
8. O'Neill, p. 101
9. Shesol, p. 40
10. Robert F. Kennedy, *Oral History,* 1964
11. Shesol, p. 66
12. February 18, 1963, pp. 33–35
13. LBJ Library, oral history
14. Schlesinger, p. 671
15. Lemann, pp. 138–139
16. Ibid.
17. Schlesinger, p. 672
18. Ibid., pp. 361–362
19. Heymann, p. 364
20. Shesol, p. 56

21. *Life,* November 18, 1966
22. Heymann, p. 364
23. Shesol, p. 100
24. RFK, *Oral History, 1964*
25. Schlesinger, p. 657
26. Califano, p. 295
27. Manchester, p. 639
28. LBJ Library, oral history
29. *The White House Tapes,* TV interview, 1999
30. Ibid.
31. Corcoran, pp. 16–18
32. RFK, *Oral History, 1964*
33. Shesol, p. 176
34. RFK, *Oral History, 1964*
35. Ibid.
36. Ibid.
37. LBJ Library, oral history
38. RFK, *Oral History, 1964*
39. LBJ Library, oral history
40. Heymann, p. 372
41. LBJ Library, oral history
42. Letter dated September 3, 1964
43. Goodwin, p. 281
44. LBJ Library, oral history
45. *Nation,* February 20, 1967, p. 226
46. Shesol, p. 366
47. Schlesinger, p. 836
48. Ibid.
49. Califano, p. 297
50. Johnson, p. 539

Chapter 10: Hoover v. King

1. Gentry, p. 572
2. Summers, p. 361
3. Ibid., p. 195
4. Halperin *et al.,* pp. 61–63
5. Sullivan, p. 136
6. Gentry, p. 501
7. Schlesinger, p. 353
8. Gentry, p. 504
9. Leon Howell, *An Interview with Andrew Young,* February 16, 1976

10. Branch, p. 791

11. Summers, p. 306

12. Ibid., p. 353

13. Sullivan to Assistant Director Alan Belmont, January 27, 1964

14. Schloredt & Brown, p. 42

15. Branch, p. 883

16. Sullivan to Belmont, August 30, 1963

17. Garrow, *The FBI and Martin Luther King,* p. 106

18. Gentry, p. 568

19. Church Committee, III, pp. 124–126

20. Gentry, p. 570

21. Church Committee, III, p. 157

22. Ibid.

23. *New York Times,* November 20, 1964

24. Gentry, p. 569

25. Sullivan to Belmont, January 27, 1964

26. Summers, p. 360

27. Ibid.

28. *Newsweek,* December 12, 1964

29. Sullivan, p. 140

30. Sullivan to Belmont, January 8, 1964

31. Garrow, *Bearing the Cross,* p. 365

32. Church Committee, III, p. 169

33. Garrow, *Cross,* p. 374

34. Summers, p. 352

35. Church Committee, II, p. 248

36. All COINTELPRO references are taken from documents obtained under Freedom of Information Act

37. King Assassination Committee, VI, p. 107

38. Gentry, p. 641

39. *Congressional Record,* House, April 5, 1971

40. Gentry, p. 721

41. Schloredt & Brown, p. 54

BIBLIOGRAPHY

N.B. Where just a city is listed, this is done because many of the older sources, particularly those from London and Edinburgh, had no publisher per se.

Chapter 1: Elizabeth I v. Mary

Anderson, James. *Collections Relating to the History of Mary of Scotland,* IV. Edinburgh: Mossman & Brown, 1728.

Bain, Joseph, ed. *Calendar of Scotland,* II. Edinburgh, 1898–1952.

Gayangos, Pascual de, ed. *Calendar of Spain.* London: Longman, 1862–1954.

Harrison, G. B., ed. *The Letters of Queen Elizabeth.* London: Cassell, 1935.

Hartley, T. E. *Proceedings in the Parliaments of Elizabeth I,* I. Leicester: University Press, 1981.

Klarwill, Victor von. *Queen Elizabeth and Some Foreigners.* London: John Lane, 1928.

Laing, David, ed. *Works of John Knox,* II. Edinburgh, 1848.

Morris, John, ed. *The Letter Books of Sir Amias Paulet.* London: Burns & Oates, 1874.

Murdin, William. *A Collection of State Papers Relating to Affairs in the Reign of Queen Elizabeth.* London: Bowyer, 1759.

Neale, J. E. *Elizabeth I and Her Parliaments.* London: Jonathan Cape, 1953.

Plowden, Alison. *Two Queens in One Isle.* Brighton: Harvester, 1984.

Pollen, J. H. *Mary Queen of Scots and the Babington Plot.* Edinburgh, 1922.

Pollen, J. H., ed. *Queen Mary's Letter to the Duke of Guise.* Edinburgh, 1904.

Somerset, Anne. *Elizabeth.* London: Fontana, 1992.

Steuart, A. Francis, ed. *Memoirs of Sir James Melville.* London: Routledge & Sons, 1929.

Tytler, P. F. *History of Scotland,* VII. Edinburgh: A. & C. Black, 1863.

Weir, Alison. *Elizabeth the Queen.* London: Jonathan Cape, 1998.

Wright, William Aldis, ed. *English Works.* Cambridge: University Press, 1904.

Chapter 2: Parliament v. Charles I

Ashworth, Leon. *Oliver Cromwell.* Bath: Cherrytree, 1997.

Blencoe, R. W., ed. *Sidney Papers.* London, 1825.

Bruce, J., ed. *The Quarrel Between the Earl of Manchester and Oliver Cromwell.* London: Camden Series, 1875.

Carlton, Charles. *Charles I.* London: Routledge, 1983.

Carlyle, Thomas. *Oliver Cromwell's Letters and Speeches,* I. London: Chapman & Hall, 1857.

Gardiner, S. R. *The History of England 1603–1642.* London: Longman & Co, 1883.

Gregg, Pauline. *King Charles I.* London: Dent, 1981.

Gregg, Pauline. *Oliver Cromwell.* London: Dent, 1988.

Hill, Christopher. *God's Englishman.* New York: Dial Press, 1970.

Notestein, W. and Relf, F. H. *Commons Debates for 1629.* Minneapolis: University of Minnesota Press, 1921.

Roots, Ivan. *The Great Rebellion.* Stroud: Alan Sutton, 1995.

Rushworth, John. *Historical Collections.* London: D. Browne, 1701.

Spence, Joseph. *Anecdotes.* London: W. H. Carpenter, 1820.

Walker, Clement. *The History of Independancy.* London: R. Royston, 1649.

Warwick, Sir Philip. *Memoirs of the Reign of King Charles.* Edinburgh, 1803.

Wedgwood, C. V. *The King's War.* London: Collins, 1961.

Chapter 3: Burr v. Hamilton

Davis, Matthew. *Burr,* II. New York: Harper & Bros., 1836.

Hendrickson, Robert. *The Rise and Fall of Alexander Hamilton.* New York: Van Nostrand Reinhold, 1981.

Jenkinson, Isaac. *Aaron Burr: His Personal and Political Relationship with Thomas Jefferson and Alexander Hamilton.* Richmond, Ind.: Cullaton & Co., 1902.

Lomask, Milton. *Aaron Burr.* New York: Farrar, Straus, Giroux, 1979.

Mitchell, Broadus. *Alexander Hamilton: A Concise Biography.* Oxford University Press, 1976.

Syrett, H. C. *Alexander Hamilton Papers,* XX1. New York: Columbia University Press, 1961.

Chapter 4: Hatfields v. McCoys

Carrington Jones, Virgil. *The Hatfields and the McCoys.* Chapel Hill: University of North Carolina Press, 1948.

Crawford, T. C. *An American Vendetta.* New York: Belford, Clarke & Co., 1889.

McCoy, Truda Williams. *The McCoys.* Pikeville, Ky.: Pikeville College Press, 1976.

Rice, Otis K. *The Hatfields and McCoys.* Lexington: University of Kentucky Press, 1978.

Simmons, James C. *Diversion Magazine.* August, 1988.

Waller, Altina. *Feud.* Charlotte: University of North Carolina Press, 1988.

Chapter 5: Stalin v. Trotsky

De Jonge, Alex. *Stalin.* New York: Quill, 1986.

Dugrand, Alain. *Trotsky in Mexico.* Manchester: Carcanet, 1992.

Lewis, Jonathan and Whitehead, Philip. *Stalin: A Time for Judgment.* London: Thames Methuen, 1990.

Medvedev, Roy. *Let History Judge.* Oxford University Press, 1989.

Trotsky, Leon. *My Life.* New York: Scribner's Sons, 1930.

Trotsky, Leon. *Stalin.* New York: Harper & Bros., 1946.

Trotsky, Leon. *Writings of Leon Trotsky.* New York: Pathfinder Press, 1970.

Volkogonov, Dmitri. *The Rise and Fall of the Soviet Empire.* London: Harper & Row, 1998.

Voroshilov, K. *Stalin and the Armed Forces.* Moscow: Foreign Languages Publishing House, 1951.

Ward, Chris. *Stalin's Russia.* London: Arnold, 1993.

Chapter 6: Amundsen v. Scott

Amundsen, Roald. *The South Pole,* I & II. London: John Murray, 1912.

Huntford, Roland. *Scott and Amundsen.* London: Hodder & Stoughton, 1979.

Preston, Diane. *A First Rate Tragedy.* London: Constable, 1997.

Scott, Robert F. *The Voyage of the Discovery,* I. London: Smith, Elder, 1905.

Thomas, D. *Scott's Men.* London: Allen Lane, 1977.

Chapter 7: Duchess of Windsor v. Queen Mother

Bloch, Michael. *The Duke of Windsor's War.* London: Weidenfeld & Nicholson, 1982.

Bryan III, J. and Murphy, Charles. *The Windsor Story.* London: Granada, 1979.

Channon, Sir Henry. *Chips: The Diaries.* London: Weidenfeld & Nicholson, 1967.

Donaldson, Frances. *Edward VIII.* London: Weidenfeld & Nicholson, 1974.

Higham, Charles. *Wallis*. London: Sidgwick & Jackson, 1989.

Hyde, H. Montgomery. *Baldwin: The Unexpected Prime Minister*. London: Hart Davis, MacGibbon, 1973.

Lesley, Cole. *The Life of Noël Coward*. London: Jonathan Cape, 1981.

Lockhart, Sir Robin Bruce. *The Diaries 1915–1938*. London: Macmillan, 1973.

Middlemass, Keith and Barnes, John. *Baldwin: A Biography*. London: Weidenfeld & Nicholson, 1969.

St. John, Adela Rogers. *The Honeycomb*. Garden City, N.Y.: Doubleday, 1969.

Soames, Mary. *Clementine Churchill*. London: Cassell, 1979.

Thornton, Michael. *Royal Feud*. London: Joseph, 1985.

Windsor, Duchess of. *The Heart Has Its Reasons*. London: Joseph, 1956.

Chapter 8: Montgomery v. Patton

Ambrose, Stephen. *The Supreme Commander*. London: Cassell, 1971.

Blumenson, Martin, ed. *The Patton Papers*, II. Boston: Houghton Mifflin, 1974.

Bradley, Omar. *A Soldier's Story*. New York: Henry Holt, 1951.

Brendon, Piers. *Ike*. London: Secker & Warburg, 1987.

Davis, Kenneth. *Soldier of Democracy*. Garden City, N.Y.: Doubleday, 1946.

Gelb, Norman, *Ike and Monty*. New York: Morrow, 1994.

Hamilton, Nigel. *Monty: Master of the Battlefield*. London: Hamish Hamilton, 1983.

Hogg, Ian V. *Patton*. London: Hamlyn, 1982.

Horne, Alistair, with David Montgomery. *Monty*. London: Macmillan, 1994.

Irving, David. *The War Between the Generals*. London: Allen Lane, 1981.

Lyon, Peter. *Eisenhower*. Boston: Little, Brown, 1974.

Miller, Merle. *Ike the Soldier.* New York: Putnam, 1987.

Oxford Dictionary of Quotations. Oxford University Press, 1996.

Chapter 9: Johnson v. Kennedy

Califano, Joseph. *The Triumph and Tragedy of Lyndon Johnson.* New York: Simon & Schuster, 1991.

Corcoran, Thomas. *Rendezvous with Democracy.* LBJ Library (private papers; not published).

Goodwin, Richard. *Remembering America.* Boston: Little, Brown, 1988.

Henggler, Paul. *In His Steps: Lyndon Johnson and the Kennedys.* Chicago: Ivan Dee, 1991.

Heymann, C. David. *RFK.* London: Heinemann, 1998.

Johnson, Lyndon Baines. *The Vantage Point.* New York: Holt, Rinehart & Winston, 1971.

Kennedy, Robert F. *Oral History.* New York: Frank Melville, Jr., Library, University of New York, 1964.

Lemann, Nicholas. *The Promised Land.* New York: Knopf, 1991.

Manchester, William. *Death of a President.* New York: Harper & Row, 1967.

O'Neill, Tip, with William Novak. *Man of the House.* New York: Random House, 1987.

Schlesinger, Arthur M. *Robert Kennedy and His Times.* Boston: Houghton Mifflin, 1978.

Shesol, Jeff. *Mutual Contempt.* New York: Norton, 1997.

Wheeler, Charles. *White House Tapes.* (TV interview) London: Channel 4, 1999.

Chapter 10: Hoover v. King

Branch, Taylor. *Parting the Waters.* New York: Simon & Schuster, 1988.

Garrow, David. *Bearing the Cross.* New York: Morrow, 1986.

Garrow, David. *The FBI and Martin Luther King*. New York: Norton, 1981.

Gentry, Curt. *J. Edgar Hoover*. New York: Norton, 1991.

Halperin, Morton H. et al. *The Lawless State*. London: Penguin, 1976.

Schlesinger, Arthur M. *Robert Kennedy and His Times*. Boston: Houghton Mifflin, 1978.

Schloredt, Valerie and Brown, Pam. *Martin Luther King*. Watford, England: Exley, 1988.

Sullivan, William. *The Bureau*. New York: Norton, 1979.

Summers, Anthony. *Official and Confidential*. London: Gollancz, 1993.

INDEX